"An excellent complement to the authors' volume on General British English. The sections on phonetic theory are wonderfully concise and precise, and the practice material with audio recordings will prove extremely useful to any student wanting to improve their American English pronunciation."

Christian Jensen, *University of Copenhagen, Denmark*

"This much-needed up-to-date description of General American phonetics with its comprehensive practice material will be welcomed by all students of American English. A fantastic achievement."

Hiroshi Miura, *Senshu University, Japan*

"The authors have succeeded in presenting complex material in a way that renders it accessible to beginners. The book's solid theoretical basis and the abundance of practice material make it a must buy for both teachers and students. I'm sure I will use it in my teaching, and I'll definitely be referring my students to this informative material."

Petr Rösel, *University of Mainz, Germany*

American English Phonetics and Pronunciation Practice

American English Phonetics and Pronunciation Practice provides an accessible introduction to basic articulatory phonetics for students of American English. Built around an extensive collection of practice materials, this book teaches the pronunciation of modern standard American English to intermediate and advanced learners worldwide.

This book

- provides an up-to-date description of the pronunciation of modern American English;
- demonstrates the use of each English phoneme with a selection of high-frequency words, both alone and in context, in sentences, idiomatic phrases, and dialogues;
- provides examples and practice material on commonly confused sounds, including illustrative pronunciation diagrams;
- is supported by a companion website featuring complete audio recordings of the practice material to check your pronunciation against;
- can be used not only for studying pronunciation in the classroom but also for independent practice.

American English Phonetics and Pronunciation Practice is essential reading for any student studying this topic.

Paul Carley is a lecturer in English at Fakeeh College for Medical Sciences, Jeddah, and has held posts at the University of Leicester, the University of Bedfordshire, and the University of Applied Sciences Utrecht. He is a regular lecturer at the UCL Summer Course in English Phonetics.

Inger M. Mees is an associate professor in the Department of Management, Society, and Communication at the Copenhagen Business School. She has formerly held lectureships at the universities of Leiden and Copenhagen. She is on the academic staff of the UCL Summer Course in English Phonetics.

American English Phonetics and Pronunciation Practice

Paul Carley and Inger M. Mees

Routledge
Taylor & Francis Group

LONDON AND NEW YORK

First published 2020
by Routledge
2 Park Square, Milton Park, Abingdon, Oxon OX14 4RN

and by Routledge
52 Vanderbilt Avenue, New York, NY 10017

Routledge is an imprint of the Taylor & Francis Group, an informa business

British Library Cataloguing-in-Publication Data
A catalogue record for this book is available from the British Library.

Library of Congress Cataloging-in-Publication Data
Names: Carley, Paul (Linguist), author. | Mees, Inger M, author.
Title: American English phonetics and pronunciation practice /
    Paul Carley and Inger M. Mees.
Description: 1. | New York : Taylor and Francis, 2019. |
    Includes bibliographical references and index.
Identifiers: LCCN 2019026217 (print) | LCCN 2019026218 (ebook) |
    ISBN 9781138588530 (paperback) | ISBN 9781138588516 (hardback) |
    ISBN 9780429492228 (ebook)
Subjects: LCSH: English language—United States—Phonetics.
Classification: LCC PE2815 .C37 2019 (print) | LCC PE2815 (ebook) |
    DDC 421/.58—dc23
LC record available at https://lccn.loc.gov/2019026217
LC ebook record available at https://lccn.loc.gov/2019026218

ISBN: 978-1-138-58851-6 (hbk)
ISBN: 978-1-138-58853-0 (pbk)
ISBN: 978-0-429-49222-8 (ebk)

Typeset in Times New Roman
by Apex CoVantage, LLC

Visit the companion website: www.routledge.com/cw/carley

Contents

English phonemic transcription key

Consonants

Voiceless			Voiced		
Plosives					
p	*pet, lap*	pɛt, læp	b	*bet, lab*	bɛt, læb
t	*town, mat*	taʊn, mæt	d	*down, mad*	daʊn, mæd
k	*cap, luck*	kæp, lək	g	*gap, lug*	gæp, ləg
Affricates					
ʧ	*chin, batch*	ʧɪn, bæʧ	ʤ	*gin, badge*	ʤɪn, bæʤ
Fricatives					
f	*fast, safe*	fæst, seɪf	v	*vast, save*	væst, seɪv
θ	*thigh, breath*	θaɪ, brɛθ	ð	*thy, breathe*	ðaɪ, brið
s	*sink, face*	sɪŋk, feɪs	z	*zinc, phase*	zɪŋk, feɪz
ʃ	*shy, wish*	ʃaɪ, wɪʃ	ʒ	*measure*	ˈmɛʒər
h	*hat*	hæt, −			
Nasals			Voiced		
			m	*meet, team*	mit, tim
			n	*nice, fine*	naɪs, faɪn
			ŋ	*−, sing*	−, sɪŋ
Approximants					
Lateral (approximant)			l	*late, sail*	leɪt, seɪl
(Median)**approximants**			j	*yes, −*	jɛs, −
			w	*wait −*	weɪt, −
			r	*red, dare*	rɛd, dɛr

Notes
1 This phonemic transcription system is, with few exceptions, the same as that in the *Routledge Dictionary of Pronunciation for Current English* (Upton and Kretzschmar 2017).
2 Examples show initial and final position. Note that /ŋ/ does not occur initially; /ʒ/ is virtually restricted to medial position; /h j w/ do not occur finally.
3 The voiceless/voiced contrast is found only in the plosives, affricates, and fricatives.
4 Stress is shown by ['] placed *before* the syllable, e.g., *open* /ˈoʊpən/, *forget* /fərˈgɛt/.
5 Syllabic consonants (Section 8.2) are shown by [ˌ] below the symbol, e.g., *apple* /ˈæpl̩/, *mission* /ˈmɪʃn̩/.
6 Tapped /t/ (Section 2.8) is shown as [t̬] e.g., *pretty* /ˈprɪt̬i/, *thirty* /ˈθərt̬i/.

Vowels

The words shown in SMALL CAPITALS are the **keywords** used throughout this book to refer to the vowels. These were first introduced in Wells (1982).

Vowel	Keyword	Additional spellings
Checked		
ɪ	KIT /kɪt/	gym, manage, busy, England, guilt
ɛ	DRESS /drɛs/	bread, friend, said, fair, vary, their
æ	TRAP /træp/	plaid
ə	schwa /ʃwɑ/	son, young, blood
ər [ɚ]	schwar /ʃwɑr/	girl, term, heard, word, journey, curry
ʊ	FOOT /fʊt/	put, would, woman
Free monophthongs		
i	FLEECE /flis/	neat, these, technique, belief, beer, weird
ɑ	PALM /pɑm/	not, swan, knowledge, start, heart, memoir
u	GOOSE /gus/	rude, soup, shoe, do, crew, tour, poor
(ɔ	THOUGHT /θɔt/	caught, saw, walk, broad)
Free diphthongs		
eɪ	FACE /feɪs/	laid, may, weigh, they, break
aɪ	PRICE /praɪs/	try, lie, buy, guide
ɔɪ	CHOICE /tʃɔɪs/	boy
oʊ	GOAT /goʊt/	nose, blow, soul, toe
[o]	SPORT /sport/	more, four, oar, door, war
aʊ	MOUTH /maʊθ/	drown
Unstressed vowels		
ə	schwa	comma, ability, useless, bonus, famous
ər [ɚ]	schwar	collar, under, forget, Virginia, capture, martyr
i	FLEECE	happy, money, hippie, mediate

Notes
1 Some American accents have an additional vowel /ɔ/, which is used instead of PALM /ɑ/ in the lexical sets THOUGHT and CLOTH (Section 5.2.1), e.g., *law, loss* /lɔ lɔs/.
2 The allophone of GOAT before /r/ is strikingly different and shown as [o], e.g., *more* [mor]. We have assigned it a separate keyword: SPORT. In accents that have an additional THOUGHT vowel, it is regarded as an allophone of THOUGHT; see Sections 5.2.1 and 5.2.2.

Phonetic symbols and diacritics

This is a list of the phonetic symbols used in this book. We have not included here the symbols used for English phonemic transcription (see previous pages).

[ç]   voiceless palatal fricative, as a realization of /hj/, e.g., *huge*
[ɦ]   voiced glottal fricative, e.g., *ahead*
[ɫ]   voiced velarized alveolar lateral approximant ("dark /l/"), e.g., *well*
[ɹ]   voiced post-alveolar approximant, e.g., *very*
[ʔ]   glottal plosive, e.g., as a realization of /t/ before consonants, *at school* [əʔ ˈskul], or glottal reinforcement of a voiceless plosive, e.g., *background* [ˈbæʔkgraʊnd]
[t̞]   tapped /t/, e.g., *city* [ˈsɪt̞i]
[̥]   devoiced consonant, e.g., *rob* [rɑb̥] (normally below the symbol, but above for descending symbols, e.g., *rag* [ræg̊])
[ʰ]   aspirated, e.g., *pie* [pʰaɪ]
[̩]   syllabic consonant, e.g., *Britain* [ˈbrɪtn̩] (normally below the symbol, but above for descending symbols, e.g., *bacon* [ˈbeɪkŋ̍])
[ˈ]   primary stress, e.g., *intend* /ɪnˈtɛnd/
[ˌ]   secondary stress, e.g., *kangaroo* /ˌkæŋɡəˈru/
/ /   phonemic transcription
[ ]   phonetic transcription
< >   orthographic form
*   incorrect or unattested form

THE INTERNATIONAL PHONETIC ALPHABET (revised to 2015)

CONSONANTS (PULMONIC)

© 2015 IPA

	Bilabial	Labiodental	Dental	Alveolar	Postalveolar	Retroflex	Palatal	Velar	Uvular	Pharyngeal	Glottal
Plosive	p b			t d		ʈ ɖ	c ɟ	k ɡ	q ɢ		ʔ
Nasal	m	ɱ		n		ɳ	ɲ	ŋ	N		
Trill	ʙ			r					ʀ		
Tap or Flap		ⱱ		ɾ		ɽ					
Fricative	ɸ β	f v	θ ð	s z	ʃ ʒ	ʂ ʐ	ç ʝ	x ɣ	χ ʁ	ħ ʕ	h ɦ
Lateral fricative				ɬ ɮ							
Approximant		ʋ		ɹ		ɻ	j	ɰ			
Lateral approximant				l		ɭ	ʎ	ʟ			

Symbols to the right in a cell are voiced, to the left are voiceless. Shaded areas denote articulations judged impossible.

CONSONANTS (NON-PULMONIC)

Clicks	Voiced implosives	Ejectives
ʘ Bilabial	ɓ Bilabial	' Examples:
ǀ Dental	ɗ Dental/alveolar	p' Bilabial
ǃ (Post)alveolar	ʄ Palatal	t' Dental/alveolar
ǂ Palatoalveolar	ɠ Velar	k' Velar
ǁ Alveolar lateral	ʛ Uvular	s' Alveolar fricative

OTHER SYMBOLS

ʍ Voiceless labial-velar fricative

w Voiced labial-velar approximant

ɥ Voiced labial-palatal approximant

ʜ Voiceless epiglottal fricative

ʢ Voiced epiglottal fricative

ʡ Epiglottal plosive

ɕ ʑ Alveolo-palatal fricatives

ɺ Voiced alveolar lateral flap

ɧ Simultaneous ʃ and x

Affricates and double articulations can be represented by two symbols joined by a tie bar if necessary.

t͡s k͡p

VOWELS

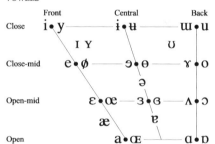

Where symbols appear in pairs, the one to the right represents a rounded vowel.

SUPRASEGMENTALS

ˈ	Primary stress	ˌfoʊnəˈtɪʃən
ˌ	Secondary stress	
ː	Long	eː
ˑ	Half-long	eˑ
̆	Extra-short	ĕ
ǀ	Minor (foot) group	
‖	Major (intonation) group	
.	Syllable break	ɹi.ækt
‿	Linking (absence of a break)	

TONES AND WORD ACCENTS

LEVEL		CONTOUR	
e̋ or ˥	Extra high	ě or ˩˥	Rising
é ˦	High	ê ˥˩	Falling
ē ˧	Mid	e᷄ ˦˥	High rising
è ˨	Low	e᷅ ˩˨	Low rising
ȅ ˩	Extra low	e᷈ ˦˨˧	Rising-falling
↓ Downstep		↗ Global rise	
↑ Upstep		↘ Global fall	

DIACRITICS Some diacritics may be placed above a symbol with a descender, e.g. ŋ̊

̥	Voiceless	n̥ d̥	̤	Breathy voiced	b̤ a̤	̪	Dental	t̪ d̪
̬	Voiced	s̬ t̬	̰	Creaky voiced	b̰ a̰	̺	Apical	t̺ d̺
ʰ	Aspirated	tʰ dʰ	̼	Linguolabial	t̼ d̼	̻	Laminal	t̻ d̻
̹	More rounded	ɔ̹	ʷ	Labialized	tʷ dʷ	̃	Nasalized	ẽ
̜	Less rounded	ɔ̜	ʲ	Palatalized	tʲ dʲ	ⁿ	Nasal release	dⁿ
̟	Advanced	u̟	ˠ	Velarized	tˠ dˠ	ˡ	Lateral release	dˡ
̠	Retracted	e̠	ˤ	Pharyngealized	tˤ dˤ	̚	No audible release	d̚
̈	Centralized	ë	~	Velarized or pharyngealized	ɫ			
̽	Mid-centralized	e̽	̝	Raised	e̝ (ɹ̝ = voiced alveolar fricative)			
̩	Syllabic	n̩	̞	Lowered	e̞ (β̞ = voiced bilabial approximant)			
̯	Non-syllabic	e̯	̘	Advanced Tongue Root	e̘			
˞	Rhoticity	ɚ a˞	̙	Retracted Tongue Root	e̙			

Preface and acknowledgments

American English Phonetics and Pronunciation Practice is unique in combining an introduction to English phonetics with extensive material for practicing English pronunciation. It presents a twenty-first-century model of educated American English, "General American" (GA), and is supported by a website containing complete recordings of all exercises. A parallel version for British English is also available (Carley, Mees, Collins 2018).

Modern corpus-based descriptions of colloquial English have been used to create materials that teach pronunciation while simultaneously practicing useful idiomatic language. Each English phoneme is demonstrated in high-frequency words in different phonetic contexts, in common phrases, in sentences, and in dialogues. Moreover, each phoneme is also extensively practiced in contrast with similar, confusable sounds in minimal pairs, phrases, and sentences.

Beyond the segmental level of vowels and consonants, considerable attention is given to the difference between strong and weak syllables, a very important component of English rhythm, and two complete chapters are dedicated to the difficult area of consonant clusters.

Learners who will benefit from the book include

- Learners of English as a foreign language
- Students of English language and linguistics
- Trainee English teachers
- Professionals wishing to speak English with clarity and accuracy

Our thanks go to Whitney Byrn for reading the manuscript and making many valuable suggestions, to Trevor Forrest for the many hours he put into making the recordings, and to Joshua S. Guenter for sharing his thoughts on certain points of analysis. Naturally, the responsibility for this work and the views expressed in it are entirely our own.

Finally, we gratefully acknowledge the patience shown and help given by our editors at Routledge – Francesca McGowan, Nadia Seemungal-Owen, and Lizzie Cox.

Paul Carley and Inger M. Mees
Jeddah and Copenhagen, May 2019

Chapter 1

Basic concepts

1.1 Pronunciation priorities

When learning to pronounce a new language, it's essential to get your priorities right. The most important sounds are the ones that can change the meaning of words. These are called **phonemes** (see Section 1.2). If you say *pin* and it sounds like *bin*, people will misunderstand you. And if you say *I hid them* and it sounds like *I hit them*, there will also be a breakdown in communication. Furthermore, you should be aware that sounds may be pronounced differently in different contexts, e.g., **pre-vocalically** (before vowels), **intervocalically** (between vowels), or **pre-consonantally** (before consonants). They may also be pronounced differently in different positions in the word – at the beginning (**initial**), in the middle (**medial**), and at the end (**final**). For instance, /p/ is more like a /b/ when it occurs after /s/, e.g., *port* vs. *sport*; /r/ sounds different in *red* and *tread*, the two /t/ sounds in *tight* are different, and the quality of <oa> is different in *goat* and *goal*. Note that when we refer to the letters in a word – as opposed to the sounds – we show them in **angle brackets**, e.g., <f> or <ie>. Phonemes are shown in **slant brackets**, e.g., /r/ or /ɛ/. The word *spread* would phonemically be shown as /sprɛd/.

Even if people can understand what you are saying, an off-target pronunciation may still sound *comical*, *irritating*, or *distracting* to listeners. For instance, if you say English /r/ with a back articulation (in your throat) instead of a front articulation (with your tongue-tip), it may sound funny to people who aren't used to it. If listeners are distracted because of a false pronunciation, they may stop concentrating on what you are trying to say. Or if they need to invest a lot of effort in deciphering what you are saying, they may lose track of your message. Furthermore, judgments of your overall ability in English are likely to be based on the impression your pronunciation makes: if you sound like a beginner, you may be treated like a beginner, even if your level is advanced in terms of grammar, vocabulary, reading, and writing.

The best approach is to aim for a pronunciation that (1) can be understood without any difficulty and (2) doesn't irritate or distract your listeners. Note that there's more to learning the pronunciation of a language than mastering the **segments** (vowels and consonants). You have to pay attention to several other points. For instance, correct use of **weak forms** (Section 8.3) helps to get the speech **rhythm** right. **Contractions**, e.g., *don't, it's, we'll*, improve the fluency. To make your pronunciation more authentic, it's important to have knowledge of **assimilation** (sounds that change under the influence of neighboring sounds, e.g., *when* becomes /wɛm/ in *when my*) and **elision** (disappearing sounds, e.g., /t/ is often lost in *facts*).

1.2 Phonemes and allophones

Some sound differences matter a great deal, whereas others are of little significance. The ones that matter most are those that can change the meaning of otherwise identical words. In English, the words *bit*, *bet*, *boat* are distinguished only by the vowels; in *bit*, *sit*, *wit*, only the initial consonant is different. In *bit*, *bill*, *bin*, it's the final consonant that brings about the change in meaning. Sounds that can distinguish meaning are called **phonemes** (adjective: **phonemic**). A *pair* of words distinguished by a single phoneme is called a **minimal pair**, e.g., *bit – hit*. The variety of English taught in this book (see Section 1.7) has 24 consonant phonemes and 13 vowel phonemes.

Not every sound difference can change the meaning of a word. Listen carefully to *feet* and *feed*. You can hear a distinct difference in the length of the two vowels. But the native English speaker interprets these vowels as two variants of the same phoneme /i/; the different vowel lengths are the result of the influence of the following consonants /t/ and /d/. Similarly, the two /k/ sounds in *keen* and *corn* are different, the first being formed more forward and the second further back in the mouth, but English speakers hear both as variants of the phoneme /k/.

When you say the /d/ in *deal*, your lips are unrounded during the consonant, but when you say /d/ in *door*, they are rounded. In *deal*, the vowel is unrounded, and in *door*, the vowel is rounded. When we say *deal* and *door*, our lips are getting ready for the vowel during the articulation of the consonant. So the lip-shape of the consonant is affected by the lip-shape of the following vowel. Each phoneme is composed of a number of such different variants. These are termed **allophones** (adjective: **allophonic**). Allophones may occur in **complementary distribution** or in **free variation**. Our *deal*/*door* example is an instance of allophones in complementary distribution. This means that the different allophones complement each other; where one occurs, the other cannot occur. In other words, we can write a rule for the occurrence of the two allophones: /d/ with rounded lips occurs before lip-rounded sounds while /d/ with unrounded lips occurs before all other sounds. Vowels are shortened before voiceless consonants like /s/ while they retain full length before voiced consonants like /z/; for example, the vowel in *face* /feɪs/ is clearly shorter than that in *phase* /feɪz/. Again, the allophones are in complementary distribution. If allophones are in free variation, their occurrence cannot be predicted from the phonetic context. An example of this would be the different possible pronunciations of /t/ in word-final position, as in *hat*. It's possible to pronounce the /t/ with or without glottal reinforcement (see Section 2.7.3). Many speakers vary between these two possibilities, and we cannot predict which of the two they are going to use. The glottally reinforced and non-glottally reinforced variants are therefore said to be in free variation.

Unfortunately for the learner, languages generally don't have the same phoneme system, and they certainly don't have the same range of allophones. So the learner has to work out the phonemic inventory of the new language and all the phonetic variants. Your first task is to make sure you never lose a phoneme contrast. This isn't easy to do in practice. Even though two phonemes may sound very similar, or identical, to the learner, to the native speaker, they are completely different. This is something native speakers and learners are often not aware of. Native speakers are frequently surprised to hear that the vowels in the English words *seat* /sit/ and *sit* /sɪt/ sound identical to speakers of most other languages, who hear them as the same vowel because they count as allophones of the same phoneme in their languages. Many learners find it difficult to separate the phonemes in *Luke* /luk/ and *look* /lʊk/. Others find it difficult to distinguish between *cat* /æ/, *cut* /ə/, and *cot* /ɑ/. Yet others can't hear and/or make the difference between the initial consonants in *three* /θ/ and *tree* /t/, or *three* /θ/ and *free* /f/, or *theme* /θ/ and *seem* /s/. In this book, we have provided exercises for 29 consonant contrasts and 17 vowel contrasts. You'll find that some of these don't pose a problem for speakers of your language while others will take a long time to master. If making a particular contrast isn't difficult for you, you can still use the contrast section as extra material to help you get the two sounds just right. Note that a full command of the contrasts involves being able to say all the different allophones of a phoneme in their appropriate contexts.

Remember that allophones can never change the meaning of words. English /t/ can be said in many different ways (i.e., there are many different allophones or variants), but if we substitute one allophone for another, the meaning remains the same. It will merely sound a bit odd. However, if we replace /t/ in *tight* by /s/, /f/, or /k/, then it turns into *sight, fight, kite*, and the result is a new word with a different meaning; /t s f k/ are therefore examples of phonemes in English. The English phoneme system is shown in the "English Phonemic Transcription Key" at the start of this book.

1.3 Spelling and sound

English **orthography** (i.e., spelling) is notoriously unreliable. For instance, the vowel /i/ can be spelled in numerous ways. All the letters underlined in the following words represent /i/: *m<u>e</u>, s<u>ee</u>, s<u>ea</u>, bel<u>ie</u>ve, rec<u>ei</u>ve, p<u>i</u>zza, p<u>eo</u>ple, k<u>ey</u>, qu<u>ay</u>, qu<u>i</u>che, Portugu<u>e</u>se*. Most other phonemes can also be spelled in many different ways, especially vowels. So instead of relying on the orthography, phoneticians use **transcription**. There are two types: (1) **phonemic transcription**, indicating phonemes only; this type, as we have seen, is normally placed inside slant brackets / /, e.g., *part* /pɑrt/. The sign – is used to show **phoneme contrasts**, e.g., *let* /lɛt/ – *met* /mɛt/; (2) **phonetic transcription**, showing more detailed allophonic distinctions, enclosed by **square brackets** [ ], e.g., *part* [pʰɑrt]. To indicate the allophonic distinctions, we often make use of **diacritics**, i.e., marks added to symbols to provide extra information, e.g., [pʰ]. The rounded allophone of /t/ is shown as [tʷ]; as /t/ said with unrounded lips is the default, there's no special symbol to denote it.

Sometimes words with different meanings are spelled completely differently but are pronounced in the same way, as in *key* and *quay* above. Such words are called **homophones** (same pronunciation, different meaning). English has a great many of these. Other examples of homophones are *wait/weight, know/no, sea/see, cite/sight/site*. To confuse matters even more, the opposite also occurs. It's possible for words that are spelled identically to be pronounced differently. The written word *row* can be said with the vowel in GOAT (when it means a "line") or the vowel in MOUTH (when it means a "quarrel"), and it's therefore impossible to tell from the spelling alone which meaning and pronunciation are intended. Words of this type are called **homographs** (same spelling, different pronunciation).

1.4 Phoneme symbols

Unfortunately, at present, there is no consensus among writers on the set of symbols used for transcribing GA. Even those, like us, who use the symbols of the International Phonetic Association's (IPA) International Phonetic Alphabet (see p. xv) don't necessarily use the same symbols in their transcriptions. The main reason for this is that while the IPA provides symbols to represent the range of speech sounds found in language, it doesn't dictate how the sound system of a language should be analyzed. A further reason is that writers have different approaches depending on whether they are writing for foreign learners, speech and language therapists, professional linguists, actors, dictionary users, and so on. In each case, there may be different traditions of transcription, differences in the linguistic knowledge of readers, different levels of tolerance for unfamiliar symbols, and different assumptions about what needs to be made explicit and what can be taken for granted in transcriptions.

In this work, we use a transcription system which is mostly phonemic but includes a small number of non-phonemic elements. We take a phonemic approach to the schwa /ə/ phoneme, using the same symbol for it in stressed and unstressed syllables (e.g., *above* /ə'bəv/; see Section 5.3) and the same symbol followed by /r/ when it is r-colored in stressed and unstressed syllables (e.g., *murmur* /'mərmər/; see Section 5.3). We take a non-phonemic approach to the SPORT [o] vowel (e.g., *four* /for/, *sort* /sort/, *story* /'stori/; see Section 5.2.2), t-tapping (e.g., *city* /'sɪt̬i/; see Section 2.8), and syllabic consonants (e.g., *kitten* /'kɪtn̩/, *rattle* /'ræt̬l̩/; see Section 1.5 and Section 8.2). In these three cases we continue to use phonemic slanted brackets in this book in order to avoid the inconvenience of constantly switching between phonemic and phonetic bracketing.

1.5 The syllable

A syllable is a group of sounds that are pronounced together. Words can consist of a single syllable, i.e., a **monosyllable** (*tight, time*) or of two or more syllables (**polysyllabic**), e.g., *waiting* (two syllables – **disyllabic**), *tomato* (three syllables), *participate* (four syllables), *university* (five syllables), and so on. A syllable nearly always contains a vowel (e.g., *eye* /aɪ/); this is called the **syllable nucleus**. The nucleus may be preceded or followed by one or more consonants (e.g., *tea, tree, stream, at, cat, cats, stamps*). The consonant or consonants preceding the nucleus are known as the **syllable onset**, and the consonants following the nucleus are called the **coda**. A group of consonants in a syllable onset or coda is known as a **cluster**. The English syllable can consist of clusters of up to three consonants in the onset (e.g., *strengths* /strɛŋθs/), and as many as four in the coda (e.g., *texts* /tɛksts/). Note that we are here concerned with *pronunciation*, so even though the word *time* looks as if it consists of two syllables because it has two vowel letters in the orthography, the word consists of only one syllable, as the second vowel letter in the spelling doesn't represent a vowel sound. A syllable that has a coda (i.e., one or more closing consonants) is called a **closed syllable**, while a syllable that ends with a vowel phoneme is called an **open syllable**.

Occasionally, a syllable consists of a consonant only, most frequently /n/ or /l/, e.g., *Britain* /'brɪtn̩/, *hidden* /'hɪdn̩/, *mission* /'mɪʃn̩/, *middle* /'mɪdl̩/, *apple* /'æpl̩/. A consonant that forms a syllable without the aid of a vowel is called a **syllabic consonant**. Note that we show a syllabic consonant by means of a small vertical mark beneath the symbol (with descending symbols, a superscript mark is used, e.g., *bacon* /'beɪkŋ̍/). A word like *apple* /'æpl̩/ consists of two syllables, but only the first contains a vowel; the second contains a syllabic consonant; see Sections 2.19, 2.23, 2.26, and 8.2.

1.6 Stress

Words consist of more than a set of segments (vowels and consonants) arranged in a certain order. Words of more than one syllable also have a distinctive rhythmic pattern depending on which syllables are pronounced with **stress** and which are not. Stressed syllables are pronounced with greater energy and effort than unstressed syllables, which results in greater

prominence, i.e., they stand out more. The first syllable in *carpet* is **stressed** and the second **unstressed**; the second syllable in *contain* is stressed and the first unstressed. Stress is indicated by means of a vertical mark placed before the stressed syllable, and unstressed syllables are left unmarked, e.g., /ˈkɑrpət/, /kənˈteɪn/. The position of stress in an English word is an important factor in word recognition, and there are even words that are distinguished by stress alone, e.g., the noun *increase* /ˈɪŋkris/ and the verb *increase* /ɪŋˈkris/.

Some words have more than one stressed syllable. In *Alabama*, the first and third syllables are stressed, while in *impossibility*, the second and fourth syllables are stressed. In these examples, as in all cases of multiple stresses, the last stress sounds more prominent than the earlier stress, and this is why the term **primary stress** has been used for the last, more prominent stress and **secondary stress** for any earlier, less prominent stresses. Primary stress is indicated with the usual stress mark and secondary stress with the same symbol at a lower level, e.g., /ˌæləˈbæmə/, /ɪmˌpasəˈbɪləṭi/. Although the terminology and transcription seem to suggest that there are three different levels of stress – primary stress, secondary stress, and unstressed – this isn't actually the case. There are only stressed and unstressed syllables, and the difference in prominence between the stresses in words such as *Alabama* and *impossibility* is due to **pitch accent**.

An accented /ˈæksɛntəd/ syllable is one that is accompanied by a change in the **pitch** of the voice. Pitch is related to the speed at which the vocal folds vibrate: faster vibration results in higher pitch and slower vibration lower pitch. When a word is pronounced in isolation, the syllable that takes primary stress is accented, i.e., accompanied by a pitch movement, usually a fall in pitch. When there's a "secondary stress" earlier in the word, this is accompanied by a step up to a relatively high pitch before the pitch movement of the "primary stress." In terms of the English sound system, the pitch movement associated with the "primary stress" is more salient than the step up in pitch associated with the "secondary stress." Thus, the distinction between primary and secondary stress is really a difference between different kinds of pitch accent rather than stress.

In this book, when individual monosyllabic words are transcribed as examples, we don't use a stress mark, which agrees with the approach taken in most dictionaries and works on English phonetics. Every word must have at least one stressed syllable when pronounced in isolation, and therefore, it's self-evident that the one and only syllable of a word is stressed. When we transcribe an individual polysyllabic word, we only indicate primary stress. When we transcribe utterances longer than a single word, we use the stress mark whenever a syllable is stressed, meaning that monosyllabic words can receive a stress mark but also that some stresses that appear when a word is said in isolation may disappear when the word is spoken in a phrase.

1.7 Pronunciation model

Every language has a number of different **accents**. An accent is a pronunciation variety characteristic of a group of people. Accents can be **regional** or **social**. In the USA, we find many different regional accents; examples are Texas, Kentucky, New York, and Boston, spoken by most of the people who live in these areas. But unless you have reasons for specifically wishing to adopt one of these regional accents, it's best for learners not to use these as a **model** for imitation. The accent of American English we recommend is one heard from educated speakers throughout the USA (and also in Canada). We shall term this social accent **General American** (abbreviated to **GA**). If you listen regularly to the American media, you're probably already familiar with this accent, since it's the variety used by the majority of American presenters. It's sometimes even called "Network English." It's either completely non-localizable (i.e., it's impossible to tell where speakers come from) or has very few regional traces. Thus, GA can be taken as the common denominator of the speech of educated Americans. When people alter their pronunciation (consciously or unconsciously) to sound less regional, they change in the direction of GA. When there's an accent spectrum within a location, those at the lower end of the social scale speak with the local accent while those toward the other end of the social scale speak with an accent progressively more like GA.

The English we describe in this book is the speech of the average modern General American speaker. Old-fashioned usages have been excluded, as have any "trendy" pronunciations that are too recent to have gained widespread acceptance.

Chapter 2

Consonants

2.1 The vocal tract and tongue

Before we discuss how the 24 English consonant phonemes are made, or **articulated**, let's familiarize ourselves with the anatomy of the **vocal tract** (Figure 2.1) and **tongue** (Figure 2.2).

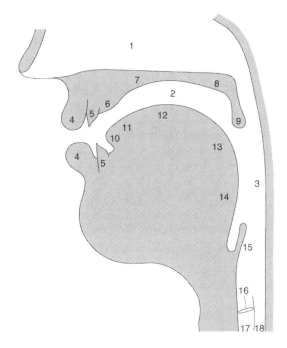

1 Nasal cavity	10 Tip of tongue
2 Oral cavity	11 Blade of tongue
3 Pharynx	12 Front of tongue
4 Lips	13 Back of tongue
5 Teeth	14 Root of tongue
6 Alveolar ridge	15 Epiglottis
7 Hard palate	16 Larynx, containing vocal folds
8 Soft palate (also termed "velum")	17 Trachea
9 Uvula	18 Esophagus

Figure 2.1 The anatomy of the vocal tract

This diagram might appear strange to you at first. The tongue may be larger or smaller than you expected. It's small in the sense that the tip does not extend much further from the place at which it's attached to the lower jaw, and it's large in the sense that it extends deep into the mouth and throat and almost completely fills the **oral cavity** (mouth).

If we start at the bottom of the diagram, we see that there are two passages. The **esophagus** /ɪˈsɑfəgəs/ (food passage) leads to the stomach, and the **trachea** /ˈtreɪkiə/ (windpipe) leads to the lungs. It's the trachea that is of most interest for our purposes. During speech, air flows up from the lungs via the trachea, and the first point of interest that it meets is the **larynx** /ˈlɛrɪŋks/. The larynx joins the trachea to the pharynx (throat), and is a box-like structure made of cartilage. It's larger in men than in women and is what makes the "Adam's apple," the lump at the front of the throat. The larynx contains the **vocal folds**, a pair of lip-like structures that can be brought together to close off the trachea and lungs. If there's a need to expel something from the lungs or trachea, the vocal folds are brought tightly together, the muscles of the chest and abdomen squeeze the lungs strongly, and then the vocal folds are abruptly separated to let the trapped air below escape in an explosion that hopefully clears the blockage. This is a cough. The vocal folds also seal off the lungs to stabilize the chest during lifting or other types of physical exertion. You will notice that before you pick up something heavy, you take a breath and trap it in your lungs by bringing the vocal folds together, and then when you put the load down, you inevitably let out a gasp as you release the air you had trapped in your lungs.

The next feature is the **epiglottis** /ɛpəˈglɑṭəs/, a flap of cartilage at the root of the tongue. It isn't involved in making speech sounds in English. Its biological function is to fold over the entrance to the larynx during swallowing in order to guide food and drink into the esophagus.

The space above the larynx and behind the root of the tongue is called the **pharynx** /ˈfɛrɪŋks/. It's smaller when the tongue is pulled back in the mouth and larger when the tongue is pushed forward.

There is then a possible fork in the road for the **airstream**. In our diagram, the **soft palate** /ˈpælət/ (also termed **velum** /ˈviləm/) and the **uvula** /ˈjuvjələ/ at its tip are shown in the lowered position, but it's also possible for the soft palate to form a seal against the back wall of the pharynx and close off the entrance to the **nasal cavity** (nose). This is known as a **velic closure**; see, e.g., Figure 2.3. Thus, the airstream can potentially enter both the oral and nasal cavities (as in Figure 2.1) or only the oral cavity (when the soft palate is raised and a velic closure is formed). There's little to be said about the nasal cavity itself because its dimensions are fixed; it's only the valve-like action of the soft palate opening and closing the entrance to it that is relevant for speech.

The oral cavity is bordered by the tongue at the bottom, the **palate** at the top, and the lips, cheeks, and teeth at the front and sides. By opening and closing the jaw and pulling the tongue back and pushing it forward, the oral cavity can be made larger or smaller. The tongue, lower teeth, and lip move with the lower jaw while the upper teeth and lip are in a fixed position.

Behind the upper front teeth is a lumpy area called the **alveolar ridge** /ælˈviələr/, and to the rear of that is the palate. The palate is divided into the soft palate and the **hard palate**. If you explore your palate with the tip of your tongue, you'll find that it's indeed hard and bony at the front and soft and fleshy at the back. At the very end of the soft palate is the uvula, which you can see hanging down when you look in the mirror.

The position shown in Figure 2.1 is actually a slightly unusual one, but it's useful for demonstration purposes. It shows the position assumed when breathing through the nose and mouth simultaneously. When not speaking, a healthy person would hold the jaws closer

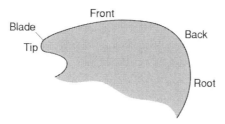

Figure 2.2 Divisions of the tongue

together with the lips and teeth touching; the tongue would fill the oral cavity, touching the roof of the mouth from the alveolar ridge to the soft palate; and the soft palate would be lowered (as in the diagram) to allow for normal breathing in and out via the nose.

The tongue has few obvious natural divisions in the way that the vocal tract does. However, phoneticians find it convenient to divide it into a number of parts when describing sounds and their articulations (see Figure 2.2).

The very point of the tongue is known as the **tip**. The part of the tongue that narrows to the tip and that lies under the alveolar ridge is the **blade** of the tongue. The part that lies under the hard palate and the part under the soft palate are called the **front** and **back** of the tongue respectively. This may seem strange at first, but front and back refer to the part of the tongue used in the articulation of vowels (see Section 5.1.1) – the front is the part of the tongue used to form front vowels and the back is the part used to form back vowels. The tip and blade remain low in the mouth and are not involved in making vowels. Finally, the part of the tongue in the pharynx is the **root**.

2.2 Describing consonants

A consonant is a speech sound that involves an obstruction of the airstream as it passes through the vocal tract. Describing a consonant involves describing the nature of the obstruction, and there are three factors to be taken into consideration: **voicing**, **place of articulation**, and **manner of articulation**.

2.2.1 Voicing

Voicing refers to the actions of the vocal folds during the articulation of a consonant. Different actions of the vocal folds produce **voiced** and **voiceless** sounds.

- For voiced sounds (i.e., vowels and the voiced consonants /b d ɡ dʒ v ð z ʒ m n ŋ l r j w/), the vocal folds are held gently together so that the airflow from the lungs causes them to vibrate.
- For voiceless sounds (i.e., the voiceless consonants /p t k tʃ f θ s ʃ h/), the vocal folds are held apart as in the position for normal breathing.

It's easiest to appreciate the voicing in sounds like /v ð z ʒ m n ŋ l r/ because these can be prolonged. Put your hand on your throat as you say them and feel the vibration. Note how the vibration stops and starts as you stop and start the consonant.

A number of English consonants come in pairs, the only difference between them being that one is voiceless and one is voiced. These pairs are: /f v/, /θ ð/, /s z/, /ʃ ʒ/, /p b/, /t d/, /k g/, and /ʧ ʤ/. Take some of the pairs that can be easily lengthened, such as /f v/ and /s z/, and alternate between the voiceless and the voiced consonants, feeling how the vibration in your larynx stops and starts.

Note that in our diagrams of consonant articulations, we use a plus sign at the larynx to indicate that the consonant is voiced and a minus sign if it's voiceless. If both signs are included (±), both voiced and voiceless articulations are possible.

2.2.2 Place of articulation

The second factor to take into account when describing a consonant is *where* in the vocal tract the obstruction is made. **Place of articulation** is described in terms of an **active articulator** that moves toward a **passive articulator**, which is in a fixed position (Table 2.1).

Table 2.1 English consonants: place of articulation

Place	Active articulator	Passive articulator	Consonants
Bilabial	Lower lip	Upper lip	/p b m/
Labio-dental	Lower lip	Upper incisors	/f v/
Dental	Tongue-tip	Upper incisors	/θ ð/
Alveolar	Tongue-tip	Alveolar ridge	/t d n s z l/
Post-alveolar	Tongue-tip	Rear of alveolar ridge	/r/
Palato-alveolar	Tongue-tip, blade, and front	Alveolar ridge and hard palate	/ʧ ʤ ʃ ʒ/
Palatal	Front of tongue	Hard palate	/j/
Velar	Back of tongue	Soft palate	/k g ŋ/
Glottal	Vocal folds	Vocal folds	/h/
Labial-velar	Back of tongue Lips	Soft palate Lips	/w/

The lip-rounding of labial-velar /w/ and positioning of the vocal folds for glottal /h/ cannot be analyzed in terms of passive and active articulators because they involve two elements moving toward each other (the corners of the mouth for /w/ and the two vocal folds for /h/). The lips and vocal folds are therefore classified as both active and passive in our table.

We refer to /r/ as post-alveolar, but see Section 2.21 for a discussion of an alternative place of articulation for this consonant.

Take some time to silently articulate the consonants listed in the table (or at least those you are confident you can correctly pronounce) in order to identify the different places of articulation.

2.2.3 Manner of articulation

Manner of articulation is the term used to describe the kind of obstruction involved in articulating a consonant. The five manners of articulation found in English are

- **Plosive**: A complete closure is formed in the vocal tract, blocking the airstream, and then released. The GA plosives are /p b t d k g/.
- **Fricative**: A narrowing is formed in the vocal tract, causing turbulence and fricative noise as the airstream is forced through. The GA fricatives are /f v θ ð s z ʃ ʒ h/.

- **Affricate**: A complete closure is formed in the vocal tract, blocking the airstream, and then released slowly, resulting in **homorganic friction** (i.e., fricative noise at the same place of articulation). The GA affricates are /ʧ dʒ/.
- **Nasal**: A complete closure is formed in the oral cavity, the soft palate is in the lowered position, and air exits via the nose. The GA nasals are /m n ŋ/.
- **Approximant**: A narrowing is formed in the vocal tract, but one not narrow enough to cause turbulence and noise as in the case of a fricative. The GA approximants are /r l j w/.

Explore what these terms really mean by articulating some of the consonants you are confident of and feeling the different manners of articulation.

2.2.4 Double and secondary articulations

English /w/ is an example of a **double articulation**, meaning that two articulations of equal magnitude (i.e., two **primary articulations**) take place at the same time – an approximant articulation between the back of the tongue and the soft palate and another approximant articulation consisting of the rounding of the lips. Other double articulations are possible but do not occur in English.

In the case of **secondary articulations**, the primary articulation is accompanied by an articulation of lesser magnitude. Examples of this in GA are the **labialization** (i.e., lip-rounding) accompanying /ʃ ʒ ʧ dʒ r/ (see Sections 2.5, 2.13, and 2.20) and the approximation of the back of the tongue to the soft palate (**velarization**) that accompanies /l/ (see Section 2.25).

2.2.5 Combining voicing, place, and manner

When we bring together the key factors of voicing, place of articulation, and manner of articulation, each English consonant phoneme has its own unique label that phoneticians use when referring to them.

/p/	voiceless bilabial plosive	/s/	voiceless alveolar fricative
/b/	voiced bilabial plosive	/z/	voiced alveolar fricative
/t/	voiceless alveolar plosive	/ʃ/	voiceless palato-alveolar fricative
/d/	voiced alveolar plosive	/ʒ/	voiced palato-alveolar fricative
/k/	voiceless velar plosive	/h/	voiceless glottal fricative
/g/	voiced velar plosive	/m/	voiced bilabial nasal
/ʧ/	voiceless palato-alveolar affricate	/n/	voiced alveolar nasal
/dʒ/	voiced palato-alveolar affricate	/ŋ/	voiced velar nasal
/f/	voiceless labio-dental fricative	/j/	voiced palatal approximant
/v/	voiced labio-dental fricative	/w/	voiced labial-velar approximant
/θ/	voiceless dental fricative	/l/	voiced alveolar lateral approximant
/ð/	voiced dental fricative	/r/	voiced post-alveolar approximant

Strictly speaking, the IPA symbol for a voiced post-alveolar approximant is [ɹ], but when making practical phonemic transcriptions for various languages, phoneticians often replace "exotic" symbols with the nearest "non-exotic" symbol for the sake of ease of printing and writing. In such cases, there's no danger of confusion because the description of the sounds is included with the symbols, as we do here.

Note that in the IPA chart (see p. xv) the term *post-alveolar* is used for /ʧ dʒ ʃ ʒ/, but we prefer the term traditionally used for English, *palato-alveolar*, because it better describes the English articulations.

2.3 The English consonants

Table 2.2 conveniently summarizes the voicing, place, and manner of articulation of the 24 English consonants. Within each cell, the sound on the left is voiceless and the one on the right is voiced.

Table 2.2 English consonant grid

	Bilabial	Labio-dental	Dental	Alveolar	Post-alveolar	Palato-alveolar	Palatal	Velar	Glottal	Labial-Velar
Plosives	p　　b			t　　d				k　　g		
Affricates						ʧ　　ʤ				
Fricatives		f　　v	θ　　ð	s　　z		ʃ　　ʒ			h	
Nasals	m			n				ŋ		
Approximants				l	r		j			w

2.4 Obstruents and sonorants

Table 2.2 reveals that consonants fall into two groups: those that typically come in voiceless and voiced pairs (obstruents) and those that do not (sonorants). Plosives, affricates, and fricatives are **obstruents** /ˈɑbstruənts/, the most consonant-like of the consonants, involving the greatest degree of obstruction to the airstream. Nasals and approximants are **sonorants** /ˈsɑnərənts/ (as are vowels) and are the least consonant-like of the consonants, involving a lesser degree of obstruction.

2.4.1 Pre-fortis clipping

Voiceless (also known as *fortis*) obstruents shorten sonorants that precede them in the same syllable. This phenomenon is termed **pre-fortis clipping** and is most often discussed in relation to vowels (see Section 5.6), but it also affects sonorant consonants, for example:

/m/	*lump* /ləmp/, *lymph* /lɪmf/
/n/	*bent* /bɛnt/, *wince* /wɪns/, *bench* /bɛnʧ/
/ŋ/	*bank* /bæŋk/
/l/	*help* /hɛlp/, *belt* /bɛlt/, *sulk* /səlk/, *belch* /bɛlʧ/, *golf* /gɑlf/, *health* /hɛlθ/, *else* /ɛls/, *Welsh* /wɛlʃ/
/r/	*sharp* /ʃɑrp/, *short* /ʃɔrt/, *fork* /fɔrk/, *march* /mɑrʧ/, *scarf* /skɑrf/, *north* /nɔrθ/, *scarce* /skɛrs/, *marsh* /mɑrʃ/

2.4.2 Obstruent devoicing

Although we have so far referred to English consonants as either voiceless or voiced, English voiced obstruents are actually only *potentially* fully voiced. Depending on the phonetic context, they are often partially or even completely **devoiced** /diˈvɔɪst/ (i.e., they partially or completely lose their voicing). For this reason, the terms **fortis** and **lenis** are sometimes used for voiceless and voiced instead. Fortis means *strong*, while lenis means *weak*, which reflects the fact that voiceless obstruents are articulated more forcefully than voiced obstruents. Force of articulation is a difficult feature to perceive, and many learners are confused by these terms because they feel that voiced sounds are louder and therefore strong, while voiceless sounds are quieter and therefore weak. It's preferable, therefore, to stick with the terms *voiceless* and *voiced*, with the understanding that when we refer to English /b d g dʒ v ð z ʒ/ as voiced obstruents, we actually mean "potentially" fully voiced.

English voiced obstruents are typically fully voiced when they occur between voiced sonorants, i.e., nasals, approximants, and vowels:

/**b**/	*rabbit* [ˈræbət]	*a boat* [ə ˈboʊt]	*rub it* [ˈrəb ɪt]
/**d**/	*colder* [ˈkoʊldər]	*a dog* [ə ˈdɑg]	*need it* [ˈnid ɪt]
/**g**/	*cargo* [ˈkɑrgoʊ]	*my gate* [maɪ ˈgeɪt]	*big oak* [ˈbɪg ˈoʊk]
/**dʒ**/	*magic* [ˈmædʒɪk]	*a joke* [ə ˈdʒoʊk]	*page eight* [ˈpeɪdʒ ˈeɪt]
/**v**/	*envy* [ˈɛnvi]	*a view* [ə ˈvju]	*move it* [ˈmuv ɪt]
/**ð**/	*clothing* [ˈkloʊðɪŋ]	*see this* [ˈsi ˈðɪs]	*loathe it* [ˈloʊð ɪt]
/**z**/	*easy* [ˈizi]	*the zoo* [ðə ˈzu]	*his own* [hɪz ˈoʊn]
/**ʒ**/	*vision* [ˈvɪʒn̩]	*a genre* [ə ˈʒɑnrə]	*beige is* [ˈbeɪʒ ˈɪz]

English voiced obstruents are typically partially or fully devoiced when they are preceded by a pause (i.e., silence) or a voiceless consonant or when a pause or voiceless consonant follows:

/**b**/	*this book* [ˈðɪs ˈb̥ʊk]	*grab some* [ˈgræb̥ ˈsəm]
/**d**/	*dog* [ˈd̥ɑg]	*load* [loʊd̥]
/**g**/	*that guy* [ˈðæt ˈg̊aɪ]	*big* [ˈbɪg̊]
/**dʒ**/	*joke* [ˈd̥ʒoʊk]	*stage fright* [ˈsteɪd̥ʒ fraɪt]
/**v**/	*eight verbs* [ˈeɪt ˈv̥ərbz]	*save time* [ˈseɪv̥ ˈtaɪm]
/**ð**/	*not that* [ˈnɑt ˈð̥æt]	*bathe* [beɪð̥]
/**z**/	*six zones* [ˈsɪks ˈz̥oʊnz̥]	*buzz* [bəz̥]
/**ʒ**/	*genre* [ˈʒ̊ɑnrə]	*beige top* [ˈbeɪʒ̊ ˈtɑp]

A devoiced consonant is normally shown by means of a subscript circle under the consonant (e.g., [b̥]), but with descending symbols, a superscript circle is used (e.g., [g̊]). In the case of fricatives, the devoicing is greater before a voiceless consonant or pause than after a voiceless consonant or pause. When devoicing occurs, the difference between pairs of voiced and voiceless obstruents is less marked, but the contrast still remains – /b d g dʒ v ð z ʒ/ do not become /p t k tʃ f θ s ʃ/.

2.5 Stops

Plosives and affricates make up the category of **stops**. They have in common a combination of a velic closure and a closure in the oral cavity that results in a complete obstruction to the airstream (hence the term *stop*).

English has three pairs of voiceless and voiced plosives at the bilabial, alveolar, and velar places of articulation.

- For /p/ and /b/, the lips come together and form a complete closure, stopping the airstream (see Figure 2.3).
- For /t/ and /d/, a complete closure is formed by the tip of the tongue against the alveolar ridge and by the sides of the tongue against the upper side teeth (see Figure 2.4).
- For /k/ and /g/, the back of the tongue forms a closure against the soft palate, and the rear of the sides of the tongue form a seal against the rear upper side teeth (see Figure 2.5).

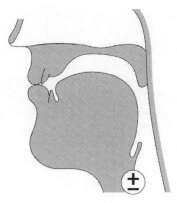

Figure 2.3 English plosives /p/ and /b/

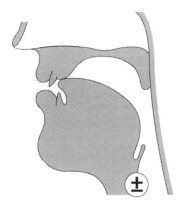

Figure 2.4 English plosives /t/ and /d/

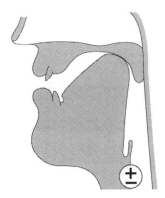

Figure 2.5 English plosives /k/ and /g/

English has a single pair of voiceless and voiced affricates at the palato-alveolar place of articulation.

- For /ʧ/ and /dʒ/, the tip and blade of the tongue form a closure against the rear part of the alveolar ridge, the front of the tongue is raised towards the hard palate, and the sides of the tongue form a seal against the upper side teeth (see Figure 2.6).
- The closure is released slowly, resulting in a brief moment of homorganic friction (Figure 2.7).
- The primary articulation is accompanied by a simultaneous secondary articulation – rounding and protrusion of the lips.

Although the phonemic symbols for the affricates consist of two elements, these phonemic affricates are single sounds, and although the first element of each symbol is the same as that used for the alveolar plosives, the place of articulation is different (as our diagrams demonstrate), the same symbols being used only for the sake of convenience.

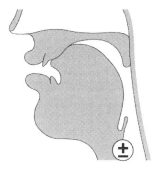

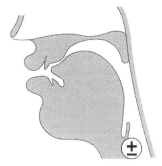

Figure 2.6 English affricates /ʧ/ and /dʒ/ showing palato-alveolar closure

Figure 2.7 English affricates /ʧ/ and /dʒ/ showing release with homorganic friction

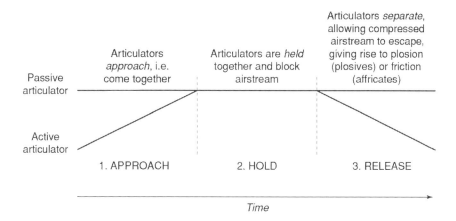

Figure 2.8 Articulation timing diagram showing the three stages of a stop

2.5.1 The stages of stops

Stops have three stages (see Figure 2.8):

1   **Approach**: The active articulator moves toward the passive articulator in order to form the closure.
2   **Hold**: The closure is made, the airstream is blocked, and pressure builds up.
3   **Release**: The active articulator moves away from the passive articulator, breaking the closure and releasing the compressed air.

The difference between plosives and affricates is that the release stage of affricates is slower, and therefore, the articulators spend a brief moment in the position for a fricative at the same place of articulation, resulting in audible friction. Another key difference is that the fricative release stage of affricates is always present while the release stage of plosives is very variable (Section 2.11).

2.6 Aspiration

When the voiceless plosives /p t k/ are at the beginning of a stressed syllable, they are released with **aspiration**. This means that there's a brief period of voicelessness between the release of the plosive and the beginning of voicing for the next sounds (see Figure 2.9).

During this period, the vocal folds remain open, and the air rushing through the vocal tract gives the impression of a short [h]; hence, aspiration is shown with the symbol [ʰ] (e.g., [tʰ]).

[pʰ]	*peas* [pʰiz]	*palm* [pʰɑm]	*pound* [pʰaʊnd]
[tʰ]	*toad* [tʰoʊd]	*tail* [tʰeɪl]	*torn* [tʰɔrn]
[kʰ]	*kind* [kʰaɪnd]	*care* [kʰɛr]	*curb* [kʰərb]

When /p t k/ are not at the beginning of a stressed syllable, they are weakly aspirated or unaspirated. This is the case at the beginning of unstressed syllables and at the end of syllables but also, quite strikingly, when preceded by /s/ at the beginning of a syllable:

[p]	*perform* [pərˈform]	*pacific* [pəˈsɪfɪk]	*pyjamas* [pəˈdʒæməz]
[t]	*today* [təˈdeɪ]	*taboo* [təˈbu]	*together* [təˈgɛðər]
[k]	*concern* [kənˈsɔrn]	*kebab* [kəˈbab]	*canal* [kəˈnæl]
[p]	*leap* [lip]	*rope* [roʊp]	*map* [mæp]
[t]	*fight* [faɪt]	*goat* [goʊt]	*rate* [reɪt]
[k]	*like* [laɪk]	*sick* [sɪk]	*cheek* [tʃik]
[pʰ]	*pin* [pʰɪn]	*pot* [pʰat]	*pie* [pʰaɪ]
[p]	*spin* [spɪn]	*spot* [spat]	*spy* [spaɪ]
[tʰ]	*tone* [tʰoʊn]	*top* [tʰap]	*till* [tʰɪl]
[t]	*stone* [stoʊn]	*stop* [stap]	*still* [stɪl]
[kʰ]	*core* [kʰor]	*kill* [kʰɪl]	*cool* [kʰul]
[k]	*score* [skor]	*skill* [skɪl]	*school* [skul]

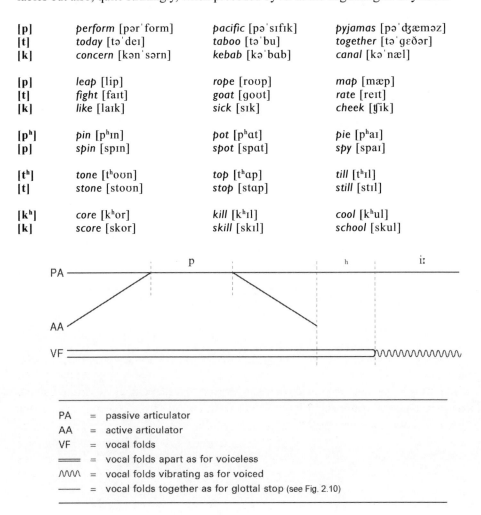

PA	=	passive articulator
AA	=	active articulator
VF	=	vocal folds
=====	=	vocal folds apart as for voiceless
ᴧᴧᴧ	=	vocal folds vibrating as for voiced
———	=	vocal folds together as for glottal stop (see Fig. 2.10)

Figure 2.9 Aspiration in English /p/ as in *pea*; the diagram shows the brief period of voicelessness after the release of the plosive and before the voicing for the vowel

When aspirated /p t k/ are followed by approximants /l r w j/, the aspiration takes place during the articulation of the approximant, partially or fully devoicing the approximant [l̥ r̥ j̊ w̥] and causing turbulence and fricative noise at the place of articulation of the approximant, for example:

/p/	play [pl̥eɪ]	print [pr̥ɪnt]	pew [pj̊u]	
/t/		treat [tr̥it]		twin [tw̥ɪn]
/k/	clay [kl̥eɪ]	cream [kr̥im]	cue [kj̊u]	queasy [ˈkw̥izi]

When /s/ precedes these clusters, there's no aspiration and therefore the approximants do not become devoiced or fricative:

/sp/	splay [spleɪ]	sprint [sprɪnt]	spew [spju]	
/sk/		scream [skrim]	skew [skju]	squeezy [ˈskwizi]

As regards aspiration and devoicing, the /str/ cluster is a little irregular. Unlike other /s/ + voiceless plosive + approximant clusters, the /r/ remains somewhat devoiced and fricative. Consequently, the /tr/ of *strap* is not very different from, or even identical to, the /tr/ of *trap*.

Because the voiced plosives are frequently partially or fully devoiced (see Section 2.4.2), the presence of aspiration is an important cue for distinguishing /p t k/ from /b d g/.

2.7 Glottal plosive [ʔ]

In addition to the bilabial /p b/, alveolar /t d/, and velar /k g/ plosives, the glottal plosive [ʔ] (often referred to as "glottal stop") also occurs in English. The closure for a glottal plosive is made by bringing the vocal folds firmly together in an articulation similar to that of a very weak cough. The vocal folds are unable to vibrate during the production of a glottal plosive and therefore the sound has no voiced equivalent. Although common, the glottal plosive is not an independent phoneme in English (though it may be in other languages). The glottal plosive has a number of uses (see the following sections).

2.7.1 Hard attack

When a word starting with a vowel is preceded by a voiceless consonant or a pause, the usual way to begin the vowel is to gently bring the vocal folds together into the position for voicing or, if the preceding sound is voiced, to continue the voicing as the articulators move into the position for the vowel. An alternative to this is to begin with a glottal plosive: irrespective of whether the vocal folds are apart for a preceding voiceless consonant or a pause or vibrating for a preceding voiced sound, the vocal folds are brought tightly together and on release immediately take up the position for voicing, giving the impression of a very abrupt start to the vowel. This is known as **hard attack** and is used for emphasis in English, although in certain other languages, this may be the most usual treatment of word-initial vowels.

Without hard attack:	*This is an apple.* [ˈðɪs ɪz ən ˈæpl̩]
With hard attack:	*This is an apple (not a pear)!* [ˈðɪs ɪz ən ˈʔæpl̩]

A similar use of the glottal plosive is to separate sequences of vowels within words. In words like *react* /riˈækt/, *cooperate* /koʊˈɑpəreɪt/, and *deodorant* /diˈoʊdərənt/, the transition from one vowel to the next usually consists of a rapid glide of the tongue from the first vowel position to the second. An alternative in emphatic speech is to insert a glottal plosive between the vowels as the tongue moves between the vowel positions. This is only possible when the second vowel is stressed (i.e., not in *serious* /ˈsiriəs/, *fluent* /ˈfluənt/, *leotard* /ˈliətɑrd/).

2.7.2 Glottal replacement

The most important occurrence of the glottal plosive in English is as an allophone of the /t/ phoneme. This is known as **glottal replacement**. Glottal replacement occurs in only a specific set of phonetic contexts. The most important of these is when /t/ is in a syllable coda, preceded by a sonorant (i.e., vowel, nasal, or approximant) and followed by another consonant:

Within words: *butler* [ˈbɔʔlər], *lightning* [ˈlaɪʔnɪŋ], *pitfall* [ˈpɪʔfɑl], *tents* [tɛnʔs]
Between words: *felt wrong* [ˈfɛlʔ ˈrɑŋ], *sent four* [ˈsɛnʔ ˈfor], *light rain* [ˈlaɪʔ ˈreɪn], *part time* [ˈpɑrʔ ˈtaɪm]

Glottal replacement is also common before a pause, e.g., *wait* [weɪʔ].

Although, in GA, [ʔ] does not occur between vowels in word-medial position, as in *meeting*, it can be heard in word-final position before a vowel in high-frequency words, for example *got a* [ˈgɑʔ ə], *met us* [ˈmɛʔ əs]; note, however, that t-tapping (see Section 2.8) is far more common in this position.

2.7.3 Glottal reinforcement

In addition to [ʔ] acting as an allophone of /t/, it can also occur together with /t/ and the other voiceless stops, /p k ʧ/, in a process known as **glottal reinforcement**. A glottal closure overlaps with the oral closure (see Figure 2.10): first the glottal closure is made; then the bilabial, alveolar, palato-alveolar, or velar closure is made; then the glottal closure is released inaudibly behind the oral closure before finally the oral closure is released; this phenomenon

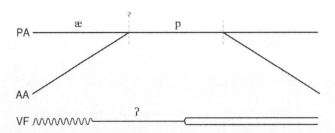

Figure 2.10 Glottal reinforcement in English /p/, as in *captive*. The reinforcing glottal plosive is formed before the hold stage of /p/ and released before the release of the bilabial plosive. (See Figure 2.9 for key to symbols.)

is sometimes also referred to as "pre-glottalization." Glottal reinforcement occurs in the same phonetic contexts as for glottal replacement of [t] (except for /ʧ/, which does not have to be followed by a consonant), and like glottal replacement, although it's common, it isn't obligatory.

captive [ˈkæʔptɪv]	*keep calm* [ˈkiʔp ˈkɑm]	
curtsey [ˈkɔrʔtsi]	*hot sauce* [ˈhɑʔt ˈsɑs]	
faultless [ˈfɑlʔtləs]	*don't know* [ˈdoʊnʔt ˈnoʊ]	
action [ˈæʔkʃn̩]	*take five* [ˈteɪʔk ˈfaɪv]	
hatchet [ˈhæʔʧət]	*catch me* [ˈkæʔʧ mi]	*catch it* [ˈkæʔʧ ɪt]

2.8 Tapping

In certain phonetic contexts, the alveolar plosives /t d/ and the alveolar nasal /n/ are articulated very rapidly. The tongue tip and blade move to and away from the alveolar ridge very quickly, and the contact between the active and passive articulators is very brief. This manner of articulation is known as a **tap**, and the IPA symbol for a voiced alveolar tap is [ɾ]. A voiced alveolar tap [ɾ] is used as the usual realization of the /r/ phoneme in many languages around the world and can also be heard in a number of English accents. Speakers who have a tap for /r/ in their language or accent of English may feel that the GA tap for /t d/ isn't quite the same as their own.

The most striking effect of tapping in GA is that /t/ becomes voiced and indistinguishable from /d/. They are both realized as a voiced alveolar tap [ɾ], and the difference between them is neutralized in tapping contexts. In contrast, the effect on the realization of /n/ is relatively minor. When tapped, /n/ is realized as a nasalized tap [ɾ̃], the equivalent of tapped /t/ or /d/ with the velum lowered. The result is a sound that isn't very different from /n/ in other contexts and that isn't easily confused with any other sound.

Some works on GA phonetics transcribe **t-tapping** with [ɾ], which emphasizes the particular type of articulation used. Other works transcribe t-tapping with [d], which demonstrates that the tapped variant of /t/ sounds to the ears of English speakers more like a variant of the /d/ phoneme than of any other phoneme. In this book, we prefer a third approach, which is used in two standard reference works: the *Longman Pronunciation Dictionary* and the *Cambridge English Pronouncing Dictionary*. The voiceless alveolar plosive symbol [t] is combined with the IPA "voiced" diacritic [̬] (t-tapping is also referred to as **t-voicing**) to give [t̬]. This symbolization has the advantage of making the transcription not too different from the orthography and of using a similar symbol for the same word in different phonetic contexts (e.g., *write* /raɪt/, *writing* /raɪt̬ɪŋ/, *writes* /raɪts/, *write it* /raɪt̬ ɪt/, *write some* /raɪt səm/). This special symbol for t-tapping makes our transcription system a little unphonemic, but for the sake of simplicity, we will continue to use phonemic slanted brackets and not switch to phonetic square brackets for every instance of t-tapping.

T-tapping occurs when /t/ is at the end of a syllable and between vowels. Within a word, the following syllable must be unstressed, but the preceding syllable can be stressed or unstressed:

Stressed:	*city* /ˈsɪt̬i/, *vitamin* /ˈvaɪt̬əmən/, *critic* /ˈkrɪt̬ɪk/, *beautiful* /ˈbjut̬əfl̩/
Unstressed:	*deputy* /ˈdɛpjət̬i/, *quality* /ˈkwɑlət̬i/, *society* /səˈsaɪət̬i/

The following syllable can also be /əl/, realized as syllabic /l/, or /ər/, realized as schwar [ɚ] (the equivalent of syllabic [ɹ], see Section 2.23) but not /ən/, realized as syllabic /n/ (where /t/ is more likely to be realized as a glottal stop):

Syllabic /l̩/:   *bottle* /ˈbɑt̬l̩/, *total* /ˈtoʊt̬l̩/, *little* /ˈlɪt̬l̩/, *fatal* /ˈfeɪt̬l̩/, *rattle* /ˈræt̬l̩/

Schwar/ər/ [ɚ]:   *letter* /ˈlɛt̬ər/, *meter* /ˈmit̬ər/, *butter* /ˈbʌt̬ər/, *water* /ˈwɑt̬ər/

Syllabic /n̩/:   *button* /ˈbʌtn̩/, *kitten* /ˈkɪtn̩/, *rotten* /ˈrɑtn̩/, *threaten* /ˈθrɛtn̩/
                button [ˈbʌʔn̩], *kitten* [ˈkɪʔn̩], *rotten* [ˈrɑʔn̩], *threaten* [ˈθrɛʔn̩]

The preceding sound doesn't have to be a vowel. It can also be /r/:

After /r/:   *dirty* /ˈdərt̬i/, *poverty* /ˈpɑvərt̬i/, *artist* /ˈɑrt̬ɪst/, *mortar* /ˈmort̬ər/, *turtle* /ˈtərt̬l̩/

When the preceding sound is /l/, tapping is variable:

After /l/:   *alter* /ˈɑltər/ or /ˈɑlt̬ər/, *guilty* /ˈɡɪlti/ or /ˈɡɪlt̬i/, *penalty* /ˈpɛnl̩ti/ or /ˈpɛnl̩t̬i/

When the preceding sound is /n/, the tendency is for the /t/ to be lost altogether, particularly in familiar, high-frequency words:

After /n/:   *twenty* /ˈtwɛni/, *winter* /ˈwɪnər/, *plenty* /ˈplɛni/, *wanted* /ˈwɑnəd/, *dentist* /ˈdɛnəst/

When t-tapping occurs between words, the following syllable does not have to be unstressed:

Unstressed: *get it* /ˈɡɛt̬ ɪt/, *visit us* /ˈvɪzət̬ əs/, *bet a lot* /ˈbɛt̬ ə ˈlɑt/, *late again* /ˈleɪt̬ ə ˈɡɛn/

Stressed: *get out* /ˈɡɛt̬ ˈaʊt/, *visit others* /ˈvɪzət̬ ˈʌðərz/, *bet everything* /ˈbɛt̬ ˈɛvriθɪŋ/, *late evening* /ˈleɪt̬ ˈivnɪŋ/

The neutralization of /t/ and /d/ in these contexts creates a number of homophones: *writer/rider*, *latter/ladder*, *parity/parody*, *atom/Adam*, *metal/medal*, *petal/pedal*.

2.9 Nasal release

The bilabial /p b/ and alveolar plosives /t d/ have the same place of articulation as the bilabial /m/ and alveolar /n/ nasals respectively. They differ only in the soft palate being in the raised position (forming a velic closure) for the plosives and in the lowered position for the nasals. Consequently, it's possible to move from /p/ or /b/ to /m/ and from /t/ or /d/ to /n/ by lowering the soft palate only and leaving the oral closure in place. This is called **nasal release** and is usual in English when plosives are followed by their nasal equivalents. It's not usual for velar plosives /k ɡ/ because the velar nasal /ŋ/ does not occur at the beginning of syllables.

/pm/	*chipmunk* /ˈtʃɪpməŋk/	*ripe melon* /ˈraɪp ˈmelən/	
/bm/	*submit* /səbˈmɪt/	*grab more* /ˈɡræb ˈmor/	
/tn/	*witness* /ˈwɪtnəs/	*got none* /ˈɡɑt ˈnən/	
/dn/	*kidney* /ˈkɪdni/	*good news* /ˈɡʊd ˈnuz/	

Nasal release often results in syllabic /n/ in unstressed syllables (see Section 8.2.2). Syllabic /m/ and /ŋ/ only occur in such contexts as the result of assimilation (see Section 12.3.1).

[tn̩]	*button* [ˈbɔtn̩]	*cotton* [ˈkɑtn̩]	*eaten* [ˈitn̩]
[dn̩]	*hidden* [ˈhɪdn̩]	*sudden* [ˈsədn̩]	*wooden* [ˈwʊdn̩]

2.10 Lateral release

A similar process to nasal release occurs when /l/ follows /t/ or /d/. It's possible to go from the /t d/ position to the /l/ position simply by lowering one or both sides of the tongue, this being the only difference in the articulation of the sounds. This is called **lateral release**.

/tl/	*atlas* /ˈætləs/	*at least* /ət ˈlist/
/dl/	*badly* /ˈbædli/	*bad luck* /ˈbæd ˈlək/

Lateral release often results in syllabic /l/ (see Sections 2.26 and 8.2.1).

[tl̩]	*bottle* [ˈbɑtl̩]	*total* [ˈtoʊtl̩]	*crystal* [ˈkrɪstl̩]
[dl̩]	*idol* [ˈaɪdl̩]	*model* [ˈmɑdl̩]	*cradle* [ˈkreɪdl̩]

When the non-alveolar plosives, bilabial /p b/ and velar /k g/, are followed by /l/, **lateral escape** occurs. This means that the tongue-tip contact for /l/ is in place during the hold stage of the bilabial and velar plosives, and when they are released, the pent-up air in the vocal tract travels around the side(s) of this obstruction.

/pl/	*topless* /ˈtɑpləs/	*stop lying* /ˈstɑp ˈlaɪɪŋ/
/bl/	*public* /ˈpəblɪk/	*grab lunch* /ˈgræb ˈlənʧ/
/kl/	*backlash* /ˈbæklæʃ/	*thick legs* /ˈθɪk ˈlɛgz/
/gl/	*burglar* /ˈbərglər/	*big lights* /ˈbɪg ˈlaɪts/

Lateral escape also often results in syllabic /l/ (see Sections 2.26 and 8.2.1).

[pl̩]	*apple* [ˈæpl̩]	*pupil* [ˈpjupl̩]	*simple* [ˈsɪmpl̩]
[bl̩]	*double* [ˈdəbl̩]	*label* [ˈleɪbl̩]	*verbal* [ˈvərbl̩]
[kl̩]	*tackle* [ˈtækl̩]	*local* [ˈloʊkl̩]	*rascal* [ˈræskl̩]
[gl̩]	*eagle* [ˈigl̩]	*legal* [ˈligl̩]	*single* [ˈsɪŋgl̩]

2.11 Stop sequences

When two identical plosives occur in sequence, the first isn't usually released. Instead, the sequence is realized as a single long plosive consisting of an approach stage followed by a long hold stage and then a release stage:

/pp/	*ripe pear* /ˈraɪp ˈpɛr/	/bb/	*grab both* /ˈgræb ˈboʊθ/
/tt/	*get two* /ˈgɛt ˈtu/	/dd/	*red door* /ˈrɛd ˈdor/
/kk/	*black car* /ˈblæk ˈkɑr/	/gg/	*big guy* /ˈbɪg ˈgaɪ/

As in the case of two identical plosives, the first plosive is also usually unreleased when the plosives have the same place of articulation but differ in voicing:

/pb/	stop by /ˈstɑp ˈbaɪ/	/bp/	rob people /ˈrɑb ˈpipl̩/
/td/	hot dinner /ˈhɑt ˈdɪnər/	/dt/	red tie /ˈrɛd ˈtaɪ/
/kg/	black gown /ˈblæk ˈgaʊn/	/gk/	big cat /ˈbɪg ˈkæt/

When plosives occur in sequence at different places of articulation, the closure for the second plosive is made before the closure for the first plosive is released. Consequently, the release of the first plosive is **inaudible** because a closure has already been made further forward in the mouth or because a closure further back in the mouth holds back the compressed air.

Second plosive further forward than first plosive:

/tp/	that part /ˈðæt ˈpɑrt/	/tb/	what beach /ˈwɑt ˈbitʃ/
/dp/	bad place /ˈbæd ˈpleɪs/	/db/	good boy /ˈgʊd ˈbɔɪ/
/kp/	black pony /ˈblæk ˈpoʊni/	/kb/	thick book /ˈθɪk ˈbʊk/
/gp/	big picture /ˈbɪg ˈpɪktʃər/	/gb/	big bang /ˈbɪg ˈbæŋ/
/kt/	lack time /ˈlæk ˈtaɪm/	/kd/	back door /ˈbæk ˈdor/
/gt/	big tip /ˈbɪg ˈtɪp/	/gd/	big dog /ˈbɪg ˈdɑg/

Second plosive further back than first plosive:

/pt/	top team /ˈtɑp ˈtim/	/pd/	strap down /ˈstræp ˈdaʊn/
/bt/	grab two /ˈgræb ˈtu/	/bd/	job done /ˈdʒɑb ˈdən/
/pk/	deep cut /ˈdip ˈkət/	/pg/	cheap gift /ˈtʃip ˈgɪft/
/bk/	drab colors /ˈdræb ˈkələrz/	/bg/	superb garden /suˈpərb ˈgardn̩/
/tk/	what car /ˈwɑt ˈkɑr/	/tg/	that guy /ˈðæt ˈgaɪ/
/dk/	sad case /ˈsæd ˈkeɪs/	/dg/	hard game /ˈhard ˈgeɪm/

When an affricate occurs as the first in a sequence of stops, it is always released. The fricative release stage of affricates is always present, for example:

Sequences of the same affricate:

/tʃtʃ/	rich cheese /ˈrɪtʃ ˈtʃiz/	/dʒdʒ/	large jaw /ˈlardʒ ˈdʒɑ/

Sequences of affricates differing in voicing:

/tʃdʒ/	which job /ˈwɪtʃ ˈdʒɑb/	/dʒtʃ/	large child /ˈlardʒ ˈtʃaɪld/

Sequences of an affricate followed by a plosive:

/tʃp/	much pain /ˈmətʃ ˈpeɪn/	/tʃb/	catch both /ˈkætʃ ˈboʊθ/
/tʃt/	each time /ˈitʃ ˈtaɪm/	/tʃd/	each day /ˈitʃ ˈdeɪ/
/tʃk/	each case /ˈitʃ ˈkeɪs/	/tʃg/	teach grammar /ˈtitʃ ˈgræmər/
/dʒp/	barge past /ˈbardʒ ˈpæst/	/dʒb/	edge back /ˈɛdʒ ˈbæk/
/dʒt/	large team /ˈlardʒ ˈtim/	/dʒd/	charge down /ˈtʃardʒ ˈdaʊn/
/dʒk/	large cuts /ˈlardʒ ˈkəts/	/dʒg/	huge grin /ˈhjudʒ ˈgrɪn/

A number of alternative realizations for the first member of a stop sequence are possible:

1   When the first stop is voiceless (i.e., /p t k ʧ/), it can undergo glottal reinforcement (see Section 2.7.3).
2   When the first stop is an alveolar plosive (i.e., /t/ or /d/), it can undergo assimilation (see Section 12.3.1), in which case /tp tb dp db/ and /tk tg dk dg/ become /pp pb bp bb/ and /kk kg gk gg/ respectively.
3   When the first stop is /t/, it can undergo glottal replacement (see Section 2.7.2), /tp tb tk tg/ becoming [ʔp ʔb ʔk ʔg].

In all three cases, the first plosive is unreleased or inaudibly released.

2.12 Affricates

So far, as is usual in phonetics textbooks, we have been using the term *affricate* a little imprecisely. There's a distinction between **phonetic affricates** and **phonemic affricates** that we should bear in mind. Phonetically, an affricate is a sound that consists of a complete closure followed by **homorganic** friction. Accordingly, English /ʧ/ and /dʒ/ are phonetic affricates because both the stop element and the fricative element are palato-alveolar. But by our definition, the alveolar sequences /ts dz/ (as in *cats*, *kids*) are also phonetic affricates. The reason we consider /ʧ/ and /dʒ/ to be phonemic as well as phonetic affricates is that they behave as single, indivisible units in the English sound system and are felt to be single sounds by native speakers. /ts dz/, in contrast, behave like sequences and are felt to be sequences by natives.

Another pair of non-phonemic phonetic affricates is formed when /r/ follows /t/ or /d/. The closure for the /t/ or /d/ is post-alveolar in anticipation of the following /r/ (see Figure 2.11), and the release into the position for /r/ results in homorganic friction. The acoustic effect of /tr/ and /dr/ is similar to that of /ʧ/ and /dʒ/, but the two sets of sounds remain distinct: *chain* /ʧeɪn/ vs. *train* /treɪn/, *Jane* /dʒeɪn/ vs. *drain* /dreɪn/.

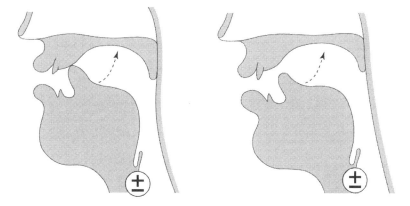

Figure 2.11 English post-alveolar (phonetic) affricates /tr/ and /dr/ [tɹ, dɹ] as in *train*, *drain*; the arrow indicates the raising of the sides of the tongue toward the back teeth

2.13 Fricatives

English has four pairs of voiceless and voiced fricatives at the labio-dental, dental, alveolar, and palato-alveolar places of articulation and a single voiceless glottal fricative.

- For /f/ and /v/, the lower lip lightly touches the upper incisors, and the airstream is forced through the gap (see Figure 2.12).
- For /θ/ and /ð/, the sides of the tongue form a seal against the side teeth, and the airstream is forced through a gap between the tongue tip and the rear of the upper incisors (see Figure 2.13). For some speakers, the articulation of /θ ð/ is interdental, i.e., made with the tongue tip projecting a little between the upper and lower incisors.
- For /s/ and /z/, the airstream is forced through a gap between the tongue tip/blade and the alveolar ridge, while the sides of the tongue form a seal against the upper side teeth (see Figure 2.14).
- For /ʃ/ and /ʒ/, the sides of the tongue form a seal against the upper side teeth, forcing the airstream through a narrow gap between the tongue tip/blade and the alveolar ridge and between the front of the tongue and the hard palate (see Figure 2.15).

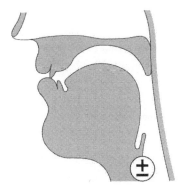

Figure 2.12 English fricatives /f/ and /v/

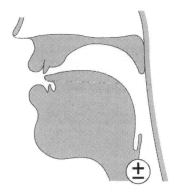

Figure 2.13 English fricatives /θ/ and /ð/

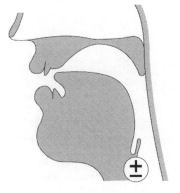

Figure 2.14 English fricatives /s/ and /z/

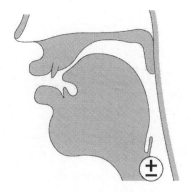

Figure 2.15 English fricatives /ʃ/ and /ʒ/

The primary articulation is accompanied by a simultaneous secondary articulation: rounding and protrusion of the lips.

•   For /h/, the airstream is forced through the vocal tract with stronger than usual pressure, resulting in friction throughout the vocal tract and particularly at the narrowest point – the **glottis**, the space between the open vocal folds.

Each fricative is accompanied by the raising of the soft palate, forming a velic closure blocking the entrance to the nasal cavity.

2.14 Sibilants

Fricatives can be divided into the sub-classes of **sibilant** fricatives /s z ʃ ʒ/ and **non-sibilant** fricatives /f v θ ð h/. The tongue assumes a longitudinal **grooved** shape for sibilants (see Figure 2.16) and a flatter shape for non-sibilants. Grooving of the tongue channels the airstream into a jet that becomes turbulent and noisy when it strikes an obstruction further forward in the mouth – the teeth. In the case of non-sibilant fricatives, the turbulence and noise is generated at the stricture itself. The jet-of-air method of producing noisy turbulence is more effective than simple narrowing of the articulators, and hence sibilants are noticeably louder than non-sibilant fricatives. In the case of the English voiced non-sibilants, /v/ and /ð/, there's often very little fricative noise, and the difference between them and their approximant equivalents can be very slight.

2.15 /h/

During the articulation of /h/, the vocal tract assumes the position for the following sound, usually a vowel, which gives /h/ the quality of a voiceless or fricative version of the following sound. Thus, when isolated, the /h/ in *heart* is noticeably different from the /h/ in *hit*, the first having the quality of [ɑ] and the second of [ɪ]. In the case of a following /j/, as in *huge*, the /h/ is usually [ç], a voiceless palatal fricative. Fricative realizations of /h/ are also sometimes heard before back vowels – pharyngeal before /ɑ/ (e.g., *hot*), uvular before [o] (e.g., *horse*), or velar before /u/ (e.g., *whose*).

    Between vowels, as in *ahead* or *a house*, a voiced glottal fricative [ɦ] is a common, but not obligatory, realization. The [ɦ] articulation involves a brief period of **breathy voice**, where the vibrating vocal folds do not fully come together as they vibrate, allowing air to escape between them and resulting in a "breathy" quality.

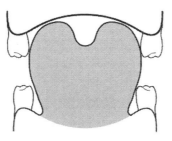

Figure 2.16 Mouth viewed from front showing grooved tongue shape for sibilants

2.16 Distribution of fricatives

Some of the fricatives are restricted in their distribution. /h/ only appears in syllable onsets before vowels (e.g., *hot*, *who*, *home*) or /j/ (e.g., *human*, *hue*), but not in syllable codas. /ʒ/ mainly occurs medially (e.g., *treasure*, *pleasure*, *vision*), being found initially and finally only in relatively recent loanwords (e.g., *genre*, *camouflage*), which often have alternative variants with /dʒ/.

2.17 Nasals

English has three nasals, all voiced, at the bilabial, alveolar, and velar places of articulation:

- For /m/, the lips come together and form a complete closure while the soft palate lowers to allow air to exit via the nose (Figure 2.17).
- For /n/, a complete closure is formed in the oral cavity by the tip of the tongue against the alveolar ridge and by the sides of the tongue against the upper side teeth. Simultaneously, the soft palate is lowered, allowing air to escape via the nose (Figure 2.18).
- For /ŋ/, the back of the tongue forms a closure against the soft palate, and the rear of the sides of the tongue form a seal against the rear upper side teeth. The soft palate is in the lowered position, allowing air to exit via the nose (Figure 2.19).

Note that these three articulations are the same as those for the bilabial /p b/, alveolar /t d/, and velar /k g/ plosives, only differing in the position of the soft palate – raised for plosives, lowered for nasals.

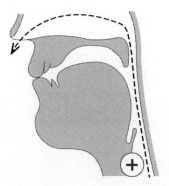

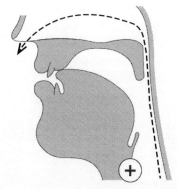

Figure 2.17 English nasal /m/; the arrow indicates the escape of the airstream through the nose

Figure 2.18 English nasal /n/; the arrow indicates the escape of the airstream through the nose

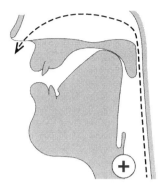

Figure 2.19 English nasal /ŋ/; the arrow indicates the escape of the airstream through the nose

2.18 Distribution of nasals

Historically, the voiced plosives /b/ and /g/ have been lost from the word-final clusters /mb/ and /ŋg/. The only voiced plosive that can occur word-finally after a nasal is /d/. All three *voiceless* plosives /p t k/, however, can occur in this position:

Bilabial /p b/:	*lump* /ləmp/	*comb* /koʊm/
Alveolar /t d/:	*count* /kaʊnt/	*hand* /hænd/
Velar /k g/:	*link* /lɪŋk/	*ring* /rɪŋ/

The preceding examples also demonstrate that within a morpheme, nasal + plosive clusters must be homorganic (i.e., have the same place of articulation). The bilabial nasal /m/ is followed by the bilabial plosive /p/, the alveolar nasal /n/ is followed by the alveolar plosives /t d/, and the velar nasal /ŋ/ is followed by the velar plosive /k/. Across a morpheme boundary, however, sequences of a nasal and a following plosive do not have to be homorganic:

Bilabial /m/ + alveolar /t d/:	*timetable* /ˈtaɪmteɪbl̩/	*someday* /ˈsəmdeɪ/
Bilabial /m/ + velar /k g/:	*tomcat* /ˈtɑmkæt/	*homegrown* /hoʊmˈgroʊn/
*Alveolar /n/ + bilabial /p b/:	*pinpoint* /ˈpɪnpɔɪnt/	*sunbed* /ˈsʌnbɛd/
*Alveolar /n/ + velar /k g/:	*springclean* /sprɪŋˈklin/	*wineglass* /ˈwaɪnglæs/
Velar /ŋ/ + bilabial /p b/:	*gangplank* /ˈgæŋplæŋk/	*songbird* /ˈsɑŋbərd/
Velar /ŋ/ + alveolar /t d/:	*Washington* /ˈwɑʃɪŋtən/	*kingdom* /ˈkɪŋdəm/

(*Note that /n/ is likely to assimilate when followed by /p b/ or /k g/; see Section 12.3.1.)

In the examples given here, although the nasal + plosive sequences are within a single word (often a compound word), they are separated by a syllable boundary, making them sequences, not true clusters (see Section 10.1). However, when verbs ending in /m/ or /n/ have their regular past/past participle form, they are followed by /d/, forming clusters, /md/ and /ŋd/, within the same syllable:

/md/:	*blamed* /bleɪmd/, *formed* /fɔrmd/, *harmed* /hɑrmd/, *named* /neɪmd/
/ŋd/:	*banged* /bæŋd/, *belonged* /bəˈlɑŋd/, *thronged* /θrɑŋd/, *wronged* /rɑŋd/

The velar nasal /ŋ/ is restricted to syllable-coda position (e.g., *sing* /sɪŋ/, *sink* /sɪŋk/) and occurs word-finally through the historical loss of /g/ from /ŋg/ at the end of words. When a suffix is added to a word ending in /ŋ/, the pronunciation remains /g/-less even though it's now in word-medial position: *ring* /rɪŋ/, *ringing* /ˈrɪŋɪŋ/; *hang* /hæŋ/, *hanger* /ˈhæŋər/; and so on. This leads to the generalization that word-medially, /ŋ/ is found at the end of morphemes (e.g., *singer*, *hanging*) and /ŋg/ within morphemes (e.g., *finger*, *angry*, *angle*, *bongo*) because in the latter words, /ŋg/ was never word-final, and therefore, /g/ was never lost. Exceptions to this rule are the words *long*, *young*, and *strong* in their comparative and superlative forms, which retain the historical /g/ lost elsewhere:

long /laŋ/	But	*longer* /ˈlaŋgər/	*longest* /ˈlaŋgəst/
young /jəŋ/	But	*younger* /ˈjəŋgər/	*youngest* /ˈjəŋgəst/
strong /straŋ/	But	*stronger* /ˈstraŋgər/	*strongest* /ˈstraŋgəst/

2.19 Syllabic nasals

The syllables /əm/, /ən/, and /əŋ/ can in certain circumstances (see Section 8.2) be realized as the syllabic consonants [m̩], [n̩], and [ŋ̩], meaning that the schwa /ə/ isn't articulated, and the nasal becomes the nucleus of the syllable (see Section 1.5). Of the three nasals, however, syllabic /n/ is much more common than the other two (see Section 8.2.2), and syllabic /ŋ/ only occurs as a result of assimilation (see Section 12.3.1). Syllabic consonants are very common in GA but not completely obligatory.

[m̩]	*chasm* /ˈkæzm̩/	*a dozen miles* /ə ˈdəzm̩ ˈmaɪlz/
[n̩]	*reason* /ˈrizn̩/	*a dozen nights* /ə ˈdəzn̩ ˈnaɪts/
[ŋ̩]	*taken* /ˈteɪkŋ̩/	*a dozen cats* /ə ˈdəzŋ̩ ˈkæts/

2.20 Approximants

English has four approximants, all voiced, at the alveolar, post-alveolar, palatal, and labial-velar places of articulation:

- For /l/, the tongue tip touches the alveolar ridge, while one or both of the sides of the tongue remain lowered, not making a seal with the side teeth and allowing air to flow around the tongue-tip contact (see Figure 2.20).
- For /r/, the tongue blade and front hollow while the tongue-tip curls slightly upward toward the rear part of the alveolar ridge (see Figure 2.21). The lips are often weakly rounded.
- For /j/, the front of the tongue moves toward the hard palate (see Figure 2.22).
- For /w/, the back of the tongue moves toward the soft palate and the lips round (see Figure 2.23).

Each approximant is accompanied by the raising of the soft palate, forming a velic closure blocking the entrance to the nasal cavity.

The double place name **labial-velar** reflects the fact that /w/ is a **double articulation** (i.e., one that involves two simultaneous articulations of equal degree – labial and velar approximants).

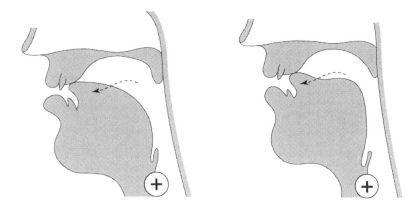

Figure 2.20 Alveolar lateral approximant /l/; left: clear /l/; right: dark /l/ showing velar-ized tongue shape; arrows indicate passage of airstream along lowered sides of tongue

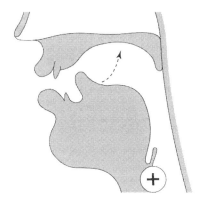

Figure 2.21 English /r/ (post-alveolar approximant); arrow indicates raising of sides of tongue toward back teeth

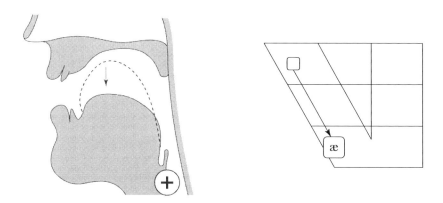

Figure 2.22 English /j/: sequence /jæ/ as in *yak*; diagram shows approximate change in tongue shape; since /j/ is a semi-vowel, it can be indicated on a vowel diagram

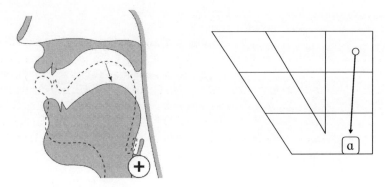

Figure 2.23 English /w/: sequence /wɑ/ as in *wasp*; diagram shows approximate change in tongue shape; since /w/ is a semi-vowel, it can be indicated on a vowel diagram

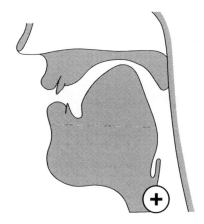

Figure 2.24 English /r/: bunched /r/

The approximants, like the nasals (and vowels), are sonorants and do not undergo the kind of devoicing that obstruents are subject to when adjacent to voiceless consonants or pauses. However, when preceded by an aspirated voiceless plosive, the aspiration takes place during the articulation of the approximant and partially or completely devoices it while the increased airflow through the approximant stricture causes friction (see Section 2.6).

2.21 Bunched /r/

So far, we have described the most common articulation of /r/, with the tongue-tip curling up toward the rear of the alveolar ridge. However, there is another relatively common way of articulating /r/ in GA, referred to as **bunched /r/**. The center of the tongue is raised (i.e., "bunched up") toward the area where the hard palate meets the soft palate (see Figure 2.24). As with the tongue-tip variant of /r/, the lips are usually weakly rounded.

2.22 Distribution of /r/: rhoticity

GA is an example of a **rhotic** accent. This means that it has retained /r/ in positions in which it has been lost in some other accents. GA has /r/ in words like *far* /fɑr/ and *farm* /fɑrm/, while **non-rhotic** accents have no /r/ in these words because historically they have lost /r/ at the ends of words and before consonants. To put it another way, in non-rhotic accents, /r/ only occurs before a vowel (i.e., in words like *red*, *bring*, *carry*, and *attract*). Scottish and Irish accents are usually rhotic, while the General British accent and nearly all the accents of Australia, New Zealand, and South Africa are non-rhotic. General American is rhotic, but the accents of New England and the American South are often non-rhotic.

2.23 Syllabic /r/

To foreign learners and speakers of other English accents, the /r/ phoneme stands out as being very characteristic of the GA accent. This is not only because GA is a rhotic accent or because the GA /r/ is an approximant (unlike the tapped or trilled /r/ of many other languages) but also because of its effect on preceding vowels, which tend to become partially r-colored in anticipation of a following /r/; see Section 5.7.2. When the preceding vowel is schwa /ə/, the whole vowel is r-colored and the phonemic sequence /ər/ is realized phonetically as [ɚ], which is known as "schwar," a very common sound in GA. An r-colored schwa [ɚ] is essentially the same as [ɹ] forming the nucleus of a syllable, and we could, therefore, analyze schwar as syllabic /r/ if we wished and transcribe *murmur*, *nurture*, and *cursor* as /ˈmr̩mr̩/, /ˈnr̩tʃr̩/, and /ˈkr̩sr̩/ instead of /ˈmərmər/, /ˈnərtʃər/, and /ˈkərsər/, but such transcriptions without vowels are difficult to read and using them systematically can be confusing to learners, so we don't use such an approach in this book. Note also that the distribution of schwar is different from the other syllabic consonants (see Section 8.2) because they only occur in unstressed syllables while schwar, as our examples demonstrate, is common in both stressed and unstressed syllables.

2.24 Median and lateral approximants

The approximants can be divided into **lateral** (/l/) and **median** approximants (/r j w/). As the names suggest, the airstream flows to the side of an obstruction for lateral approximants and along the midline of the oral cavity for the median approximants. You can test this by putting your tongue in the position for /l/ and breathing in deeply. You'll notice that one or both sides of your tongue feel cold because of the lateral airflow. Since /l/ is the only lateral approximant, it's often simply called a "lateral," and since all other English approximants are median, the label "median" isn't usually included for them.

2.25 Velarized /l/

Since only tongue-tip contact with the alveolar ridge is necessary for the articulation of /l/, the rest of the tongue, a very flexible articulator, is able to take up a range of different shapes. Different languages and different accents of English have different habits regarding the position of the body of the tongue during the articulation of /l/. Sometimes, the tongue shape is relatively neutral, rather flat (see Figure 2.20, left) or merely anticipates the position of a following vowel. Sometimes the front of the tongue is raised toward the hard palate, creating a **palatalized** [l] or the back of the tongue is raised toward the soft palate (the velum), creating a **velarized** [l] (see Figure 2.20, right). In some languages, velarized or palatalized [l] contrasts phonemically with non-velarized or non-palatalized [l], the two sounds counting as different phonemes. In other languages or accents, different varieties of [l] occur in different phonetic contexts and count as variants of the same /l/ phoneme. In GA, the tendency is for /l/ to be velarized in all positions, especially at the end of words (e.g., in *hill*, *doll*, and so on) and before consonants (e.g., in *help*, *build*, and so on). Velarization and palatalization are types of secondary articulation (see Section 2.2.4). Velarized /l/ is also known as **dark /l/** and has the IPA symbol [ɫ], while non-velarized /l/ is often referred to as **clear /l/**.

2.26 Syllabic /l/

The syllable /əl/ is very often realized as syllabic /l/ (i.e., [l̩] (see Section 8.2.1)). The articulators move directly from the preceding consonant to /l/, the schwa /ə/ isn't articulated, and the /l/ becomes the nucleus of the syllable. Syllabic /l/ is the most common syllabic consonant in GA, occurring in a greater range of contexts than syllabic /n/.

Syllabic /l/:   *people* [ˈpipl̩], *devil* [ˈdɛvl̩], *satchel* [ˈsætʃl̩], *camel* [ˈkæml̩], *giggle* [ˈgɪgl̩]

2.27 Semi-vowels

Another way of grouping the approximants is according to the part of the tongue involved in their articulation, giving the terms **semi-vowel** (/j/ and /w/) and **non-semi-vowel** (/l/ and /r/). The semi-vowels are articulated with the part of the tongue that is used to articulate vowels – the front, center, and back. The position for /j/ and /w/ are the same as for the [i] and [u] vowels respectively. [j] and [i] both consist of an approximation of the front of the tongue to the hard palate, and [w] and [u] both consist of an approximation of the back of the tongue to the soft palate accompanied by simultaneous lip-rounding. Thus, [j] and [w] are glides from these vowel positions to a vowel of longer duration. The non-semi-vowels /l/ and /r/ involve the tip and blade of the tongue, which are not used in the articulation of vowels.

2.28 Distribution of approximants

The semi-vowels /j/ and /w/ only occur in syllable onsets in English (e.g., *young* /jəŋ/, *unit* /ˈjunət/, *few* /fju/, *one* /wən/, *wax* /wæks/, *twin* /twɪn/). Learners from other language backgrounds may feel that /j/ and /w/ can also occur in syllable codas, but in English, such non-onset glides toward the [i] and [u] positions are best analyzed as part of the syllable nucleus, forming diphthongs (see Section 5.5):

FACE:	*cake* /keɪk/	*sail* /seɪl/	*day* /deɪ/
PRICE:	*like* /laɪk/	*ride* /raɪd/	*try* /traɪ/
CHOICE:	*voice* /vɔɪs/	*coin* /kɔɪn/	*boy* /bɔɪ/
GOAT:	*oak* /oʊk/	*rose* /roʊz/	*no* /noʊ/
MOUTH:	*shout* /ʃaʊt/	*clown* /klaʊn/	*plow* /plaʊ/

The lateral approximant /l/ occurs in both syllable onsets and codas, and since GA is a rhotic accent (see Section 5.7), /r/ also occurs freely in these positions.

2.29 Yod-dropping

We've seen that /j/ only occurs in syllable onsets, but even in onsets, /j/ tends to be lost after certain consonants in stressed syllable-initial positions. This phenomenon is known as **yod-dropping**, "yod" being a name for the palatal approximant [j]. Historically, /j/ occurred with /u/ in words, where /u/ has a spelling that includes <u> or <w>, but has been lost after palato-alveolar consonants:

/ʃ tʃ dʒ/:   chute /ʃut/, chew /tʃu/, juice /dʒus/

After approximants:

/r l/:   rude /rud/, blue /blu/, crew /kru/, lute /lut/, allude /əˈlud/

And after alveolar and dental fricatives:

/s z θ/:   suit /sut/, assume /əˈsum/, /z/ presume /prəˈzum/, enthusiasm /ɪnˈθuziæzm̩/

Most GA speakers, in contrast to speakers of some other English accents, have also lost /j/ after alveolar plosives and the alveolar nasal:

/t d n/:   tune /tun/, duke /duk/, news /nuz/

After the remaining consonants, /j/ is retained (i.e., after labio-dentals, bilabials, velars, and /h/):

/f v/:   few /fju/, fuse /fjuz/, feud /fjud/, view /vju/
/p b/:   pew /pju/, puny /pjuni/, putrid /ˈpjutrəd/, beauty /ˈbjuti/, abuse /əˈbjus/
/k g/:   cute /kjut/, cue /kju/, accuse /əˈkjuz/, argue /ˈɑrgju/, legume /ˈlɛgjum/
/h/:   human /ˈhjumən/, huge /hjudʒ/, hew /hju/

In the case of the /hj/ cluster, the /h/ is sometimes dropped by GA speakers, giving *human* /ˈjumən/, *huge* /judʒ/, and so on. It is not necessary for learners to imitate this, however.

Immediately following a stressed syllable, /j/ is retained after /n l/ and variable after /r/, while /tj dj sj zj/ have coalesced over time to yield /tʃ dʒ ʃ ʒ/ respectively. The original /u/ has sometimes been replaced by schwa /ə/, which is typical of unstressed vowels in English.

/n l/:   venue /ˈvɛnju/, annual /ˈænjuəl/, value /ˈvælju/, volume /ˈvɑljum/
/r/:   erudite /ˈɛrədaɪt/ or /ˈɛrjədaɪt/, virulent /ˈvirələnt/ or /ˈvirjələnt/
/tj dj sj zj/:   statue /ˈstætʃu/, module /ˈmɑdʒul/, issue /ˈɪʃu/, visual /ˈvɪʒuəl/

2.30 Inflections

The pronunciation of the **-s** suffix (ending), occurring in plurals (e.g., *cats*), third person present tense endings (e.g., *thinks*), and possessives (e.g., *John's*), is determined by the preceding sound. It's pronounced /əz/ following sibilants, /s/ following all other voiceless consonants, and /z/ following all other voiced sounds:

/əz/:	*buses, Alice's, seizes, Rose's, wishes, churches, catches, judges, George's, camouflages*
/s/:	*stops, lips, hats, Pete's, thinks, Mike's, laughs, Jeff's, myths, Beth's*
/z/:	*Bob's, needs, bags, leaves, breathes, seems, Kevin's, things, Jill's, cars, bees, Sue's, bras, ways, Joe's, lies, cows, toys, Hilda's*

The same rule applies in contractions involving auxiliary *has* and *is* (see Sections 8.6.3 and 8.7.2):

has:	*What's happened?* /ˈwɑts ˈhæpənd/, *Mike's left.* /ˈmaɪks ˈlɛft/, *Who's gone.* /ˈhuz ˈgɑn/
is:	*That's good.* /ˈðæts ˈgʊd/, *It's difficult.* /ɪts ˈdɪfəkəlt/, *Where's Pete?* /ˈwɛrz ˈpit/

The pronunciation of the past tense ending -ed (e.g., *talked*) is also governed by the preceding sound. It's pronounced /əd/ following /t/ or /d/, /t/ following all other voiceless consonants, and /d/ following all other voiced sounds, both consonants and vowels:

/əd/:	*waited, needed*
/t/:	*stopped, thanked, watched, laughed, unearthed, kissed, wished*
/d/:	*robbed, begged, judged, saved, breathed, used, seemed, frowned, banged, sailed, starred, played, showed, sighed, allowed, employed*

Note that certain adjectives (e.g., like *crooked, dogged, naked, -legged, wicked*) take the /əd/ ending.

Chapter 3

Practice

Individual consonants

3.1 Stops: practice

The following sections provide practice in pronouncing the English consonants and their various allophones. The exercise material includes the target sounds in different positions in the word or syllable, in words and phrases where they occur multiple times, in sentences, and in dialogues.

3.1.1 Summary of key features

The stops consist of the plosives /p b t d k g/ and affricates /ʧ dʒ/. Their key features are:

1   With the soft palate raised, a closure is formed in the oral cavity and the airstream is blocked completely; see Section 2.5.
2   In the case of affricates, the release stage is obligatory and is slower than that of plosives, resulting in homorganic friction; see Section 2.5.1.
3   The release stage for plosives is variable. It may be absent when a homorganic stop follows, inaudible when a non-homorganic stop follows, nasal when a nasal follows or lateral when /l/ follows; see Sections 2.11, 2.9, and 2.10.
4   Together with fricatives, the stops are obstruents and behave similarly in the following ways:

   a)   they come in voiceless and voiced pairs; see Section 2.4;
   b)   voiced stops are typically devoiced when adjacent to voiceless sounds or a pause and only usually fully voiced between voiced sounds; see Section 2.4.2;
   c)   voiceless stops shorten preceding sonorants (nasals, approximants, and vowels) in the same syllable; see Sections 2.4.1 and 5.6.

5   Aspiration accompanies voiceless plosives /p t k/ at the beginning of stressed syllables. In other contexts, they are weakly aspirated. When preceded by /s/, they are completely unaspirated; see Section 2.6.
6   Approximants following aspirated /p t k/ become devoiced and fricative. They remain voiced when /p t k/ are preceded by /s/ at the beginning of a syllable; see Section 2.6.
7   The voiceless stops /p t k ʧ/ can optionally undergo glottal reinforcement; see Section 2.7.3.
8   /t/ can optionally undergo glottal replacement; see Section 2.7.2.
9   /t/ can be tapped at the end of syllables between sonorants; see Section 2.8.

10   /t/ is often dropped from the /nt/ cluster when it occurs between vowels; see Section 2.8.
11   The sequences /tr/ and /dr/ form phonetic affricates at the post-alveolar place of articulation; see Section 2.12.

3.2 Voiceless bilabial plosive /p/

3.2.1 Description

Voiceless bilabial plosive. With the soft palate raised, the lips come together to form a complete closure, blocking the airflow through the vocal tract. The tongue is free to anticipate the position of a following consonant or vowel.

3.2.2 Spelling

<p> pay, apart, space, stop
<pp> happy, puppy, stopped
Note that <p> is silent in certain words, e.g., coup, corps, cupboard, raspberry, receipt, pneumonia, pneumatic, psychology, psychological, psychiatrist, psychotic, pterodactyl, psalm, pseudo.

3.2.3 Aspirated

a) Stressed syllable-initial

pack, page, paint, pale, pan, park, part, pass, pat, path, paw, pay, pea, peace, peach, peak, peg, pen, pick, pie, piece, pig, pile, pill, pin, pinch, pine, pink, pint, pit, point, pole, pond, pool, port, post, pot, pound, pour, pull, punch, purse, push, put; apart, apology, appear, disappoint, opinion, repeat, report, superb, suppose

b) Before /r/, /l/, and /j/

precious, press, pretty, price, pride, print, prize, problem, profit, promise, proof, proper, practice; place, plan, planet, plank, plant, plaster, plastic, plate, play, pleasant, please, pleasure, plenty, plot, plow, plug, plum, plumber, plural, plus; pew, pewter, puny, pupil, pure, putrid

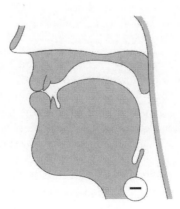

Figure 3.1 English /p/ (hold stage)

3.2.4 Unaspirated or weakly aspirated

a) Syllable-final (potential pre-glottalization)

cap, cheap, chip, chop, clap, cope, cup, deep, dip, gap, grape, grip, group, heap, hip, hoop, hop, hope, keep, lap, leap, lip, loop, map, mop, ripe, rope, shape, sharp, sheep, ship, shop, sip, skip, slap, sleep, slip, slope, snap, soap, soup, steep, swap, tap, tip, top, type, up, weep, whip, wipe, wrap

b) Syllable-final, word-medial (never pre-glottalized)

capital, carpenter, carpet, copper, copy, happy, leopard, open, rapid, stupid, super, supper, topic, typical

c) Unaspirated after /s/: /sp/, /spr/, /spl/, /spj/

space, spare, spark, speak, spear, special, speech, speed, spell, spend, spice, spill, spin, spinach, spine, spirit, spit, spite, spoil, sponge, spoon, sport, spot, spy; sprain, sprawl, spray, spread, spring, sprinkle, sprint, sprout; splash, spleen, splendid, splice, splinter, split, splutter; spew, spurious

d) Unstressed syllable-initial

particular, pathetic, patrol, peculiar, percent, perform, persist, police, polite, position, potato, precise, predict, prefer, protect, provide

3.2.5 Multiple

pamper, paper, parsnip, pauper, peep, people, pepper, perhaps, pickpocket, pimple, pineapple, pipe, plump, pompous, poppy, popular, prepare, proper, pump, pupil, puppy, purple, purpose

3.2.6 Phrases

a profound apology, keeping up appearances, apple pie, bumper to bumper, an Olympic champion, a pork chop, a paper clip, a copper pipe, a spare copy, a happy couple, a piece of gossip, purple grapes, an appeal for help, a paper napkin, pots and pans, wrapping paper, post a parcel, spare parts, a surprise party, pea soup, peer pressure, a sharp pencil, sleeping pills, a police report, an opinion poll, proof of purchase, a jump rope, a slippery slope, a picnic spot, step by step, a shopping trip, paint stripper, scrap paper

3.2.7 Sentences I

(1) Pass me the pepper please, Paul. (2) She wrapped his present in purple paper. (3) Pauline's performance is just past its prime. (4) Patricia put a piece of apple pie on the plate. (5) The patient proved to be susceptible to hypnosis. (6) This place specializes in maps, posters, and prints. (7) They weren't prepared to compromise their principles. (8) Percy's completely dependent on his parents for support. (9) He played an important part in shaping European policies. (10) Patrick adopted a pragmatic approach to this complex topic.

Sentences 2

(1) She couldn't appreciate the deeper implications of the poem. (2) They took precautionary steps to prevent the spread of polio. (3) Pete stopped punching to avoid crippling his sparring partner. (4) The most important passage in the pamphlet is the opening paragraph. (5) After he'd dropped off the Polish passengers, he picked up the Portuguese. (6) Particular groups are disproportionately represented among the poor population. (7) She was disappointed that her patient experienced post-operative complications. (8) The press put a positive spin on the pessimistic report that appeared in September. (9) Philip gave an inspiring PowerPoint presentation on how to prepare a paper for publication. (10) He's keeping his options open, hoping that unexpected opportunities might present themselves.

3.2.8 Dialogue

A: Perhaps Peter could propose a plan.
B: But all Peter's previous plans have been completely preposterous.
A: Stop picking on poor Peter. He can't help pitching peculiar proposals.
B: I suppose so. But please oppose any project involving leopards, pumas, pandas, or puppies.
A: Yes, Peter needed police protection after the last episode!

3.3 Voiced bilabial plosive /b/

3.3.1 Description

Voiced bilabial plosive /b/. With the soft palate raised, the lips come together to form a complete closure, blocking the airflow through the vocal tract. The tongue is free to anticipate the position of a following consonant or vowel.

3.3.2 Spelling

<b> back, sober, verb
<bb> rabbit, robber

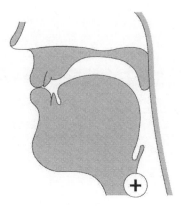

Figure 3.2 English /b/ (hold stage)

<b> is silent in certain words (e.g., *debt, doubt, subtle*) and also in inflected forms (e.g., *debtor, doubtful*). Note in particular silent <b> in final <mb> (e.g., *aplomb, bomb, climb, comb, crumb, dumb, lamb, limb, numb, plumb, succumb, thumb, tomb, womb*) and derived forms (e.g., *bomber, climber, dumbest, plumbing*). Otherwise, medial <mb> is pronounced (e.g., *amber, limbo, lumber, timber*).

3.3.3 Word-initial

back, bad, badge, bag, bake, bald, ball, band, bang, bank, bar, barn, bat, bath, bay, beach, bead, beak, bean, beard, beat, bed, bee, beef, beer, beg, bell, belt, bench, bend, best, bet, big, bike, bin, bird, bit, bite, board, boast, boat, boil, bone, book, boot, boss, both, bounce, box, boy, bull, bump, bunch, burn, bush, buy

3.3.4 Word-medial

above, abroad, acrobat, alphabet, cabbage, cabin, cucumber, cupboard, debate, exhibition, habit, harbor, hobby, labor, neighbor, orbit, rabbit, ribbon, robber, robot, rubber, sober, tobacco, tribute

3.3.5 Word-final

globe, grab, herb, jab, job, curb, knob, mob, probe, proverb, pub, robe, rub, scrub, shrub, slab, snob, sob, stab, superb, tab, throb, tribe, tub, tube, verb, web

3.3.6 Multiple

absorb, baby, backbone, bamboo, barbecue, barber, bribe, bubble, bumblebee, cobweb, probably, rhubarb, suburb

3.3.7 Phrases

a burning ambition, a baby boy, a bean bag, a bunch of bananas, a brass band, the big bang, a bank robber, a breakfast bar, a beer barrel, back to basics, a baseball bat, bubble bath, a bitter battle, a beautiful beach, amber beads, a bushy beard, bed and breakfast, as blind as a bat, a rubber band, a broken bone, rubber boots, brown bread, bad breath, blood brothers, a book club, a boring job, a double bed, bread and butter

3.3.8 Sentences I

(1) Toby has both brains and brawn. (2) Their baby boy was born in Boston. (3) Bob's blatant fibs are beyond belief. (4) Barbara banged her elbow on the table. (5) Her book was published as a paperback. (6) His labored breathing was barely audible. (7) I believe he broke every bone in his body. (8) My brother's a member of a debating club. (9) Bill's bald but has bushy eyebrows and a beard. (10) Is it possible to borrow albums from the library?

Sentences 2

(1) Phoebe's husband's job is their bread and butter. (2) Abigail was deliberately ambiguous about her birthdate. (3) The rebels were based along the border with Bangladesh. (4) The

bilingual brochures are now available for distribution. (5) Bob and Betty bought a bunga-low in a respectable suburb. (6) The building was beset with problems from the beginning. (7) Rechargeable batteries are better than disposable batteries. (8) He brought the business back from the brink of bankruptcy. (9) Isobel had an unshakeable belief in the importance of personal liberty. (10) The bluebells burst into bloom, and there were bumblebees in the bushes.

3.3.9 Dialogue

A: How's your brother Bob doing in Boston?
B: He's gotten a job brewing beer, and his bank account's getting bigger and bigger.
A: Brewing beer to bring home the bacon? Fabulous!
B: He's been brewing beer since he bought the brewery in Buzzards Bay.

3.4 Voiceless alveolar plosive /t/

3.4.1 Description

Voiceless alveolar plosive. With the soft palate raised, the tip of the tongue forms a closure at the alveolar ridge; the sides of the tongue form a closure against the upper side teeth, block-ing the airflow through the vocal tract. The lips are free to take the position for a following vowel or consonant.

3.4.2 Spelling

<t> tea, waiter, stop, bet
<tt> pretty, letter, bottle
<th> Esther, Thames, Thomas, Thai, thyme
<z, tz, zz> = /ts/ schizophrenia, blitz, chutzpah, spritzer, Ritz, pizza
<ed> in inflections (see Section 2.30) hoped, wished
Note that <t> is silent in <tle> (e.g., *apostle, bristle, bustle, castle, hustle, nestle, rustle, this-tle, whistle, wrestle*) and in <sten> (e.g., *fasten, glisten, listen, moisten, soften*). <t> is also silent in *Christmas* and *mortgage*, and in recent French loans, e.g., *bouquet, ballet, buffet,*

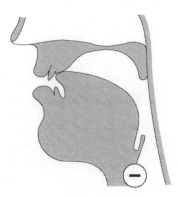

Figure 3.3 English /t/ (hold stage)

cachet, chalet, crochet, depot, sachet, ragout. The word *often* is said both with and without /t/ (even by the same speaker).

3.4.3 Aspirated

a) Stressed syllable-initial

take, tale, tall, tank, tap, tape, task, tax, tea, team, teeth, tell, ten, time, tin, tiny, tip, toe, tongue, tool, tooth, top, torch, touch, tough, tour, toy, tube, tune, turn, type; antique, attack, competition, contain, material, return

b) Before /r/ and /w/

track, trade, traffic, train, trap, tray, treasure, treat, tree, trick, trip, trouble, truck, true, trunk, trust, truth, try, control; between, twang, tweak, tweezers, twelve, twice, twenty, twig, twilight, twin, twinkle, twirl, twist

3.4.4 Word-medial

a) Tapping at the end of a stressed syllable

atom, beautiful, bottom, citizen, city, committee, cottage, creative, critic, duty, exotic, item, lettuce, motto, motive, native, naughty, notice, petty, photo, pity, pretty, quota, satisfy, suitable, vitamin; better, butter, computer, daughter, latter, letter, litter, matter, Saturday, scatter, shatter, slaughter, sweater, utter, waiter, water; battle, bottle, brittle, brutal, cattle, fatal, little, metal, rattle, settle, vital

b) Tapping at the end of an unstressed syllable

ability, anxiety, authority, cavity, charity, community, deputy, dignity, facility, humanity, majority, priority, quality, reality, relative, security, society, variety, vicinity; senator, theater; capital, hospital

c) Tapping after /r/

artist, article, assertive, charter, courtesy, dirty, forty, liberty, mortal, party, portable, reporter, shortage, sporty, thirty

d) Voiceless /t/ vs. tapped /t/

beat/beating, bite/biting, bright/brighter, chat/chatty, cheat/cheater, date/dating, defeat/defeated, delete/deleted, dirt/dirty, eat/eating, flat/flatter, float/floating, forget/forgettable, great/greater, heat/heating, hot/hotter, invite/invited, late/later, meet/meeting, note/notable, port/portable, pot/potty, regret/regrettable, repeat/repeated, seat/seating, short/shorter, shut/shutter, support/supporter, visit/visitor, write/writer

3.4.5 Unaspirated or weakly aspirated

a) Syllable-final (potential pre-glottalization)

bet, boat, cat, coat, court, debt, doubt, flat, flight, float, foot, fruit, gate, hate, heart, height, hurt, hut, kite, knot, late, light, net, night, note, nut, pet, plate, plot, quite, rat, root, sheet, shirt, shout, smart, sort, sweet, thought, weight, wet, white

b) Unaspirated after /s/ (except in /str/)

stab, staff, stage, stain, stamp, stand, star, stare, starve, station, steam, steep, steer, step, stick, stiff, still, stone, stop, store, storm, story, studio, stupid, stuff, disturb; straight, strange, strap, straw, stream, street, stress, stretch, strict, strike, string, stripe, strong, struggle, destroy

c) Unstressed syllable-initial

taboo, tobacco, today, tomato, tomorrow, toward

3.4.6 Multiple /t/ (tapped /t/ underlined)

appetite, architect, assistant, automatic, contact, distant, important, instant, instinct, instrument, intelligent, irritate, protect, start, state, status, street, straight, substitute, tablet, talent, target, taste, tent, test, text, ticket, tight, title, toast, toilet, total, tourist, traitor, treat, trust, twist, attitude, competitor, contributor, gratitude, imitator, integrity, intuitive, motivate, repetitive, spectator, stutter, turtle

3.4.7 Phrases (tapped /t/ underlined)

tight-fisted, a table for two, tall tales, a water tank, tea for two, rotten teeth, a tennis racket, a wet towel, a stray cat, ten minutes late, a photo shoot, sit still, as white as a sheet, an irritating habit, top secret, a return ticket, nuts and bolts, a gentle giant, a subtle hint, test results, a shooting star, caught in a trap, twin sisters, a complete waste of time, an anxiety attack, breathtaking beauty, a bitter taste, a bottle top, a lottery ticket, a metal detector, a flat tire, heartfelt gratitude, a silent letter, a hot-water bottle, static electricity, two left feet, first and foremost, hit the jackpot, a heart of stone, a tower of strength, a sweet tooth, nine times out of ten, salt water, a theater critic, little by little, pretty dirty

3.4.8 Sentences I (tapped /t/ underlined)

(1) Tom's parents taught him the tricks of the trade. (2) The most important titles are printed in italic type. (3) Aunt Tracy bought me a knitted turtleneck sweater. (4) The meeting was a complete and utter waste of time. (5) Peter was determined to get to the root of the matter. (6) Is it true that bottled water tastes better than tap water? (7) Most of the students completed the assignment on time. (8) It turns out he was a secret agent for British intelligence. (9) Victoria told us that she was still waiting for the test results. (10) Ted was not in a fit state to take part in the tennis tournament.

Sentences 2 (tapped /t/ underlined)

(1) I felt just a twinge of guilt as I left her standing on the platform. (2) I was truly grateful to Patrick for taking the trouble to write to me. (3) Apparently, Betty dropped out of university when she was twenty. (4) They fought a bitter battle over the custody of their daughter Natasha. (5) It's difficult to alter the habits of a lifetime without continued support. (6) Visitors can expect to be treated with respect and courtesy by our staff. (7) Efforts are being made to appoint part-time teachers in different subjects. (8) Robert wanted to get an apartment that was within commuting distance of the city center. (9) We rented a beautiful little cottage in the country and invited my twin sister to stay with us. (10) Yesterday, we took our first tentative steps toward establishing contact with potential clients.

3.4.9 Dialogue (tapped /t/ underlined)

A: There are twenty-two letters on the table awaiting your attention.
B: Twenty-two Valentine's cards from twenty-two secret admirers, you meant to say. Tell me how many you got, Tony.
A: I'm not interested in trite platitudes and tacky greeting cards.
B: I'll take that to mean you got exactly twenty-two fewer than I got.

3.5 Voiced alveolar plosive /d/

3.5.1 Description

Voiced alveolar plosive. With the soft palate raised, the tip of the tongue forms a closure at the alveolar ridge; the sides of the tongue form a closure against the upper side teeth, blocking the airflow through the vocal tract. The lips are free to take the position for a following vowel or consonant.

3.5.2 Spelling

<d> day, shadow, mad
<dd> sudden, wedding, address, add

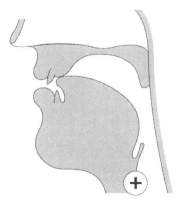

Figure 3.4 English /d/ (hold stage)

3.5.3 Word-initial

damp, dance, dare, dark, dart, date, day, deaf, deal, debt, deep, desk, die, dig, dime, dirt, dish, ditch, dive, do, dog, doll, door, dose, dot, doubt, down, duck, dull, dump, dust

3.5.4 Word-medial

adopt, audition, body, comedy, corridor, edit, freedom, idea, idiom, ladder, lady, melody, murder, powder, predict, product, ready, ridiculous, shadow, spider, study, tradition, widow

3.5.5 Before /r/

draft, drag, drain, draw, dread, dream, dreary, dress, drift, drill, drink, drive, drone, drop, drown, drug, drum, dry

3.5.6 Word-final

add, bad, beard, bed, bird, bread, bride, broad, card, cloud, code, fade, feed, flood, food, glad, good, grade, guard, guide, hard, head, hide, load, loud, mood, mud, need, odd, proud, red, ride, road, sad, seed, shade, side, speed, spread, weed, weird, wide, wood, word

3.5.7 Multiple

daffodil, dead, decide, dedicate, deed, defend, demand, depend, divide

3.5.8 Phrases

an added advantage, sound advice, a reddish beard, a dead body, an ideal candidate, widespread damage, today's date, dead and buried, a good deed, a deep desire, the dish of the day, a bad dream, a drunk driver, from dawn to dusk, food and drink, a stupid idiot, a needle and thread, shoulder blades, the speed of sound, double standards, weird and wonderful, words of wisdom, the good old days

3.5.9 Sentences I

(1) Did it happen by accident or by design? (2) The ducks are paddling like mad around the pond. (3) By Friday, news of the scandal had spread worldwide. (4) The farmhands toiled in the fields from dawn to dusk. (5) My friend's understanding made a world of difference. (6) Richard was an ideal candidate for the board of directors. (7) The gold pendant is studded with diamonds and emeralds. (8) They drove down the dead-end road and then turned around. (9) Linda needed a friendly word of advice to provide some direction. (10) Outdated words and idioms should be excluded from the dictionary.

Sentences 2

(1) Suddenly a deafening sound of thunder could be heard in the distance. (2) These Scandinavian designers deserve credit for daring to be different. (3) The document concluded that

the incident had been handled adequately. (4) I can recommend this comedy if you don't mind suspending your disbelief. (5) Appendix D describes the data and the methodology adopted for this study. (6) They endeavored to remedy the fundamental design defects in the building. (7) My husband ordered the dish of the day, and I had a delicious seafood salad. (8) The doctors admitted that the medical records had been accidentally destroyed. (9) Danny's daughter dreams of spending her birthday in Disney World in Orlando, Florida. (10) The head of the department decided to include on the agenda a discussion of academic freedom.

3.5.10 Dialogue

A: Did Dean do the dishes yesterday?
B: He said he would, but in the end, Fred had to do them.
A: I told you so, didn't I? I said you should definitely doubt Dean's word.
B: I decided to find out for myself, and he indeed proved to be a devious devil and avoided washing the dirty dishes after dinner.

3.6 Voiceless velar plosive /k/

3.6.1 Description

Voiceless velar plosive. The back of the tongue forms a closure against the soft palate, which is raised, and the rear sides of the tongue form a closure against the rear upper side teeth, blocking the airflow through the vocal tract. The lips, tongue tip, blade, and front are free to take the position for a following vowel or consonant.

3.6.2 Spelling

<c> cost, country
<ch> chaos, character, scheme, school, echo, ache; also in derived forms: aching, chaotic, characteristic, and so on
<cc (+a/o/u)> occasion, account, occur
<ck> tricky, back, stick

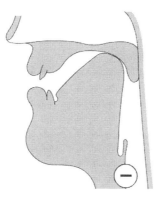

Figure 3.5 English /k/ (hold stage)

<k> keep, awake, speaker, work
<kk> trekking
<qu, cqu> = /kw/ quick, acquaintance
<x> = /ks/ box, fix, suffix
Note that initial <k> is silent in words like *knack, knapsack, knave, knead, knee, kneel, knell, knew, knickers, knife, knight, knit, knob, knock, knot, know, knowledge, knuckle.*

3.6.3 Aspirated

a) Stressed syllable-initial

cab, cake, call, camp, car, card, care, case, catch, cause, coach, coast, code, cold, comb, come, cook, cool, copy, cost, count, course, cow, cup, curl, curse, cut, keen, keep, key, kind, king, kiss, kit; accomplish, accountant, become, education

b) Before /r/, /l/, /j/, and /w/

crab, crack, craft, crash, cream, credit, creep, crime, crisis, critic, cross, crowd, crude, crumb, cry; claim, clap, class, clay, clean, clear, clever, click, client, cliff, clip, clock, cloth, cloud, clover, clown, club, clue; cube, cue, cure, curious, cute; choir, quack, quaint, quality, quantity, quarrel, queen, question, quick, quiet, quilt, quit, quite, quiz, quote

3.6.4 Unaspirated or weakly aspirated

a) Syllable-final (potential pre-glottalization)

back, black, block, book, chalk, check, dark, duck, hike, hook, joke, knock, lake, leak, like, lock, look, luck, make, mark, neck, oak, pack, park, pick, rock, shake, shock, sick, smoke, snake, sneak, soak, sock, speak, stick, take, talk, thick, track, trick, wake, walk, work

b) Syllable-final, word-medial (never pre-glottalized)

baker, broken, bucket, chicken, circus, echo, focus, hockey, jacket, market, packet, second, token, turkey

c) Unaspirated after /s/: /sk/, /skj/, /skw/, and /skr/

discussion, escape, scheme, school, score, skate, sketch, skill, skin, skirt, sky; skew, skewer; squad, squalid, squander, square, squash, squat, squeak, squeeze, squelch, squid, squint, squirrel, squirt; scrape, scratch, scream, screen, screw, scribble, scrounge, scrub

d) Unstressed syllable-initial

canal, canoe, career, casino, cathedral, command, condition, collect, compare, complain, complete, computer, concern, consider, contain

3.6.5 Multiple

academic, acoustic, architect, backache, bookcase, cactus, cake, calculate, character, chemical, classic, click, clinic, clock, coconut, communicate, conclusion, conquer, cook, cork, correct, creak, critic, croak, expect, kick, kiosk, mechanic, picnic, quick, skunk, technique, toxic

3.6.6 Phrases

a close acquaintance, a broken ankle, background music, a bank account, a picnic basket, the black market, a plastic bucket, carrot cake, a wake-up call, a company car, a deck of cards, a magic carpet, a cause for concern, crystal clear, a cuckoo clock, black coffee, a topic for discussion, a quick drink, cause and effect, a close encounter, a quick fix, a clove of garlic, next of kin, a panic attack, a parking ticket, a rescue worker, a fraction of a second, keep a secret, an electric shock

3.6.7 Sentences 1

(1) Michael speaks with a thick Kentucky accent. (2) Frank comes from a working-class background. (3) Kate's cold came complete with a hacking cough. (4) We kept the school equipment under lock and key. (5) Keith was scared he'd panic and go completely blank. (6) We had black coffee and chocolate cake at the corner café. (7) The couple couldn't accept the consequences of their actions. (8) The crying kid came to me for a comforting kiss and a cookie. (9) Christine looked frantically for the ticket in her jacket pocket. (10) Rebecca shook back her dark curls and looked into the camera.

Sentences 2

(1) The seconds ticked by on the clock at the back of the classroom. (2) After a brisk walk, we cuddled up on the couch with a cup of cocoa. (3) The secret of his success is dedication and his incredible work ethic. (4) The experiments were conducted under strictly controlled conditions. (5) Is there a connection between academic skills and workplace productivity? (6) They discussed the security considerations that had to be taken into account. (7) Mark successfully completed his college education without encouragement. (8) There's no justification for the scathing remarks Ken directed at his colleagues. (9) The catalog contains color reproductions of the pictures with accompanying text. (10) There was a complete breakdown in communication between the company and the client.

3.6.8 Dialogue

A: Colin was caught copying chemical equations from a concealed crib sheet during the chemistry exam.

B: Can they kick him out of the course for academic misconduct?

A: He's making excuses, and it looks like he could escape with a warning.

B: He's quite a character, our Colin. He's as cunning as a fox when copying in class and as cool as a cucumber when caught and questioned.

3.7 Voiced velar plosive /g/

3.7.1 Description

Voiced velar plosive. The back of the tongue forms a closure against the soft palate, which is raised, and the rear sides of the tongue form a closure against the rear upper side teeth, blocking the airflow through the vocal tract. The lips, tongue tip, blade, and front are free to take the position for a following vowel or consonant.

3.7.2 Spelling

<g> game, eager, again, dog
<gg> luggage, trigger
<gh> aghast, ghastly, ghost, spaghetti, gherkin, ghetto
<gu, -gue> guard, guide, vague, league (but note *figure* with /gj/: /ˈfɪgjər/)
<x> = /gz/ exact, exam, exaggerate, exist
<xh> = /gz/ exhaust, exhaustion, exhilarate, exhilaration, exhort
<g> + <e/i/y> may either be /g/ or /dʒ/ (e.g., get vs. gel, gift vs. gin, gynecologist vs. gypsy)
Note that <g> is silent in words like *diaphragm, paradigm, phlegm, gnarled, gnaw, gnome, align, assign, benign, campaign, champagne, cologne, design, foreign, reign, resign, sign.*
<gh> = silent in the following words
although, bough, bought, borough, breakthrough, brought, bright, caught, daughter, dough, doughnut, drought, eight, fight, fought, fraught, fright, haughty, height, high, light, might, mighty, naughty, neighbor, night, ought, right, sigh, sight, slaughter, sleigh, sought, straight, taught, thigh, thorough, though, thought, through, weigh, weight

3.7.3 Word-initial

game, gap, gas, gasp, gate, gauge, gaunt, gaze, gear, get, ghost, gift, girl, give, go, goal, goat, gold, golf, good, goose, guard, guess, guest, guide, gum, gun

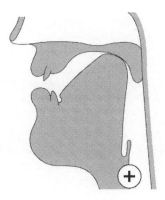

Figure 3.6 English /g/ (hold stage)

3.7.4 Word-medial

again, agony, arrogant, asparagus, bargain, beggar, begin, burger, cigar, dagger, dragon, eager, figure, forget, forgive, haggard, logo, luggage, meager, negative, organ, slogan, sugar, target, tiger, together, trigger, vinegar, wagon, yoga

3.7.5 Word-final

bag, beg, big, dog, drag, drug, egg, flag, fog, frog, hug, jog, jug, leg, log, mug, peg, pig, plague, rag, rug, shrug, smug, snag, snug, tug, twig, vague, wig

3.7.6 Multiple

gag, gargle, giggle

3.7.7 Phrases

a doggie bag, a guide dog, an illegal drug, a good figure, forgive and forget, gold nuggets, a golf bag, green grass, a good guess, a regular guest, a big hug, a legal obligation, a group photograph, as good as gold, gain ground

3.7.8 Sentences 1

(1) Give Douglas my kind regards. (2) Megan got a degree in English linguistics. (3) Get your grubby fingers off my glass mug! (4) Regrettably, I forgot to give them their gifts. (5) Are you going to go big game hunting again? (6) She wasn't eager to give up her ill-gotten gains. (7) My grandparents are going to Portugal in August. (8) The guest extinguished his cigarette on the ground. (9) The grass is growing and gradually getting greener. (10) He guarantees that the grapes are organically grown.

Sentences 2

(1) The gangster had his finger on the trigger of the gun. (2) Gordon said goodbye to Margaret, giving her a big hug. (3) They negotiated an agreement with the Greek government. (4) I'm good at forgiving and forgetting – I don't hold grudges. (5) My grandmother was engrossed in her gardening magazine. (6) Graham's gaze lingered on the photograph of his girlfriend. (7) There's a significant degree of ambiguity in your argument. (8) This was a flagrant disregard of the examination regulations. (9) Give Agnes and Greg our congratulations on their engagement. (10) A great big dog was growling at the girls who were gathered in our garage.

3.7.9 Dialogue

A: What an elegant gown, Gwen! What a gorgeous figure you've got!
B: Gary's going to be flabbergasted when he gets a glimpse of what he gave up.
A: Agreed. You're too good for that guy.
B: I'll never forgive the greedy geek for going off with that grotesque magnate's grand-
    daughter and forgetting me, his gorgeous girlfriend.

3.8 Voiceless palato-alveolar affricate /ʧ/

3.8.1 Description

Voiceless palato-alveolar affricate. With the soft palate raised, the tip, blade, and front of the tongue form a closure with the alveolar ridge and the front of the hard palate, and the sides of the tongue form a closure with the upper side teeth, completely blocking the airflow. Air is compressed behind the closure and released relatively slowly, resulting in homorganic friction. The lips are rounded and protruded.

3.8.2 Spelling

<ch> child, achieve, teacher, touch
<tch> catch, watch, kitchen
<ti> congestion, exhaustion, question, suggestion
<tu> following a stressed syllable (e.g., century, future, mutual, statue)

Unusual spellings

cello, concerto, Czech
   Note that <ch> is pronounced /k/ in scholarly words of Greek origin (e.g., *archaeology, chaos, charismatic, chasm, hierarchy, psychology*); <ch> is silent in *yacht* /jɑt/.

3.8.3 Word-initial

chain, chair, chalk, chance, change, chant, charge, charm, chart, chase, chat, cheap, cheat, check, cheek, cheer, cheese, chess, chest, chew, chief, child, chill, chip, choice, choose, chop, chore

3.8.4 Word-medial

achieve, adventurous, bachelor, butcher, feature, fortune, future, kitchen, mutual, nature, orchard, situation, statue, teacher, virtue

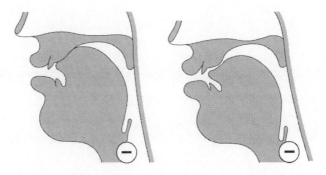

Figure 3.7 Left: English /ʧ/ showing palato-alveolar closure; right: release with homorganic friction; note trumpet-shaped lip-rounding

3.8.5 Word-final

arch, beach, bench, bleach, branch, brooch, bunch, catch, coach, couch, each, fetch, itch, march, match, much, patch, peach, pitch, reach, rich, scorch, scratch, screech, sketch, snatch, speech, stretch, such, switch, teach, torch, touch, watch, witch, church

3.8.6 Phrases

a challenging question, matching chairs, an intellectual challenge, a torture chamber, a chunk of cheese, a bunch of cherries, a chess champion, catch a chill, chocolate chips, eye-catching features, a change of fortune, scratch an itch, a catch-22 situation, a charcoal sketch, cheddar cheese, a spiritual teacher

3.8.7 Sentences I

(1) I had chicken enchiladas for lunch. (2) Rachel reached out to touch his cheek. (3) Add chocolate chips to the mixture. (4) The chimp let out a high-pitched screech. (5) She teaches Chinese literature and culture. (6) These mid-century kitchen chairs are charming. (7) I munched a peach and a whole bunch of cherries. (8) How much did the butcher charge for those chops? (9) If the temperature changes, you might catch a chill. (10) The adventurers eventually reached Chile in March.

Sentences 2

(1) He saw the chance for a change in their future fortune. (2) We approached the eye-catching statues on the beach. (3) The coach congratulated them on the victory over China. (4) This charcoal sketch of Charlie Chaplin is worth a fortune. (5) I watched the chess championship with my friend Chad. (6) He preaches the virtues of a contextual approach to research. (7) The child chose the chocolate cheesecake. (8) That cheerful guy with the chiseled features is our French lecturer. (9) You have a choice of cheddar cheese or chicken in your sandwich. (10) We tried to catch snatches of the exchange between Richard and Chuck.

3.8.8 Dialogue

A: Mitch chose cheap cheddar cheese and chips for lunch.
B: I'm itching for a change. Cheese and chips daily is a challenge.
A: In the future, you can reach into your own pocket and choose your own lunch – chicken, pork chops, fresh cherries, peaches . . .
B: Maybe cheddar cheese and chips isn't such a bad choice after all. Break me off a chunk of cheddar, would you?

3.9 Voiced palato-alveolar affricate /ʤ/

3.9.1 Description

Voiced palato-alveolar affricate. With the soft palate raised, the tip, blade, and front of the tongue form a closure with the alveolar ridge and the front of the hard palate, and the sides

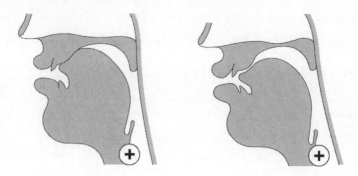

Figure 3.8 Left: English /ʤ/ showing palato-alveolar closure; right: release with homorganic friction; note trumpet-shaped lip-rounding

of the tongue form a closure with the upper side teeth, completely blocking the airflow. Air is compressed behind the closure and released relatively slowly, resulting in homorganic friction. The lips are rounded and protruded.

3.9.2 Spelling

<j> jam, joke
<g+<e/i/y> gentle, ginger, gym, suggest, danger, logic, apology, rage (This spelling can also represent /g/; see Section 3.7.2).
<dg> badge, budget, edge
<di, dj> soldier, adjourn, adjust
<du> following a stressed syllable (e.g., gradual, procedure)
<gg> suggest(ion), exaggerate, exaggeration

Unusual spellings

margarine /ˈmɑrdʒərən/

3.9.3 Word-initial

jail, general, gentle, genuine, giant, gin, ginger, gym, jab, jacket, jade, jam, jar, jaw, jazz, jealous, jelly, jet, job, join, joke, jolly, journal, joy, juice, jump, junk, jury, just, judge

3.9.4 Word-medial

agenda, agent, allergy, analogy, angel, apology, budget, danger, energy, fragile, gadget, imagine, intelligent, legend, logic, magic, major, margin, origin, pigeon, procedure, pajamas, region, rigid, suggest, surgeon, teenager, urgent, ginger

3.9.5 Word-final

age, badge, barge, bridge, cabbage, cage, charge, college, courage, damage, dodge, edge, emerge, hedge, huge, image, knowledge, language, large, luggage, manage, marriage, merge, message, nudge, package, page, rage, ridge, sausage, stage, storage, urge, verge, village, voyage, wage, grudge

3.9.6 Phrases

an intelligence agent, an abject apology, a large budget, a huge challenge, a gradual change, psychological damage, a jagged edge, an energy shortage, a jet engine, a gentle giant, average intelligence, a twinge of jealousy, a challenging job, jump for joy, a junior manager, an urgent message, a gentle nudge, a surgical procedure, a jealous rage, the average wage, a bungee jump

3.9.7 Sentences 1

(1) This region's ecologically fragile. (2) The orange juice is in the fridge, Judy. (3) Joan's engaged to Jeff, a project manager. (4) The images were arranged chronologically. (5) Angela hugely enjoyed her voyage to Egypt. (6) Eugene gradually got the gist of the message. (7) Benjamin's allergic to oranges and tangerines. (8) We stock a large range of engines for generators. (9) It's a major technological challenge for our engineers. (10) Jean jumped for joy when the surgeon discharged her.

Sentences 2

(1) How dangerous is bungee jumping in terms of injuries? (2) D'you know the average age range for college students? (3) Gerald and Jane tried to salvage their damaged marriage. (4) We have a generous budget for our journey to Argentina. (5) The teenagers were enraged when their luggage was damaged. (6) Jenny urged him to reject the outrageous suggestions for change. (7) Jessica encouraged me to buy her cottage at the edge of the village. (8) Marjorie's vegetarian sausages and ginger-fried vegetables were gorgeous. (9) George has a huge knowledge of languages, including German and Japanese. (10) I can just imagine how jealous Gemma must have been when John got the job in Geneva.

3.9.8 Dialogue

A: Would you suggest to Jim that he enjoy his jazz music more gently?
B: I've urged him to jump around less energetically, but he just doesn't get the message.
A: If Reggie flies into a rage and charges at him, not even Jim's agile jaw will dodge his giant fists.
B: Apart from his jazz jam sessions, Jim's a good lodger, but his outrageous gymnastics are no joke.

3.10 Fricatives: practice

3.10.1 Summary of key features

There are nine fricatives /f v θ ð s z ʃ ʒ h/. Their key features are:

1   With the soft palate raised, the articulators move close together to form a narrow gap. Forced through this stricture, the airstream becomes turbulent, resulting in audible friction; see Sections 2.2.3 and 2.13.

2   Together with stops, fricatives make up the obstruent class of consonants and therefore behave similarly in the following ways:

  a)   they come in voiceless and voiced pairs (except /h/) (see Section 2.13);
  b)   voiced fricatives are typically devoiced when adjacent to voiceless sounds and pauses – more so when followed by voiceless sounds or silence than when preceded by them – and are only reliably fully voiced between voiced sounds (see Section 2.4.2);
  c)   voiceless fricatives shorten sonorants (nasals, approximants, and vowels) preceding them in a syllable (see Sections 2.4.1 and 5.6).

3   [ɦ], a voiced allophone of /h/, is possible between voiced sounds; see Section 2.15.
4   The fricatives can be divided into sibilants /s z ʃ ʒ/ and non-sibilants /f v θ ð h/:

  a)   sibilants involve a longitudinal groove in the tongue channeling the airstream into a jet that produces turbulence and fricative noise when it hits an obstruction further along the vocal tract (the teeth) (see Section 2.14);
  b)   non-sibilant fricatives involve no grooving of the tongue and consequently their fricative noise is due to turbulence at the stricture itself (see Section 2.14);
  c)   the fricative noise produced by the sibilants is strong, while the non-sibilants produce rather weak fricative noise, especially the voiced ones, which sometimes verge on being approximants (see Section 2.14).

5   During the glottal fricative /h/, friction is not only produced at the glottis but also throughout the whole vocal tract, and since the articulators take the position for the following vowel during the articulation of /h/, there are as many allophones of /h/ as there are vowels (see Section 2.15).
6   The glottal fricative /h/ only occurs in syllable onsets (see Section 2.16).

3.11 Voiceless labio-dental fricative /f/

3.11.1 Description

Voiceless labio-dental fricative. The lower lip makes a light contact with the upper incisors. The soft palate is in the raised position. The air escapes with labio-dental friction. The tongue is free to anticipate the position of a following sound.

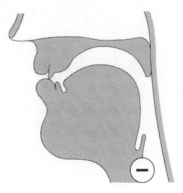

Figure 3.9 English /f/

3.11.2 Spelling

<f> fail, force, benefit, brief
<ff> coffee, staff
<ph> photo, philosophy, graph
<gh> laugh, enough, rough

Unusual spellings

have to /ˈhæf tə/

3.11.3 Word-initial

face, fact, fade, fail, faint, fair, fake, fall, false, fan, far, farm, fast, fat, fate, fault, fear, feed, feel, fence, fetch, fight, file, fill, film, find, fine, fire, firm, first, fish, fist, fit, five, fix, fog, foil, fold, food, fool, foot, force, fork, form, four, fox, full, fun, fur, phone

3.11.4 Word-medial

afford, before, benefit, buffalo, coffee, defeat, defend, define, differ, difficult, effort, muffin, nephew, offer, office, perform, prefer, professor, profit, qualify, refer, suffer, trophy, uniform

3.11.5 Word-final

beef, belief, brief, chief, cliff, cough, deaf, enough, grief, half, knife, laugh, off, proof, relief, roof, rough, safe, scarf, sniff, staff, stiff, stuff, thief, tough, wife

3.11.6 Multiple

faithful, falafel, falsify, fanfare, fearful, fifteen, fifty, firefly, fluff, forefinger, fulfil, funfair, philosophy, photograph

3.11.7 Phrases

a familiar face, facts and figures, fear of failure, fame and fortune, family and friends, a lifelong fan, a fruit farm, an awful fate, a film festival, a fair fight, official figures, freshwater fish, as fit as a fiddle, difficult to follow, frozen food, forgive and forget, a knife and fork, a faithful friend, a coughing fit, half and half, a flat roof, the phonetic alphabet, fresh coffee, a futile effort, a free gift, the facts of life, a father figure

3.11.8 Sentences I

(1) This colorful floral fabric's fabulous. (2) A fond farewell to our faithful friends! (3) Humphrey had a fierce frown on his face. (4) Jennifer stuffed herself with comfort food. (5) I infinitely prefer fresh fruit to frozen fruit. (6) Daphne was profoundly deaf in her left ear. (7) Don't forget that a first draft isn't a final draft. (8) There were four or five familiar faces on the staff. (9) We found the perfect gift for our unforgettable friend. (10) Fiona and her fiancé had terrific fun at the folk festival.

Sentences 2

(1) Phoebe suffered from whooping cough at the age of four. (2) Fortunately, there was a friendly atmosphere in the office. (3) Philip feared that they would laugh in his girlfriend's face. (4) Frank's former wife finds it difficult to forgive and forget. (5) Ralph's photos of the butterflies and flowers are beautiful. (6) To Fred's relief, there was a brief bibliography in the pamphlet. (7) Christopher was grateful when we offered him a lift to Memphis. (8) The conference facilities were first class, and the food was fantastic. (9) My father intensified his efforts to find sufficient funds to finance the deficit. (10) We had hoped to find fresh footprints the following afternoon but failed to do so.

3.11.9 Dialogue

A: Enough is enough. I'm finished with fatty foods forever.
B: Muffins? French fries? Fudge? Fried fish? Fast food?
A: I'm off fat forever. From now on, it's coffee and cigarettes for me. I'll be as fit as a fiddle.
B: That's far-fetched.
A: It's the famous coughing diet.
B: The infamous coffin diet is more like it.

3.12 Voiced labio-dental fricative /v/

3.12.1 Description

Voiced labio-dental fricative. The lower lip makes a light contact with the upper incisors. The soft palate is in the raised position. The air escapes with labio-dental friction. The tongue is free to anticipate the position of a following sound.

3.12.2 Spelling

<v> van, avoid, ever, give

Unusual spellings

of

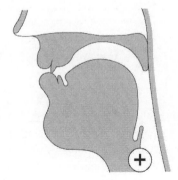

Figure 3.10 English /v/

3.12.3 Word-initial

vague, valid, value, vampire, van, vandal, vanilla, vanish, vary, vegetable, verb, verse, vest, vibrate, victim, victory, village, vinegar, violent, violin, virus, vision, visit, voice, volcano, volume, volunteer, vomit, vote, voucher, vowel, voyage

3.12.4 Word-medial

available, avenue, average, avid, avoid, clever, clover, cover, deliver, develop, device, devote, discover, divide, divorce, event, ever, fever, flavor, gravy, harvest, heavy, ivy, navy, nervous, over, poverty, prevent, private, provide, reveal, revenge, reverse, river, savage, service, severe, shiver, survey, universe

3.12.5 Word-final

above, achieve, active, alive, approve, arrive, attractive, behave, believe, brave, cave, curve, deserve, dive, drive, expensive, five, give, glove, improve, leave, love, massive, move, observe, olive, prove, receive, remove, reserve, save, serve, shave, shove, starve, wave

3.12.6 Multiple

inventive, involve, overactive, overview, revive, revolve, survive, valve, velvet, verve, vindictive, vivacious, vivid

3.12.7 Phrases

vice versa, an impressive achievement, an attractive alternative, above average, aggressive behavior, a private conversation, an undercover detective, a voyage of discovery, a lovely evening, develop a fever, a distinctive flavor, a harvest festival, a private individual, a massive investment, silver knives, a clever maneuver, a brave move, a rave review, a devoted servant, a time-saving device, a viable alternative, a detective novel

3.12.8 Sentences 1

(1) The removal van'll arrive at twelve. (2) Voting behavior never varies very much. (3) We have a variety of pullovers and vests. (4) Vernon's like a vulture hovering overhead. (5) Sylvia's novel received very favorable reviews. (6) This gives them a positive advantage over their rivals. (7) Microwave ovens are marvelous time-saving devices. (8) Steven and Veronica live in a lovely village in Virginia. (9) Oliver vowed he'd never leave his beloved Venice Beach. (10) Our services are reserved exclusively for private individuals.

Sentences 2

(1) You leave me with no alternative but to reveal your motives. (2) These progressive views were virtually universal in the 1770s. (3) Clive swerved violently to avoid driving into the delivery van. (4) Olivia's survey involved interviews with seventy-seven veterans. (5) Kevin discovered that we have several living relatives in Vermont. (6) Remove the vegetables from the oven and serve them with the veal. (7) Vanilla's prohibitively expensive, as harvesting it

is so labor-intensive. (8) Vicki makes every endeavor to provide them with advice on visiting Vietnam. (9) While Val lived in Bratislava, she developed an extensive vocabulary in Slovak. (10) The television viewers were given live coverage of Slovenia's victory over Bolivia.

3.12.9 Dialogue

A: I'm very versatile. I've done a variety of volunteer jobs.
B: Have you ever handled doves?
A: I love doves. They're very attractive birds.
B: You'll be serving the doves to the vipers. Have you developed a resistance to venom? If not, our vet can provide vials of anti-venom. Our lovely vipers are very mischievous little savages.

3.13 Voiceless dental fricative /θ/

3.13.1 Description

Voiceless dental fricative. The tip of the tongue is raised toward the rear of the upper incisors forming a narrow gap. The sides of the tongue form a seal against the upper side teeth. Unlike /s z/, there's no groove along the center of the tongue so that the air escapes diffusely over the whole surface of the tongue.

3.13.2 Spelling

<th> think, author, month, with
Note that <th> is often pronounced /ð/ (see Section 13.14.2). It is silent in *asthma* and *isthmus*.

3.13.3 Word-initial

thank, thaw, theater, theft, theme, theory, therapy, thesis, thick, thief, thigh, thimble, thin, thing, think, third, thirsty, thirty, thistle, thorn, thorough, thought, thousand, thread, threat, three, thriller, throat, throng, through, throw, thug, thumb, thump, thunder

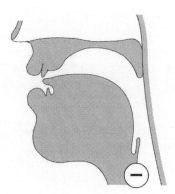

Figure 3.11 English /θ/

3.13.4 Word-medial

anything, apathy, authentic, author, authority, cathedral, empathy, ethics, ethos, every-thing, Gothic, hypothesis, method, nothing, orthodox, orthography, pathetic, sympathetic, sympathy

3.13.5 Word-final

bath, beneath, birth, both, breath, broth, cloth, death, earth, faith, froth, growth, hearth, heath, henceforth, length, math, mirth, moth, mouth, myth, north, oath, path, smith, south, teeth, tooth, truth, worth, wreath, youth

3.13.6 Phrases

death threats, diphthongs and monophthongs, a Gothic cathedral, healthy growth, a math-ematical theory, mouth-to-mouth, an orthodox theory, from strength to strength, through thick and thin, something to think about, a threat to health, a length of cloth

3.13.7 Sentences I

(1) Theo was in the throes of death. (2) It's Thelma's thirty-third birthday. (3) The death threats strengthened his faith. (4) Are there any panthers in Ethiopia? (5) Elizabeth brings warmth and empathy. (6) This strengthened the author's hypothesis. (7) What's the length and breadth of the cloth? (8) He threw himself into mathematical theories. (9) I think you should do something about your teeth. (10) She thinks Agatha Christie's thrillers are enthralling.

Sentences 2

(1) Kenneth needed therapy and time to think things through. (2) Matthew and Meredith are both enthusiastic about the theater. (3) This author doesn't think much of the orthodox theory of growth. (4) Arthur was healthy and wealthy and had the enthusiasm of youth. (5) Dorothy wants to be a goldsmith, and Gareth is an enthusiastic athlete. (6) Keith was faithful to Judith and stayed with her through thick and thin. (7) How are the monophthongs and diphthongs shown in the orthography? (8) Ethnographic methods are sometimes used in anthropological research. (9) Thaddeus authored three lengthy works on the theory of political myth. (10) Her health was threatened from the fourth to the sixth month of her pregnancy. (11) One of the themes of Elizabeth Gaskell's *North and South* is rebellion against an authority.

3.13.8 Dialogue

A: There's been a theft from the theater.
B: I thought I heard something about some threatening thugs.
A: They climbed through a window on the fourth floor.
B: Did the thieves take anything worth much?
A: They stole my thunder!

3.14 Voiced dental fricative /ð/

3.14.1 Description

Voiced dental fricative. The tip of the tongue is raised toward the rear of the upper incisors, forming a narrow gap. The sides of the tongue form a seal against the side teeth. Unlike /s z/, there's no groove along the center of the tongue so that the air escapes diffusely over the whole surface of the tongue.

3.14.2 Spelling

It is <th> word-initially in grammatical words such as *this, them, those*; medially in native words like *brother, father, mother, either, other, northern, southern*; and in a small number of words in final position (e.g., *smooth*). Otherwise, <th> tends to be /θ/.
Final <the> clothe, breathe, soothe

3.14.3 Word-initial

the, this, that, these, those, they, them, then, thus, there, theirs, though, than

3.14.4 Word-medial

another, bother, brother, clothing, dither, either, farther, father, feather, further, gather, heather, lather, leather, mother, neither, nevertheless, other, scathing, slither, smoothie, soothing, together, wither, worthy

3.14.5 Word-final

bathe, breathe, clothe, loathe, smooth, soothe

3.14.6 Phrases

mother and father, gather together, the Netherlands

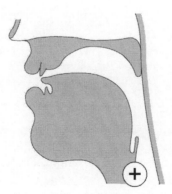

Figure 3.12 English /ð/

3.14.7 Sentences 1

(1) I can't fathom this weather. (2) His forefathers were heathens. (3) My brother sheathed the scythe. (4) It's a rather monotonous rhythm. (5) Wuthering Heights is worthy literature. (6) My godmother lives in the Netherlands. (7) My stepfather was at the end of his tether. (8) No denim or leather clothing may be worn. (9) My grandfather gathered his relatives together. (10) Those two are as featherbrained as each other.

Sentences 2

(1) They went hither and thither gathering heather. (2) Neither my mother nor my father will be there. (3) I'm putting together a menu for a get-together. (4) Heather has a soothing influence on my brother. (5) He didn't smother her or breathe down her neck. (6) He was a Southerner born in Weatherford, Texas. (7) Her grandmother gave these clothes to my mother. (8) Could I bother you for directions to the smoothie bar? (9) I loathe his scathing remarks and holier-than-thou attitude. (10) It was inlaid with mother-of-pearl and wreathed with feathers.

3.14.8 Dialogue

A: My brother's mother's rather bothersome.
B: Your brother's mother? That's *your* mother.
A: No. My brother's mother and my father got together after my mother ran off with my father's brother.
B: Ah, so your father's your brother's father, but your mother isn't your brother's mother.
A: Yes, he's my brother from another mother.

3.15 Voiceless alveolar fricative /s/

3.15.1 Description

Voiceless alveolar fricative. The tip and blade of the tongue are raised in the direction of the alveolar ridge forming a narrow gap. The sides of the tongue are held against the upper side teeth. There's a clear groove along the center of the tongue.

3.15.2 Spelling

<s> six, basic, yes
<se> sense, case, grease
<sce, sci> coalesce, scissors, condescend, scene, scent, fascinating, science
<ss> classic, assist, loss
<c (+e/i/y)> cell, circle, bicycle, race, receive, source, excellent, except
<x> = /ks/ box, expand
Note that <s> is silent in *aisle, isle, island, viscount, chassis, debris, précis, corps* /kor/, *rendezvous, chamois.*

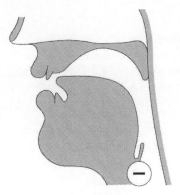

Figure 3.13 English /s/

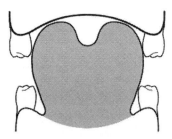

Figure 3.14 Mouth viewed from front showing grooved tongue shape for /s/

3.15.3 Word-initial

sad, safe, salt, same, sand, saw, say, sea, search, see, seem, self, sell, send, sick, side, sight, sign, sing, sink, sit, size, soap, sob, sock, soft, soil, son, song, sore, sort, sound, soup, south, suit, sun

3.15.4 Word-medial

basic, bossy, classic, conversation, decide, essay, gossip, impressive, jealousy, massive, possible, receive, reception, recipe

3.15.5 Word-final

base, bus, case, chase, chess, choice, class, course, cross, dress, face, fierce, force, glass, grease, guess, hiss, horse, house, kiss, less, loss, mess, nice, pass, place, plus, press, price, purse, race, twice, voice, worse, yes

3.15.6 Multiple

access, assess, assistance, basis, circus, consist, crisis, discuss, distance, insist, precise, process, sauce, science, sense, sentence, serious, service, silence, since, sister, six, slice, source, space, spice, sponsor, status, stress, success, suggest, surface, system, useless

3.15.7 Phrases

accept responsibility, a serious accident, sensible advice, a precise answer, a personal assistant, a false assumption, a gasp of astonishment, a savage beast, a Christmas bonus, a confidence boost, a case study, a star-studded cast, a center of excellence, customer service, a sense of decency, a unanimous decision, a stroke of genius, a ghost story, a safe guess, a spelling mistake, false modesty, bits and pieces, a recipe for success, a dress rehearsal, a sign of respect, bursting at the seams, a split second, a false sense of security, a stainless steel sink, a slippery slope, the speed of sound, suffer in silence, better safe than sorry

3.15.8 Sentences I

(1) Scott's face creased into a smile. (2) Sally tossed and dressed the salad. (3) Steven sat sipping a glass of whisky. (4) My sister missed the last bus yesterday. (5) The task was beyond the grasp of our son. (6) Selena sewed the seam with small stitches. (7) Sports are a constant source of fascination for us. (8) The selection process takes place next Saturday. (9) Spelling mistakes can be embarrassing and costly. (10) Samuel sprinkled the steak with a teaspoon of salt.

Sentences 2

(1) It's sometimes impossible to escape one's destiny. (2) Simon protested his innocence throughout the case. (3) Tess spoke without the slightest sign of nervousness. (4) Several scientists were conspicuous by their absence. (5) Laurence couldn't suppress the excitement in his voice. (6) The police arrested suspects during the house-to-house search. (7) Her relentless pursuit of artistic excellence is an inspiration to us. (8) The house faces southwest and overlooks the surrounding countryside. (9) The industrious students succeeded in grasping the basics of the science. (10) The security forces collapsed in the face of recent assaults by the militants.

3.15.9 Dialogue

A: I missed the bus yesterday. It didn't stop for us at the bus stop.
B: When it's stuffed full, they say you must wait for the next one.
A: So the season passes I buy are for standing at the bus stop getting soaked and not for sitting on a seat inside going to my destination?
B: Face facts. The bus service stinks. Save your sanity and take a taxi.

3.16 Voiced alveolar fricative /z/

3.16.1 Description

Voiced alveolar fricative. The tip and blade of the tongue are raised in the direction of the alveolar ridge forming a stricture of close approximation. The sides of the tongue are held against the upper side teeth. There's a clear groove along the center of the tongue.

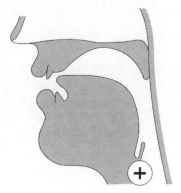

Figure 3.15 English /z/

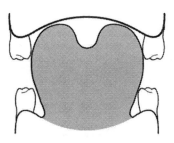

Figure 3.16 Mouth viewed from front showing grooved tongue shape for /z/

3.16.2 Spelling

<z> zoo, bizarre, lazy, quiz
<ze> blaze, freeze, prize
<zz> dizzy, jazz, buzz
<s, se> pleasant, always, museum, rise, wise, houses (but /s/ in blouse and erase)
<x> xenophobia, xylophone, anxiety
<x, xh> = /gz/ exam, exact, exist, exhilarate, exhausted
Also in -s endings, e.g., dogs, sees, John's (see Section 2.30)
After <pre-, de-, re->, e.g., preserve, desert, resist

Unusual spellings

<ss> possess, dissolve, scissors, dessert

3.16.3 Word-initial

zealous, zest, zinc, zip, zone, zoo, zoom

3.16.4 Word-medial

bizarre, busy, closet, cozy, crazy, daisy, deposit, deserve, design, desire, dessert, disaster, dissolve, dizzy, drowsy, easy, fizzy, hazy, hesitate, laser, lazy, miser, museum, music, physics, resist, scissors, visit

3.16.5 Word-final

accuse, always, amaze, amuse, apologize, breeze, bruise, buzz, cause, cheese, choose, cruise, daze, freeze, gaze, jazz, maze, news, noise, nose, pause, phrase, please, prize, quiz, realize, revise, rose, size, sneeze, squeeze, suppose, surprise, tease, wise

3.16.6 Multiple

disease, enthusiasm, lazybones, measles, mesmerize, scissors, trousers, zigzag

3.16.7 Phrases

a pleasant breeze, business studies, Parmesan cheese, a reasonable compromise, surprisingly easy, jazz music, a buzzing noise, the laws of physics, easy to please, rose petals, a surprise visit, a pleasant surprise

3.16.8 Sentences I

(1) Please excuse my clumsy words. (2) These tools are surprisingly easy to use. (3) She grows herbs like basil, rosemary, and chives. (4) Elizabeth's cheesecake with hazelnuts is tantalizing. (5) Brussels sprouts with Parmesan cheese sounds bizarre. (6) He has master's degrees in tourism and business studies. (7) Alexandra adores flowers like azaleas, zinnias, and roses. (8) My cousin holds a position as a career adviser in Arizona. (9) She sounds exhausted and miserable although she denies it. (10) Why does she refuse what seems a reasonable compromise?

Sentences 2

(1) I'm amazed that anxiety can cause these physical symptoms. (2) Liz knows many words and phrases in Brazilian Portuguese. (3) They apologized to the passengers for the delays and cancellations. (4) I was surprised that they chose me to represent their values and ideas. (5) His findings aren't implausible and deserve to be examined exhaustively. (6) When James opens the browser, he hears a buzzing noise in his headphones. (7) He loves visiting the zoo and observing animals like zebras and chimpanzees. (8) My husband appears to be losing his enthusiasm for his jazz music magazines. (9) In the mornings and evenings, there was always a pleasant breeze from the mountains. (10) Our offices are closed on Tuesday and Wednesday but will resume business on Thursday.

3.16.9 Dialogue

A: The zoo's closed on Tuesdays, Wednesdays, and Thursdays.
B: How surprising! Is it wise to stay closed during the holidays?

A: The owner's very lazy and prefers an easy life to a busy one.
B: How bizarre! Surely, he feeds and cares for the animals when the zoo's closed to visitors anyway.

3.17 Voiceless palato-alveolar fricative /ʃ/

3.17.1 Description

Voiceless palato-alveolar fricative. The tip, blade, and front of the tongue are raised in the direction of the alveolar ridge and the front of the hard palate, forming a narrow gap. The sides of the tongue are held against the upper side teeth. A groove is formed along the center of the tongue. The groove is shallower than for /s z/ and also further back. The lips are rounded and protruded.

3.17.2 Spelling

<sh> ship, sushi, cash
<ti> station, portion, education
<ch> machine, brochure, chef, champagne
<su> sure, insure
<ssu> assure, pressure
<ci> special, precious
<si> following a consonant letter (e.g., controversial, compulsion, passion, expansion)
<sci> conscious, conscience
<x> = /kʃ/ anxious, obnoxious, luxury

Unusual spellings

ocean

3.17.3 Word-initial

chef, shake, shame, shape, share, shark, sharp, shave, sheep, sheet, shelf, shell, shield, shift, ship, shirt, shock, shoe, shoot, shop, short, shot, shout, shove, show, shut, shy, sugar, sure

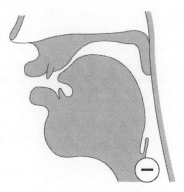

Figure 3.17 English /ʃ/; note trumpet-shaped lip-rounding

3.17.4 Word-medial

action, ambition, ancient, auction, audition, beneficial, bishop, caption, caution, connection, delicious, edition, emotion, fashion, fiction, issue, lotion, magician, mission, motion, mushroom, ocean, passion, portion, ration, session, station

3.17.5 Word-final

ambush, astonish, banish, blush, brush, bush, cash, clash, crash, crush, dash, English, establish, finish, fish, flash, flesh, fresh, hush, leash, push, rash, rush, smash, splash, squash, varnish, wash, wish

3.17.6 Multiple

appreciation, initiation, negotiation, sheepish, shellfish

3.17.7 Phrases

cherish an ambition, a shaving brush, a cash machine, short of cash, a champagne reception, fresh fish, a controversial issue, shampoo and conditioner, sheep shearing, fresh sheets, a makeshift shelter, a fresh shirt, shoe polish, a fashion shoot, a shoe shop, a fashion show

3.17.8 Sentences 1

(1) He shrank back into the shadow of a shrub. (2) Joshua polished his shoes until they were shiny. (3) Are there any sugar plantations in Bangladesh? (4) Sharon and Sean went shark fishing in the ocean. (5) The fashion show was shot on location in Chicago. (6) An ancient ship washed up on the shores of Croatia. (7) They wished to publish a special issue on education. (8) He rode roughshod over the wishes of the shareholders. (9) Our destination was a sheep-shearing station in the bush. (10) We specialize in pashmina ponchos and crocheted shawls.

Sentences 2

(1) If you're short of cash, there's a cash machine at the station. (2) The optician refurbished his old-fashioned shop in Nashville. (3) I'm partial to sherry, but I find traditional British cider atrocious. (4) Ashley's dish was garnished with mushrooms and fresh radishes. (5) Sheila shrugged her shoulders impatiently and shivered with repulsion. (6) Shirley was anxious that her shorts would shrink in the washing machine. (7) Natasha has an astonishing collection of Chopin, Schubert, and Schumann. (8) We took exception to his wishy-washy positions on this contentious issue. (9) We have a sensational selection of shampoos and conditioners on our shelves. (10) We had fish and shrimp washed down with Danish schnapps and champagne.

3.17.9 Dialogue

A: I wish you'd shut up about fashion.
B: I wish you'd shut up about fishing.

A: Your collection of shiny shoes should be sent to the garbage dump.
B: Your fishing contraptions should be shoved into the ocean.

3.18 Voiced palato-alveolar fricative /ʒ/

3.18.1 Description

Voiced palato-alveolar fricative. The tip, blade, and front of the tongue are raised in the direction of the alveolar ridge and the front of the hard palate, forming a narrow gap. The sides of the tongue are held against the upper side teeth. A groove is formed along the center of the tongue. The groove is shallower than for /s z/ and also further back. The lips are rounded and protruded.

/ʒ/ virtually only occurs in intervocalic position, e.g., *treasure*, though it's sometimes found initially and finally in recent French loanwords, e.g., *genre, beige, prestige*. In many cases, there are alternative pronunciations with /dʒ/.

3.18.2 Spelling

<si> following a vowel, e.g., confusion, decision, collision, occasion
<su> pleasure, casual, usual
<g(+e/i)> genre, regime, prestige
<zu> seizure, azure

3.18.3 Word-medial

allusion, casual, closure, collision, composure, corrosion, confusion, conclusion, decision, delusion, diffusion, elision, enclosure, erosion, exclusion, excursion, explosion, exposure, illusion, intrusion, invasion, leisure, measure, occasion, persuasion, pleasure, precision, profusion, provision, regime, revision, seizure, television, treasure, usual, vision

3.18.4 Word-final

barrage, beige, camouflage, collage, entourage, espionage, massage, rouge, sabotage

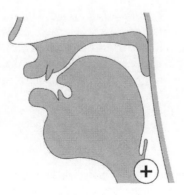

Figure 3.18 English /ʒ/; note trumpet-shaped lip-rounding

3.18.5 Sentences I

(1) The road closure led to confusion. (2) The explosion caused few casualties. (3) This added to the prestige of the genre. (4) The regime's measures were sabotaged. (5) Is it some sort of mirage or visual delusion? (6) There was a profusion of casual leisure wear. (7) Standard deviation's a measure of precision. (8) The results led to a revision of the conclusion. (9) We can make a corsage that fits any occasion. (10) The soldiers were dressed in beige camouflage.

Sentences 2

(1) The star was surrounded by his usual entourage. (2) Work's an unwelcome intrusion on my leisure time. (3) People with visual impairment experience exclusion. (4) The damages may be caused by corrosion or erosion. (5) Beaujolais was the preferred wine of the bourgeoisie. (6) He accepted the treasurer's decision with composure. (7) It was such a pleasure to read Jane Austen's *Persuasion*. (8) He was met by a barrage of questions on the failed invasion. (9) He was arrested for espionage and collusion with the Russians. (10) It's debatable whether too much exposure to television is harmful.

3.18.6 Dialogue

A: I spend my leisure time searching for lost treasure.
B: There's been a profusion of treasures uncovered with all the erosion.
A: I'm taking an excursion with my entourage to dig for more.
B: That sounds like a fun occasion. Exposure of ancient artifacts could bring you prestige.

3.19 Voiceless glottal fricative /h/

3.19.1 Description

Voiceless glottal fricative. The vocal folds are slightly narrowed, producing friction at the glottis. In addition, there is friction throughout the vocal tract. /h/ can be considered a strong voiceless beginning to the following sound (/j/ or a vowel), having the quality of a voiceless version of the following sound.

3.19.2 Spelling

<h> hand, home, perhaps
<wh> who, whose, whole, whore, wholesale, wholehearted, wholesome
Note that <h> is silent in words like *herb, hour, honest(y), honor(able), heir(ess), annihilate, exhibit, exhaust, exhilarate, rhapsody, rhinoceros, rhotic, rhyme, rhythm, shepherd, silhouette, vehicle, vehement, vehemence.*
For words containing silent <gh>, as in *thought, through*, see Section 3.7.2.

3.19.3 Word-initial

hair, half, hall, ham, hand, hard, harm, hat, hate, head, hear, heart, heat, hell, help, hide, high, hike, hill, hip, hiss, hit, hold, hole, home, hook, hope, horn, horse, host, hot, house, hug, hunt, hurt, whole

3.19.4 Word-medial

alcohol, apprehend, beehive, behalf, behavior, behind, coherent, comprehensive, enhance, inherit, perhaps, rehearse

3.19.5 Multiple

half-hearted, haphazard, headhunter, hitchhike, hobbyhorse, household, whole-hearted

3.19.6 Phrases

a happy childhood, a horrible habit, half and half, a huge hall, hard to handle, a hard hat, a health hazard, the head of the household, a heavy heart, a head for heights, a childhood hero, a huge hit, a holiday home, high hopes

3.19.7 Sentences 1

(1) Heidi's hairstyle's hideous. (2) Hilary has no head for heights. (3) Hubert hasn't got a hope in hell. (4) A heat haze hung over the harbor. (5) Harry hung his head in humiliation. (6) Helen held her hands over her head. (7) Humphrey was headhunted by Harvard. (8) We heard that the hurricane had hit Ohio. (9) Is Henry Higgins a hero or an anti-hero? (10) His workaholic behavior harms his health.

Sentences 2

(1) He had a happy and wholesome childhood. (2) Here the husband was head of the household. (3) He hiked up a high hill in Haiti during his holidays. (4) Hugo held out his hand to his childhood sweetheart. (5) They were held hostage by the hot-headed hooligans. (6) The hound was howling its head off outside the house. (7) We helped ourselves to the heavenly hake and haddock. (8) Hugh is handsome with his hazel hair and high forehead. (9) The helicopter hovered above the house where he was hiding. (10) Harriet was so heavily dehydrated that she had to go to a hospital.

3.19.8 Dialogues

A: I can hardly hear Hugh's history lecture.
B: He's half asleep and hung over.
A: His alcohol habit is harming his career.
B: It's harming his home life too. A heavy drinker makes a horrible husband.

A: I half hoped to have the whole holiday here.
B: Henry, my husband, is happy here at the harbor too.
A: Perhaps hiking in the hills would be too hard.
B: In this heat, it'd be horrible, hellish!

3.20 Nasals: practice

3.20.1 Summary of key features

There are three nasals, /m n ŋ/. Their key features are:

1   A complete closure is formed in the oral cavity while the soft palate is in the lowered position, allowing the airstream to exit via the nose; see Sections 2.2.3 and 2.17.

2   The complete closures formed for /m n ŋ/ are identical to those for the bilabial /p b/, alveolar /t d/, and velar plosives /k g/. The difference is in the position of the soft palate: raised for the plosives, lowered for the nasals (see Section 2.17).

3   Together with approximants (and vowels), nasals are sonorants and act similarly in the following ways:

a)   they don't come in voiceless and voiced phonemic pairs (see Section 2.4);
b)   they aren't devoiced when adjacent to voiceless sounds or a pause (see Section 2.4.2);
c)   they are shortened by following voiceless consonants in the same syllable (see Section 2.4.1).

4   In word-final position, the alveolar nasal can be followed by both voiceless and voiced alveolar plosives – /nt/ and /nd/. Bilabial and velar nasals can only be followed by voiceless bilabial and velar plosives in these positions – /mp/ and /ŋk/ (see Section 2.18).

5   Within a morpheme, nasals can only be followed by plosives that are homorganic (see Section 2.18).

6   In certain circumstances, nasals, particularly /n/, can become syllabic and form the nucleus of a syllable (see Section 2.19).

7   The velar nasal /ŋ/ doesn't occur in syllable onsets (see Section 2.18).

8   Apart from a small number of exceptions, /ŋg/ occurs within morphemes and /ŋ/ at the end of morphemes (see Section 2.18).

3.21 Voiced bilabial nasal /m/

3.21.1 Description

Voiced bilabial nasal. The soft palate is lowered; the lips form a closure, thus preventing the airstream from exiting via the mouth and allowing it to escape through the nose. The vocal folds vibrate throughout the articulation.

3.21.2 Spelling

<m> map, amazing, human, aim
<mm> command, hammer

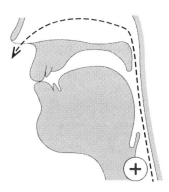

Figure 3.19 English /m/; the arrow indicates the escape of the airstream through the nose

<mb> climb, lamb, comb, plumber
<mn> hymn, solemn, condemn
<gm> paradigm, phlegm, diaphragm
Note that in the word *mnemonic* <m> is silent.

3.21.3 Word-initial

main, make, man, map, march, mark, mask, mat, match, mate, math, may, maze, meal, mean, melt, mend, merge, mess, mild, mile, milk, mind, mine, miss, mist, mix, moan, month, mood, moon, mouth, move, much, mud, mug

3.21.4 Word-medial

amazing, among, amount, climate, comic, comma, command, comment, common, customer, damage, demand, domestic, drama, element, familiar, glamour, grammar, hammer, human, humor, image, lemon, limit, promise, rumor, stomach, summer, woman

3.21.5 Word-final

a) Full length

aim, bomb, calm, climb, comb, cream, crime, crumb, dim, dream, farm, firm, flame, foam, form, frame, game, gem, gloom, gum, ham, harm, home, jam, name, numb, room, same, seem, shame, slim, steam, storm, sum, swim, team, time, warm, zoom

b) Clipped

bump, chimp, clump, jump, lump, pump, stamp, stump, swamp, trump

c) Full length vs. clipped

cam/camp, clam/clamp, cram/cramp, dam/damp, dumb/dump, hem/hemp, hum/hump, lamb/lamp, limb/limp, plum/plump, ram/ramp, slum/slump, thumb/thump

3.21.6 Multiple

commitment, compromise, embarrassment, mainstream, mammoth, maximum, measurement, medium, member, memo, memory, mermaid, mime, minimum, moment, movement, mumble, murmur, museum, premium, remember, sometimes

3.21.7 Phrases

an impressive achievement, a smoke alarm, a modest ambition, the maximum amount, the animal kingdom, a common assumption, a time bomb, a famous composer, commit a crime, permanent damage, a simple diagram, a moment of drama, a family member, a team game, doom and gloom, a meager income, a musical instrument, plum jam, a time limit, a family man, man-made materials, a simple meal, an elementary mistake, a memorable moment, tomorrow morning, a complete mystery, a malicious rumor, a lump sum, a farm animal

3.21.8 Sentences 1

(1) The moment's come to make a move. (2) That makes it something of a minor miracle! (3) Mary embraced the system with enthusiasm. (4) The maritime museum's marked on the map. (5) Mandy admitted she'd made a major mistake. (6) My family gave the newcomers a warm welcome. (7) Marilyn was completely immune to Tom's charms. (8) This matter was uppermost in my mind at the time. (9) A monument's been commissioned in his memory. (10) Malcolm made himself comfortable in an armchair.

Sentences 2

(1) The computer comes with a comprehensive manual. (2) Mass media are an important means of communication. (3) Emily supplemented her income with part-time journalism. (4) By this time tomorrow, the temperature will have plummeted. (5) Moira's a member of the management team for my company. (6) Max aimed to cause the maximum amount of embarrassment. (7) Cameras were employed to monitor the movement of animals. (8) The musician demonstrated complete mastery of his instrument. (9) The government embarked on an ambitious program of economic reforms. (10) Michael had no problem with his long-term memory, but his short-term memory was damaged.

3.21.9 Dialogue

A: My mate's merely a mediocre musician who hammers away on his instrument for money.
B: You might make him mad with your grim assessment of his competence.
A: It's Mike's own assessment, not mine. He moans and moans about his drums.
B: Then maybe he should make music with the tambourine.

3.22 Voiced alveolar nasal /n/

3.22.1 Description

Voiced alveolar nasal. The tip of the tongue forms a closure with the alveolar ridge and the sides of the tongue with the side teeth. The soft palate is lowered, allowing air to escape through the nose. The vocal folds vibrate throughout the articulation.

3.22.2 Spelling

<n> name, unite, money, burn
<nn> funny, tennis
<kn> knack, knee, kneel, know, knight, knife, knock, knob, knowledge, knit
<gn> gnaw, reign, sign, align, campaign, champagne, design, foreign (also derived forms, e.g., *assignment, foreigner, designer*)

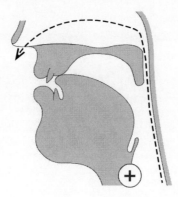

Figure 3.20 English /n/; the arrow indicates the escape of the airstream through the nose

<pn> pneumonia
Note that <n> is silent in final <mn> (e.g., *column, condemn, damn, hymn, solemn*).
/n/ often returns in derived forms (e.g., *autumnal, condemnation, columnist,* and so on).

3.22.3 Word-initial

knee, knife, knob, knock, knot, know, naked, name, nap, narrow, nasty, nature, near, neck, needle, neighbor, nerve, next, nice, night, no, nose, normal, note, nothing, now, number, nurse

3.22.4 Word-medial

animal, corner, dinner, funny, honey, honor, manner, many, minor, money, owner, panic, piano, planet, pony, spinach, tennis, unite

3.22.5 Word-final

a) Full length

bean, bin, brown, burn, can, chain, chin, coin, dawn, down, drown, fan, fine, gain, green, grin, keen, lawn, learn, line, loan, main, man, men, mine, moon, pain, pan, pen, phone, pin, queen, scan, shine, skin, spin, strain, sun, thin, tone, town, train, tune, turn, twin, warn, win, zone

b) Clipped

aunt, blunt, count, dent, front, glint, grant, hint, hunt, mint, point, print, slant, want; month; bounce, chance, dance, glance, once, prince, rinse, sense; bench, branch, bunch, inch, launch, lunch, munch, pinch, punch, trench, wrench

c) Full length vs. clipped

complained/complaint, joined/joint, mend/meant, mound/mount, pained/paint, send/sent, spend/spent, tend/tent, tinned/tint, vend/vent, nine/ninth, ten/tenth, lunge/lunch

3.22.6 Multiple

abandon, accountant, announce, banana, cannon, confident, consonant, contain, engine, genuine, ignorant, innocent, napkin, nineteen, nonsense, noon, noun, onion, opinion, suntan

3.22.7 Phrases

a foreign accent, a sunny afternoon, brains and brawn, none of your business, the turn of the century, a change of scene, common sense, genuinely funny, a gin and tonic, moan and groan, a gentle hint, turn down an invitation, a blunt knife, behind enemy lines, a no-nonsense manner, friends and neighbors, a bundle of nerves, a handwritten note, a punch on the nose, a brain scan, a banana skin, a tennis tournament, a train of events, vintage wine, a sense of destiny

3.22.8 Sentences I

(1) Only one question remains unanswered. (2) Nicholas grinned and nodded in confirmation. (3) Don't let the discussion end on a negative note. (4) Nancy doesn't have an ounce of common sense. (5) One of the men had a pronounced Southern accent. (6) The students insisted that no offence was intended. (7) Cynthia's no-nonsense manner inspires confidence. (8) They'd confessed their sins and done their penance. (9) The parents confirmed that their son was born blind. (10) The town center has changed beyond all recognition.

Sentences 2

(1) The next of kin have been informed about the accident. (2) The panel of scientists was drawn from the universities. (3) A nationwide hunt was launched for the dangerous gunman. (4) Simon and Jenny invested their money in government bonds. (5) Kenneth went from a no-win situation to a win-win situation. (6) Norman evidently wanted to be in control of his own destiny. (7) You'll need to be patient, as change doesn't happen overnight. (8) His friend's experiences remained at the forefront of his mind. (9) None of the participants understood the meaning of the sentence. (10) Dominic eventually managed to convince them of his innocence.

3.22.9 Dialogue

A: No more nouns and pronouns!
B: We want to know about consonants – approximants, nasals, obstruents, and sonorants.
A: Enough of determiners, tenses, inflections, and inversion!
B: We demand to learn about the sounds of spoken English – phonetics!

3.23 Voiced velar nasal /ŋ/

3.23.1 Description

Voiced velar nasal. The back of the tongue forms a closure with the soft palate and the rear of the sides of the tongue with the rear side teeth. The soft palate is lowered, allowing air to escape through the nose. Note that this means that there's a velar closure but no velic closure. The vocal folds vibrate throughout the articulation.

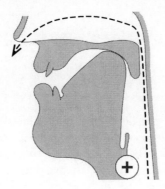

Figure 3.21 English /ŋ/; the arrow indicates the escape of the airstream through the nose

3.23.2 Spelling

<ng> singer, king, young
<nk> = /ŋk/ ankle, sink
<nc> = /ŋk/ uncle, zinc
<ng> = /ŋg/ anger, longer
<nx> = /ŋks/ lynx, larynx (but note *anxious* /ˈæŋkʃəs/ and *anxiety* /æŋˈzaɪəti/)
<nq> = /ŋk/ banquet, tranquil

3.23.3 Word-final

a) Full length

along, among, belong, cunning, during, evening, fling, gang, gong, hang, king, lightning, long, lung, morning, nothing, oblong, pang, ring, slang, song, spring, string, strong, swing, tongue, wrong, young

b) Clipped

blank, blink, drink, drunk, frank, ink, jinx, junk, link, mink, monk, plank, prank, punk, rink, shrink, sink, thank, trunk, zinc

c) Full length vs. clipped

bang/bank, bring/brink, cling/clink, ping/pink, rang/rank, sang/sank, sing/sink, sting/stink, stung/stunk, tang/tank, thing/think, wing/wink

3.23.4 Word-medial

a) Word-medial before /k/

anchor, ankle, blanket, bunker, conquer, crinkle, donkey, hanker, monkey, sprinkle, tinker, tinkle, tranquil, trinket, twinkle, uncle, wrinkle

b) Word-medial, before /g/

anger, angle, angry, anguish, bingo, English, finger, hunger, hungry, jingle, jungle, kangaroo, linger, mango, mingle, mongrel, penguin, single, strangle, tangle, tango, tingle, longer, stronger, younger, longest, youngest, strongest

3.23.5 Multiple

angling, banging, belongings, bringing, clinging, hanging, inkling, longing, ping-pong, ringing, singing, spring-cleaning, stinging, swinging; banking, blinking, drinking, linking, ranking, shrinking, sinking, thanking, thinking, twinkling, winking; jingling, lingering, mingling, strangling, tingling

3.23.6 Phrases

growing anger, a wedding banquet, a boxing ring, on the brink of extinction, an imposing building, the wrong conclusion, a refreshing drink, a spring evening, a sinking feeling, a surprising finding, hunger pangs, language learning, the missing link, a punctured lung, an angry meeting, shocking pink, a wedding ring, a younger sibling, a drinking song, a length of string, a long think, swimming trunks, a knowing wink

3.23.7 Sentences I

(1) It's a tranquil setting for a relaxing evening. (2) I've been feeling strong hunger pangs all morning. (3) We encourage you to be punctual for the meetings. (4) Angus was worrying about getting the timing wrong. (5) My siblings are playing ping-pong in the dining room. (6) My uncle was looking forward to his posting in Beijing. (7) We were dying to sing along with the best-selling songs. (8) Congratulations to Duncan and Bianca on getting engaged! (9) Think about cycling or walking to work instead of driving. (10) Surprisingly, she wasn't wearing a wedding ring on her finger.

Sentences 2

(1) I'm considering wearing long dangling earrings to the banquet. (2) Her findings were fascinating, but her conclusion was misleading. (3) It was so disappointing that they weren't willing to sing an encore. (4) We're moving from a crumbling building to a charming bungalow. (5) We were getting the hang of understanding Cockney rhyming slang. (6) He's trying to bring pink flamingos back from the brink of extinction. (7) The youngsters were traveling from Washington, DC, to Rock Springs. (8) I'll be studying English language and linguistics in Hong Kong next spring. (9) He was hoping he could relinquish the nagging anxiety that was weighing him down. (10) Learning to distinguish the diphthongs of Hungarian was proving to be a challenging undertaking.

3.23.8 Dialogue

A: Gangs of youngsters have been ringing my doorbell and running away.
B: I'd like to strangle those pranksters.

A: It's ruining my tranquil evenings.

B: I think I'll bring my dog over. He's an angry mongrel with long fangs.

3.24 Approximants: practice

3.24.1 Summary of key features

There are four approximants /l r j w/. Their key features are:

1   With the soft palate raised, the articulators move toward each other to form a gap wider than that for fricatives and not narrow enough to cause turbulence and fricative noise (see Sections 2.2.3 and 2.20).

2   Together with nasals (and vowels), approximants are sonorants and act similarly in the following ways:

   a)   they don't come in voiceless and voiced phonemic pairs (see Section 2.4);
   b)   they aren't devoiced when adjacent to voiceless sounds or a pause (see Section 2.4.2);
   c)   they are shortened by a following voiceless consonant in the same syllable (see Section 2.4.1).

3   /j/ and /w/ and are semi-vowels. They are articulated with parts of the tongue used to articulate vowels and are in essence glides from the [i] and [u] positions respectively (see Section 2.27).

4   While all other English phonemes involve the airstream traveling down the midline of the vocal tract, the lateral approximant /l/ forms a closure in the center of the mouth and causes the airstream to flow on one or both sides of it (see Section 2.24).

5   When following aspirated voiceless plosives /p t k/, the aspiration takes place during the articulation of the approximants, causing them to become devoiced and fricative (see Section 2.6).

6   Two of the four approximants, /j w/, only occur in syllable onsets (see Section 2.28).

7   /l/ is velarized and especially so before consonants or a pause (see Section 2.25).

3.25 Voiced palatal approximant /j/

3.25.1 Description

Voiced palatal median approximant. With the soft palate raised, the front of the tongue approaches the hard palate but not close enough to result in friction. This is the same articulation as for a close front unrounded vowel, and therefore, [j] can alternatively be described as a glide from the [i] vowel position. If the following vowel is open, the approximation to the hard palate is less close, equating to a glide from an opener vowel position, for example [ɪ].

3.25.2 Spelling

<y> year, yellow, youth
<u> = /ju/ unit, useful, music
<ue> = /ju/ argue, value, venue
<ew> = /ju/ few, pew

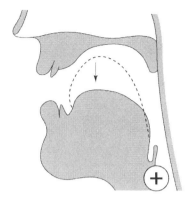 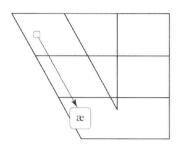

Figure 3.22 English /j/: sequence /jæ/ as in *yak*; diagram shows approximate change in tongue shape; since /j/ is a semi-vowel, it can be indicated on a vowel diagram

<eu> = /ju/ feud, Eugene, therapeutic
<i> behavior, dominion, savior, onion

Unusual spellings

beautiful, Houston

3.25.3 Word-initial

unicorn, uniform, union, unique, unit, unite, universe, university, USA, useful, usual, utensil, utility, yacht, yard, yawn, year, yearn, yeast, yell, yellow, yes, yesterday, yet, yoga, yogurt, yolk, young

3.25.4 Word-medial

accurate, ambulance, argument, beauty, behavior, calculate, canyon, circulate, companion, confusion, deputy, executive, fabulous, failure, feud, few, formula, fuel, funeral, fuse, future, huge, human, humid, humor, immaculate, interview, manipulate, monument, museum, music, occupy, opinion, particular, popular, review, spectacular, stimulate, view, volume

3.25.5 Multiple

accumulate, uvula, yoyo

3.25.6 Phrases

a popular venue, yell abuse, argue furiously, a useful attribute, human behavior, the undisputed champion, regular communication, a useful contribution, a miraculous cure, the usual excuse, humiliating failure, a user's manual, beautiful music, popular opinion, an annual review, make yourself useful, a huge yawn

3.25.7 Sentences 1

(1) Sonia looked cute in her yellow uniform. (2) Yasmin and Samuel are like yin and yang. (3) My nephew's only a year younger than me! (4) Muriel refuses to speculate about the future. (5) There was a spectacular view from the pavilion. (6) There's no excuse for this continued inhumanity. (7) This beautiful volume is a tribute to Cuban music. (8) Hugo's a fabulous interviewer and communicator. (9) His manuscript was particularly popular in Europe. (10) This doesn't excuse his unusual behavior yesterday.

Sentences 2

(1) He contributed regularly to the *Communist Review*. (2) Emmanuel was yearning to use his Italian vocabulary. (3) Matthew attributes his miraculous cure to acupuncture. (4) This computer manual's particularly useful for seniors. (5) The document was distributed to the youthful population. (6) William's first year at the University of Houston was a failure. (7) Hubert calculated it meticulously and executed it scrupulously. (8) The monument was obscured from our view by a huge museum. (9) Bartholomew made a valuable contribution to the future of our community. (10) My nephew did manual work for years before becoming a communications executive.

3.25.8 Dialogue

A: The yoga instructor you recommended is useless.
B: Useless? She's fabulous! A spectacular yogic beauty!
A: Youth and beauty alone aren't a formula for yogic excellence.
B: Okay. You do your yoga with your corpulent old guru, and I'll continue with my cute young instructor.

3.26 Voiced labial-velar approximant /w/

3.26.1 Description

Voiced labial-velar median approximant. With the soft palate raised, the back of the tongue approaches the soft palate but not close enough to cause friction, and simultaneously, the lips

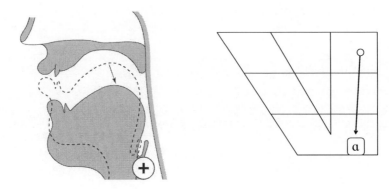

Figure 3.23 English /w/: sequence /wɑ/ as in *wasp*; diagram shows approximate change in tongue shape; since /w/ is a semi-vowel, it can be indicated on a vowel diagram

round. This is the same articulation as for a close back rounded vowel, and therefore, [w] can alternatively be described as a glide from the [u] position. If the following vowel is open, the approximation to the soft palate is less close, equating to a glide from an opener position, for example [ʊ]. /w/ is a double articulation consisting as it does of two strictures of equal rank: velar and labial approximants.

3.26.2 Spelling

<w> wait, world, awake
<wh> whale, white, whether, what, where, when, which, why
<qu> = /kw/ quite, query, acquire
<ngu> = /ŋgw/ anguish, language, linguistics
<su> = /sw/ assuage, persuade, suede, suite
Note that <w> is silent in *who, whose, whole, whore, answer, sword, two*. <w> in initial <wr> is also silent (e.g., *wrack, wrangle, wrap, wrath, wreak, wreath, wreck, wreckage, wren, wrench, wrest, wrestle, wretch, wretched, wriggle, wring, wrinkle, wrist, write, writer, writhe, wrong, wrote, wrought, wrung, wry*).

3.26.3 Word-initial

one, wage, wait, wake, walk, wall, want, war, warm, wash, wasp, watch, water, wave, way, web, well, went, west, wet, wheel, while, whip, white, why, wide, wife, wig, wild, will, win, wine, wipe, wire, wish, witch, wolf, wood, wool, word, work, world, worm, worse

3.26.4 Word-medial

awake, award, aware, away, equal, farewell, firewood, highway, kiwi, leeway, liquid, microwave, motorway, otherwise, paperwork, penguin, reward, seaweed, sequence, squad, square, squash, squeeze, sweet, swallow, swim, swan, swap, swear, sweat, swing

3.26.5 Multiple

one-to-one, quick-witted, swimwear, twenty-one, walkway, wall-to-wall, watchword, wayward, well-worn, werewolf, westward, whirlwind, whitewash, wickerwork, wigwam, wishy-washy, woodwind, woodwork, woodworm, worthwhile

3.26.6 Phrases

words of wisdom, wide awake, win an award, a farewell banquet, liquid waste, a qualified midwife, an awkward question, a white swan, a quick swim, a walk-in wardrobe, wonderfully warm weather, wise words, lukewarm water, the way forward, a white wedding, weird and wonderful, a wishing well, a wealthy widow, white wine, wit and wisdom, word for word, a swear word

3.26.7 Sentences I

(1) Why worry about the weather, Edward? (2) Gwen wore a wig at the awards banquet. (3) When it's wet, wear waterproof rainwear. (4) William was wounded twice in World War I.

(5) Wayne would do well to watch his language. (6) I frequently quoted my wife's words of wisdom. (7) We watched the whales with wide-eyed wonder. (8) Wendy's unquestionably a woman of the world. (9) The women wept and wailed when he went away. (10) We watched them weave their way through the swamp.

Sentences 2

(1) We were wondering why she quarreled with the midwife. (2) Woolen sweaters should be washed with lukewarm water. (3) Gwyneth was woken up by the squeak of the wagon wheels. (4) The quality of his work's without equal in the Western world. (5) We went to a one-week workshop on language and linguistics. (6) The walkers watched the white-crested waves sweep towards them. (7) The watermelons were sweet, mouth-watering, and thirst-quenching. (8) While wearing a white swimsuit, she waded waist-deep into the water. (9) Walter switched between wanting to be a waiter and a welfare worker. (10) Watching wildlife in the wonderful tranquility of the woods was rewarding.

3.26.8 Dialogue

A: Why won't you wear the wool sweater I made you?
B: Itchy wool is the worst thing in the world.
A: It's wonderfully warm on windy days.
B: Well, if you want, I'll wait until winter and wear it then.

3.27 Voiced alveolar lateral approximant /l/

3.27.1 Description

Voiced alveolar lateral approximant. With the soft palate raised, the tip of the tongue forms a central closure with the alveolar ridge. One or both sides of the tongue are lowered, allowing the airstream to pass around the central obstruction. /l/ is typically velarized (i.e., the back of the tongue is raised towards the soft palate), especially when a consonant or pause follows.

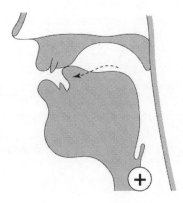

Figure 3.24 English /l/ showing velarized tongue shape; arrow indicates airstream escapes over lowered sides of tongue

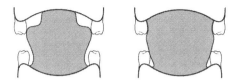

Figure 3.25 Mouth viewed from front; left: tongue's sides lowered for lateral /l/; right: tongue's sides raised for non-lateral consonants

3.27.2 Spelling

<l> look, alone, elephant, build, bold
<le> little, saddle, tackle, vile
<ll> vanilla, bullet, wall
Note that <l> is silent in *colonel, half, salmon, balk, chalk, folk, talk, walk, yolk,* and often in *calm, palm, almond.* <l> is also silent in *could, should, would.* Otherwise, <l> is pronounced (e.g., *cold, field, told, milk, silk*).

3.27.3 Pre-vocalic

lake, lamb, lamp, land, lane, large, last, late, laugh, law, leaf, leak, leap, learn, leave, left, lend, lid, life, lift, light, like, line, lip, list, load, lock, long, look, lose, loss, loud, love, luck

3.27.4 Pre-consonantal

album, balcony, bald, bold, build, bulb, child, cold, culture, elbow, field, film, fold, gold, guilty, healthy, mild, old, result, shelf, shelter, silver, solve, vulgar, wild, world

3.27.5 Pre-pausal

all, appeal, ball, bill, boil, bull, call, cool, crawl, curl, doll, drill, dull, fall, feel, file, fool, girl, hall, hill, howl, ill, meal, mile, nail, oil, owl, pale, pearl, pill, pull, roll, rule, seal, sell, small, smell, smile, spell, still, style, tail, tall, tell, thrill, tool, trail, wall, well, wheel, while

3.27.6 Clipped

gulp, help, pulp, scalp, yelp, belt, fault, melt, result, salt, bulk, hulk, milk, silk, belch, zilch, elf, golf, self, wolf, filth, health, wealth, pulse

3.27.7 Full length vs. clipped

build/built, bold/bolt, falls/false, guild/guilt, killed/kilt, shelve/shelf

3.27.8 Multiple

absolutely, alcohol, calculate, fulfil, leaflet, legal, level, likely, lilac, lilt, lily, little, lively, local, lollipop, lonely, lovely, multiply

3.27.9 Phrases

install an alarm, mentally alert, call an ambulance, a letter of apology, polite applause, fall asleep, a golf ball, a commonly held belief, a light bulb, a burglar alarm, lovely and clean, loud and clear, live in exile, full of flavor, feel like a fool, a call for help, manual labor, learn a language, a silent letter, flashing lights, swallow a pill, a helicopter pilot, learn to relax, build a shelter, a wall of silence, solid silver, tall and slim, a cold spell, a bulging wallet

3.27.10 Sentences 1

(1) Oliver's planted fields full of sunflowers. (2) The local police were placed on full alert. (3) Malcolm was too lazy to consult the manual. (4) He lives in a sleepy little village in Alabama. (5) Luke told me he'd fill me in on the details later. (6) The tail of Allan's plane was filled with bullet holes. (7) The level of alcohol in his blood was below the legal limit. (8) These animals will curl up or roll into a ball when it's cold. (9) Carol volunteered to help children with learning difficulties. (10) Nicola chuckled softly to herself and then lapsed into silence.

Sentences 2

(1) Please familiarize yourselves with all the rules and regulations. (2) Michael has the ability to tackle problems from unusual angles. (3) Lesley published a collection of scholarly articles on linguistics. (4) The walls of the local library were lined with black steel shelves. (5) It was a cold-blooded killing of a defenseless eleven-year-old girl. (6) The old building was badly vandalized and eventually demolished. (7) Lucy felt overwhelmed with guilt for leaving her family in the lurch. (8) In this lesson, the children will learn about the life cycle of the butterfly. (9) The town council apologized for the delay in replying to Linda's complaint. (10) Dylan's accumulated wealth allowed him to live a life of luxury and leisure.

3.27.11 Dialogue

A: I'd like a little less salt and garlic in my meal next time, please.
B: Certainly. You clearly have a delicate palate.
A: I've lived for eleven years on salad and mineral water.
B: Well, that's healthy but slightly bland. Help yourself to apple crumble. It's delicious. It'll blow your mind!

3.28 Voiced post-alveolar approximant /r/

3.28.1 Description

Voiced post-alveolar approximant. With the soft palate in the raised position, the tip of the tongue approaches the rear of the alveolar ridge, but doesn't get close enough to cause turbulence. The center of the tongue is lowered, giving rise to the distinct hollowing of the tongue characteristic of /r/, and the sides are held in contact with the upper back teeth. Weak lip-rounding is also frequently present. An alternative realization, bunched /r/, is also common. The center of the tongue is raised (i.e., "bunched up") toward the area where the hard palate meets the soft palate. This is also usually accompanied by weak lip-rounding.

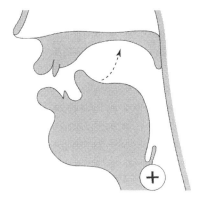

Figure 3.26 English /r/ (post-alveolar approximant); arrow indicates raising of sides of tongue toward back teeth

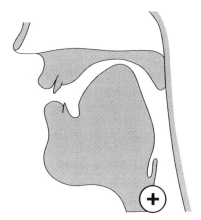

Figure 3.27 English /r/: bunched /r/

GA is a rhotic accent, which means /r/ is pronounced wherever it occurs in the spelling (before a vowel, a consonant, and a pause), e.g., *red, card, car*; see Sections 2.22 and 5.7.

3.28.2 Spelling

<r> rich, horizon, very
<rr> terrific, carrot, worry, error
<wr> wrap, write, wrong, playwright
<rh> rhyme, rhubarb, rhotic, rhythm, rhapsody, rhinoceros

3.28.3 Word-initial

rabbit, race, radio, rain, raise, random, rate, reach, ready, reason, receive, recent, recipe, reckon, red, reduce, reflection, region, relative, relax, release, relief, rely, remind, remove, rent, repeat, resign, respect, rest, result, revenge, rhyme, ribbon, rice, rich, ride, right, rigid, ring, ripe, road, rob, roof, room, root, rope, rose, rough, round, rub, rude, rug, rule, run, rush

3.28.4 Word-medial

afraid, agree, appearance, area, arid, arrange, arrest, arrive, arrogant, arrow, boring, borrow, carrot, carry, cereal, charity, cherry, correct, corrupt, curry, diary, encourage, ferry, foreign, forest, giraffe, guarantee, hero, horizon, hungry, jury, kangaroo, merry, miracle, narrow, orange, parade, parallel, parent, parrot, perish, safari, scary, series, sorry, story, terrific, weary

3.28.5 Word-final

air, bar, bear, beer, blur, bore, car, care, chair, cheer, choir, clear, core, dare, ear, fair, far, fare, fear, fire, flair, floor, flour, for, four, fur, gear, hear, heir, hour, jar, jeer, liar, more, near, par, poor, rare, roar, scar, sir, smear, sneer, sore, sour, spear, steer, swear, tar, war, wear, wire, year, your

3.28.6 Pre-consonantal

hard, scarf, charge, torch, cork, arm, barn, scarce, north, snarl, heart, starve, stairs

3.28.7 Full-length vs. clipped

heard/hurt, serve/surf, surge/search, card/cart, hard/heart, ward/wart, sword/sort

3.28.8 Phonetic affricates /tr dr/

track, trade, traffic, tragic, trail, train, traitor, tramp, trance, trap, travel, tray, treason, treasure, treat, tree, trek, trench, trend, tribe, trick, trip, trolley, trophy, trouble, true, trust, truth, try, attract, patrol; draft, drag, dragon, drain, draw, dread, dream, dress, dribble, drill, drink, drip, drive, drone, drop, drown, drug, drum, dry

3.28.9 Multiple

refrigerator, airport, radar, rare, rear, repair, roar, referee, regret, report, reward, rhubarb, career, corridor, prepare, warfare, barbarian, bravery, carnivore, dartboard, ordinary, remark, rigorous, teardrop, dreary, fragrant, frustration, grapefruit, paragraph, primary, program, referee, regret, represent

3.28.10 Phrases

an art gallery, a practical approach, an area of interest, an arrest warrant, bread and butter, a broken arrow, fresh bread, a promising career, a charity worker, careful consideration, a contradiction in terms, red cherries, bribery and corruption, correct an error, dark brown, ripe fruit, room for improvement, a journey of discovery, juniper berries, raw materials, bricks and mortar, peer pressure, proud parents, a piercing scream, purple grapes, a progress report, private property, torrential rain, free of charge, friends and relations, a mark of respect, rest and relaxation, a rose garden, a rude remark, red roses, short of breath, sour cream, a reign of terror, work in progress, warm regards, arts and crafts, a breath of fresh air

3.28.11 Sentences 1

(1) Robert's red hair was smeared with grease. (2) The newspapers are distributed free of charge. (3) This morning, we reaped the first fruits of our labor. (4) We heard a crack of thunder before it started pouring. (5) After the war, the church was restored to its former glory. (6) Unfortunately, Carol's car brakes aren't working properly. (7) Teenagers are frequently vulnerable to peer group pressure. (8) Gregory ignored Peter's harsh remarks and words of reproach. (9) Carol was the first to arrive and start warming up for her workout. (10) Charlotte's a fiery redhead, and Eleanor has naturally dark-brown hair.

Sentences 2

(1) This report provides further information on current research in literacy. (2) The workshop was a true journey of discovery for everyone concerned. (3) Percy agreed to be Mary's bridge partner at the tournament on Thursday. (4) Erica cried tears of relief when she learned that her daughter was unharmed. (5) This player has an incredible energy and enormous powers of concentration. (6) There was a tremendous variety of mushrooms under the gnarled roots of the tree. (7) There's no guarantee that the emergency measures will produce the desired result. (8) Catherine adores gardening and is particularly proud of her wonderful rose garden. (9) We've experienced unforeseen problems and don't have the resources to overcome them. (10) We stress that our primary concern is for the welfare of the children who are entrusted to our care.

3.28.12 Dialogue

A: My friends have peculiar cars. Robert, for instance, drives around in a purple car. Can you credit it?

B: I sure can. My friend Peter's car is bright maroon, and our manager's is dark green with red stripes.

A: My neighbor's overloaded truck is dangerous, and Rebecca's cramped supermini is really uncomfortable. It's truly microscopic.

B: Personally I prefer riding my motorbike. I feel free as a bird.

A: And my favorite means of transportation is my daughter's electric scooter!

Chapter 4

Practice

Consonant contrasts

This chapter provides practice in distinguishing between pairs of consonants that learners tend to confuse. The exercise material includes minimal pairs demonstrating the contrast in word-initial, word-medial, and word-final positions and in words, phrases, and sentences containing both sounds. The numbers in the table indicate the sections containing the contrasts.

4.1 /p/ vs. /b/	4.11 /s/ vs. /θ/	4.21 /dʒ/ vs. /ʒ/
4.2 /t/ vs. /d/	4.12 /z/ vs. /ð/	4.22 /p/ vs. /f/
4.3 /k/ vs. /g/	4.13 /s/ vs. /ʃ/	4.23 /b/ vs. /v/
4.4 /ʧ/ vs. /dʒ/	4.14 /z/ vs. /ʒ/	4.24 /t/ vs. /θ/
4.5 /f/ vs. /v/	4.15 /n/ vs. /ŋ/	4.25 /d/ vs. /ð/
4.6 /θ/ vs. /ð/	4.16 /r/ vs. /w/	4.26 /v/ vs. /w/
4.7 /s/ vs. /z/	4.17 /l/ vs. /r/	4.27 /dʒ/ vs. /j/
4.8 /ʃ/ vs. /ʒ/	4.18 /t/ vs. /ʧ/	4.28 /h/ vs. zero
4.9 /f/ vs. /θ/	4.19 /d/ vs. /dʒ/	4.29 /ŋk/ and /ŋg/ vs. /ŋ/
4.10 /v/ vs. /ð/	4.20 /ʧ/ vs. /ʃ/	

4.1 Voiceless bilabial plosive /p/ vs. voiced bilabial plosive /b/

4.1.1 Minimal pairs with /p/ and /b/

a) Word-initial

pack/back, pad/bad, pair/bare, pan/ban, park/bark, pat/bat, patch/batch, path/bath, pay/bay, pea/bee, peach/beach, peak/beak, peg/beg, pest/best, pet/bet, pie/buy, pig/big, pill/bill, pin/bin, pit/bit, pole/bowl, post/boast, pride/bride, pull/bull, pump/bump, punch/bunch, push/bush

b) Word-final

cap/cab, cup/cub, hop/hob, lap/lab, mop/mob, rip/rib, pup/pub, rope/robe, slap/slab, swap/swab, tap/tab, tripe/tribe

c) Word-medial

ample/amble, crumple/crumble, dapple/dabble, nipple/nibble, simple/symbol, staple/stable

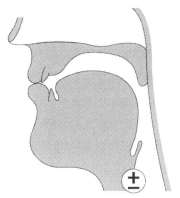

Figure 4.1 English /p/ and /b/ (hold stage)

4.1.2 Words with /p/ and /b/

acceptable, backup, battleship, beep, bishop, blueprint, bump, capable, clipboard, disposable, hipbone, paintbrush, paperback, pebble, placebo, portable, possible, postbox, powerboat, probe, problem, prohibit, proverb, public, publish, scrapbook, superb

4.1.3 Phrases with /p/ and /b/

a humble apology, a baseball cap, a broken cup, a bunch of grapes, a park bench, a birthday party, a bus pass, a bald patch, bits and pieces, break a promise, the push of a button, sleep like a baby, a bus stop, back pain, a paper bag, a picnic basket, a bird of prey, pitch black, deep blue, a paperback book, a copper tube

4.1.4 Sentences with /p/ and /b/

(1) Pete's behavior's simply beneath contempt. (2) Belinda responded with a barely audible whisper. (3) Patrick bought bananas, pears, and a bunch of grapes. (4) This report's based on people's subjective experiences. (5) My husband's mobility has improved by leaps and bounds. (6) Reasonable expenses will be reimbursed by your employer. (7) Betty dabbed some perfume on her temples and collarbone. (8) The company embarked on a program to help the disabled. (9) Would you prefer baked or boiled potatoes with your pork chops? (10) This appealing book bears the unmistakable stamp of personal observation.

4.2 Voiceless alveolar plosive /t/ vs. voiced alveolar plosive /d/

4.2.1 Minimal pairs with /t/ and /d/

a) Word-initial

tangle/dangle, tank/dank, tart/dart, ten/den, tense/dense, tie/die, time/dime, tin/din, tip/dip, tire/dire, toe/dough, tomb/doom, ton/done, town/down, train/drain, trawl/drawl, tread/dread, trench/drench, trip/drip, trout/drought, trudge/drudge, true/drew, trunk/drunk, try/dry, two/do

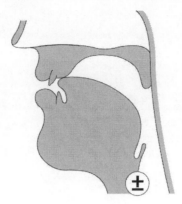

Figure 4.2 English /t/ and /d/ (hold stage)

b) Word-final

bat/bad, beat/bead, bent/bend, bet/bed, bit/bid, bright/bride, brought/broad, built/build, cart/card, court/cord, coat/code, debt/dead, eight/aid, fate/fade, feet/feed, great/grade, greet/greed, grit/grid, hat/had, heart/hard, height/hide, hit/hid, hurt/heard, knot/nod, mat/mad, rate/raid, right/ride, root/rude, rot/rod, seat/seed, set/said, sight/side, slight/slide, sort/sword, squat/squad, threat/thread, tight/tide, wait/wade, wheat/weed, white/wide, write/ride

4.2.2 Words with /t/ and /d/

accident, astounding, attend, attitude, bandit, bloodshot, contend, contradict, dart, date, debt, decorate, defeat, delicate, dent, department, determined, dictator, diet, dirt, disaster, distant, donate, dot, doubt, dust, edit, gratitude, idiot, instead, intend, introduce, meltdown, modest, standard, teddy, tedious, tidy, timid, tired, toad, today, trade, tradition

4.2.3 Phrases with /t/ and /d/

a dinner table, a sad tale, a team leader, crocodile tears, tooth decay, dead tired, from head to toe, garden tools, today's date, as fit as a fiddle, a fruit salad, neat and tidy, a red carpet, bread and butter, drinking water, a dead end street, a cloud of dust, a reading list, the distant past, a gifted child, a tap dancer, day and night, attention to detail, cast a shadow, wit and wisdom

4.2.4 Sentences with /t/ and /d/

(1) The two methods yielded identical results. (2) After dinner, we headed to the historic city center. (3) It happened in the distant past and is best forgotten. (4) My elder sister's as blind as a bat and as deaf as a doorknob. (5) The leadership team decided to treat it as an isolated incident. (6) What's the difference between word stress and sentence stress? (7) Katie and her husband, Peter, are in the middle of a bitter divorce. (8) Hundreds of students have benefited from Derek's wit and wisdom. (9) Donald got a master's degree in statistics at Delaware State University. (10) For breakfast, we were served a delicious fruit salad and homemade bread with nuts.

4.3 Voiceless velar plosive /k/ vs. voiced velar plosive /g/

4.3.1 Minimal pairs with /k/ and /g/

a) Word-initial

cage/gauge, came/game, cane/gain, cap/gap, card/guard, cause/gauze, cave/gave, class/glass, clue/glue, coal/goal, coast/ghost, coat/goat, cold/gold, come/gum, cot/got, could/good, crab/grab, craft/graft, crane/grain, crate/great, crave/grave, crease/grease, crew/grew, crime/grime, crow/grow, curl/girl

b) Word-final

back/bag, buck/bug, muck/mug, peck/peg, pick/pig, pluck/plug, rack/rag, sack/sag, snack/snag, stack/stag, tack/tag, tuck/tug, wick/wig

c) Word-medial

anchor/anger, ankle/angle, decree/degree, mucky/muggy, tinkle/tingle, vicar/vigor

4.3.2 Words with /k/ and /g/

backgammon, backlog, cardigan, cargo, catalog, cog, colleague, congratulate, foxglove, kangaroo, keg, kilogram, agriculture, eggcup, exact, exotic, galaxy, garlic, geek, graphic, magnetic, neglect, organic

4.3.3 Phrases with /k/ and /g/

gain confidence, forget to ask, a dog blanket, a card game, close together, a mug of coffee, regular contact, a golf course, hugs and kisses, beginner's luck, a gap in the market, a rock garden, a closely guarded secret, work in progress, a weak argument, a stomach bug, key figures, sticky fingers, a gas leak, a security guard, a lucky guess, a catchy slogan, sugar cubes

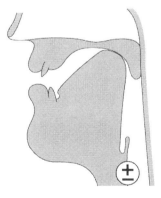

Figure 4.3 English /k/ and /g/ (hold stage)

4.3.4 Sentences with /k/ and /g/

(1) Agnes just scraped through her chemistry exam. (2) Gary caught a glimpse of the cat burglar in action. (3) The candidates must have a good command of English. (4) We recommend the guided walk through the botanical gardens. (5) She picked up a copy of a yoga magazine at the local supermarket. (6) Gwen was commissioned to think of a catchy slogan for the golf club. (7) Keith compiled a comprehensive bibliography in cognitive linguistics. (8) I've been asked to give a lecture at the School of Agriculture in August. (9) Chris comported himself with great dignity and integrity during the crisis. (10) Secret negotiations were conducted between the kidnappers and the government.

4.4 Voiceless palato-alveolar affricate /ʧ/ vs. voiced palato-alveolar affricate /ʤ/

4.4.1 Minimal pairs with /ʧ/ and /ʤ/

a) Word-initial

chain/Jane, char/jar, cheer/jeer, cherry/jerry, chess/Jess, chest/jest, Chester/jester, chew/Jew, chin/gin, chive/jive, choice/Joyce, choke/joke, chunk/junk

b) Word-final

batch/badge, cinch/singe, etch/edge, H/age, larch/large, lunch/lunge, march/Marge, match/Madge, perch/purge, retch/Reg, rich/ridge, search/surge

4.4.2 Words with /ʧ/ and /ʤ/

challenge, charge, congestion, conjecture, digestion, gesture, stagecoach, suggestion

4.4.3 Phrases with /ʧ/ and /ʤ/

a cheerful subject, a branch manager, a cabbage patch, a challenging question, a champion jockey, a change of strategy, a charming cottage, cultural heritage, a digital watch, a gentle

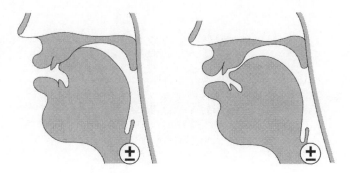

Figure 4.4 English /ʧ/ and /ʤ/; left: hold stage; right: release with homorganic friction; note trumpet-shaped lip-rounding

touch, a huge challenge, a job search, a juicy cherry, a large batch, a major change, a strange mixture, cottage cheese, free-range chicken, Punch and Judy, change the subject, choose a jury, launch a project, a huge statue

4.4.4 Sentences with /ʧ/ and /ʤ/

(1) Richard's major subject's cultural anthropology. (2) Jeff was a branch manager for a regional furniture chain. (3) Jim wouldn't budge an inch until Charlie had apologized. (4) They launched a research project on agricultural drainage. (5) The teenagers were charged with cheating in a geography project. (6) We checked in our luggage and then trudged to the departure lounge. (7) Judith cringed when she approached the torture chambers and dungeons. (8) Gemma has a thatched roof cottage in a picturesque village in Massachusetts. (9) There was a large beech hedge around the vegetable patch and the charming peach orchard. (10) Joe indulged in a chicken and spinach sandwich, while Gina munched on the juicy, sumptuous cherries.

4.5 Voiceless labio-dental fricative /f/ vs. voiced labio-dental fricative /v/

4.5.1 Minimal pairs with /f/ and /v/

a) Word-initial

fail/veil, fairy/vary, fan/van, fast/vast, fat/vat, fault/vault, fear/veer, ferry/very, feud/viewed, few/view, file/vile, final/vinyl, fine/vine, fuse/views

b) Word-final

belief/believe, calf/calve, grief/grieve, half/halve, leaf/leave, proof/prove, safe/save, shelf/shelve, strife/strive, surf/serve, thief/thieve, wafer/waiver

c) Word-medial

confection/convection, infest/invest, reference/reverence, refuse/reviews, rifle/rival, safer/saver, shuffle/shovel, sniffle/snivel, surface/service, wafer/waiver

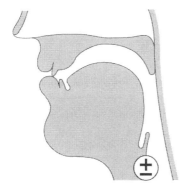

Figure 4.5 English /f/ and /v/

4.5.2 Words with /f/ and /v/

aftershave, defensive, definitive, effective, favor, festive, fever, five, flavor, forever, forgive, offensive, hovercraft, overdraft, verify

4.5.3 Phrases with /f/ and /v/

family values, a grave face, feel very faint, a devoted fan, live in fear, a moveable feast, wave a flag, reveal a flaw, invest in the future, a carving knife, living proof, a vast difference, a valiant effort, an attractive offer, free advice, a safe alternative, a fascinating conversation, drive carefully, full of flavor, a love affair, a fast-flowing river, perfect vision

4.5.4 Sentences with /f/ and /v/

(1) Frank's funeral service was very moving. (2) It's November, and the leaves are falling fast. (3) My friend Valerie finally finished her first novel. (4) It's a fascinating film about love and forgiveness. (5) We deliver fresh fruit and vegetables in refrigerated vans. (6) My boyfriend and I visited the dolphins on Friday evening. (7) The university professors eventually resolved their conflict. (8) It definitely isn't difficult to find vegetarian food in Vietnam. (9) Phil vented his frustration at their failure to develop an effective vaccine. (10) It was painfully obvious to everyone that Phoebe had given false evidence.

4.6 Voiceless dental fricative /θ/ vs. voiced dental fricative /ð/

4.6.1 Minimal pairs with /θ/ and /ð/

thigh/thy, loath/loathe, sheath/sheathe, teeth/teethe, wreath/wreathe

4.6.2 Phrases with /θ/ and /ð/

gather strength, breathe through your mouth, rather pathetic, further south, gather your thoughts

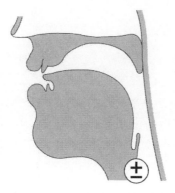

Figure 4.6 English /θ/ and/ð/

4.6.3 Sentences with /θ/ and /ð/

(1) Matthew and his grandfather withdrew from the throng. (2) Pleather's a type of synthetic leather made from polyethylene. (3) Without further thought, Dorothy ruthlessly threw out all her clothes. (4) Catherine made a healthy smoothie to soothe Elizabeth's throbbing throat. (5) Edith gathered the strength to tell Martha the truth about her father's death. (6) The three of us loathed his pathetic blather about the ethics of youth athletics. (7) Further north, a path threads its way through a wealth of heather-covered heath. (8) It's healthiest to breathe in through the nose and to breathe out through the mouth. (9) It's her mother's seventieth and her brother's thirty-fifth birthday on the thirteenth. (10) That godfather of yours is economical with the truth; in fact, he lies through his teeth.

4.7 Voiceless alveolar fricative /s/ vs. voiced alveolar fricative /z/

4.7.1 Minimal pairs with /s/ and /z/

a) Word-initial

sack/Zack, sink/zinc, sip/zip, sown/zone, sue/zoo

b) Word-final

advice/advise, bus/buzz, cease/seize, device/devise, dose/doze, face/phase, fuss/fuzz, grace/graze, hearse/hers, hiss/his, loose/lose, price/prize, race/raise, rice/rise

c) Word-medial

looser/loser, muscle/muzzle

4.7.2 Words with /s/ and /z/

business, centralize, citizen, criticize, customize, despise, disaster, disclose, dispose, emphasize, exercise, fantasize, possess, residence, resist, salesman, scales, scissors,

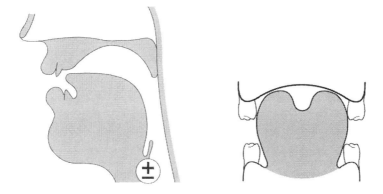

Figure 4.7 Left: English /s/ and/z/; right: mouth viewed from front showing grooved tongue shape

season, seize, series, size, sneeze, snooze, sometimes, squeeze, summarize, supervise, surprise, zealous, zest

4.7.3 Phrases with /s/ and /z/

easy access, a surprise announcement, a blessing in disguise, a prison cell, deserve a chance, a wise choice, a cause for concern, hazard a guess, repossess a house, a recipe for disaster, a poisonous snake, a serious accusation, a fierce blaze, a sea breeze, Swiss cheese, a basic design, a strong desire, a contagious disease, pass an exam, a jealous husband, a jazz singer, a famous phrase, past and present, a jigsaw puzzle, the voice of reason, a massive raise

4.7.4 Sentences with /s/ and /z/

(1) This mysterious disease spreads easily. (2) Steve raised his glass to propose a toast. (3) Zoe listens to classical music for relaxation. (4) This was my first tantalizing glimpse of the islands. (5) James seized the chance to present his ideas to his boss. (6) The rise in taxes caused widespread resentment among investors. (7) Sebastian still hasn't paused to consider the reasons for these rules. (8) Zack suffered serious cuts and bruises after the accident last Thursday. (9) The owners took pains to stress that there were no plans to close the restaurant. (10) The lecturers and students expressed surprise at the news of the dean's resignation.

4.8 Voiceless palato-alveolar fricative /ʃ/ vs. voiced palato-alveolar fricative /ʒ/

4.8.1 Minimal pairs with /ʃ/ and /ʒ/

Aleutian/allusion, Confucian/confusion

4.8.2 Phrases with /ʃ/ and /ʒ/

a national treasure, a partial closure, a rash decision, a foolish delusion, social divisions, a population explosion, radiation exposure, a special measure, malicious pleasure, a special regime, an unusual shape, national television, a special occasion

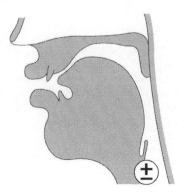

Figure 4.8 English /ʃ/ and /ʒ/; note trumpet-shape lip-rounding

4.8.3 Sentences with /ʃ/ and /ʒ/

(1) This collection's a national treasure. (2) Elision's the deletion or omission of a sound. (3) Make a donation in celebration of a special occasion. (4) Mesh was inserted into the Caucasian patient's incision. (5) Overfishing led to the partial closure of the recreation area. (6) The conclusion is that education and working conditions are crucial. (7) The justification of this action was the prevention of sabotage and espionage. (8) There was substantial opposition to the introduction of commercial television. (9) The revision included the provision of information on legislation and regulations. (10) Schadenfreude is the satisfaction or malicious pleasure felt at somebody else's hardship.

4.9 Voiceless labio-dental fricative /f/ vs. voiceless dental fricative /θ/

4.9.1 Minimal pairs with /f/ and /θ/

fin/thin, first/thirst, fought/thought, Fred/thread, free/three, freeze/threes, frill/thrill; deaf/death, oaf/oath, roof/Ruth

4.9.2 Words with /f/ and /θ/

afterbirth, aftermath, afterthought, facecloth, faith, filthy, footpath, fourth, froth, mouthful, thankful, thief, thoughtful, youthful

4.9.3 Phrases with /f/ and /θ/

thin fabric, false enthusiasm, monthly fees, a fight to the death, fit and healthy, thick fog, healthy food, lethal force, worth a fortune, a faithful friend, thick fur, go through a phase, three and a half, a thatched roof, nothing to be afraid of, a different author, freeze to death, life on earth, farming methods, follow a path, a funny thing, thoughts and feelings, nothing to offer

4.9.4 Sentences with /f/ and /θ/

(1) Cathy filled three thermos bottles with coffee. (2) Follow the path on the south side of the cliff. (3) This French Gothic cathedral's breathtakingly beautiful. (4) My friend Judith will

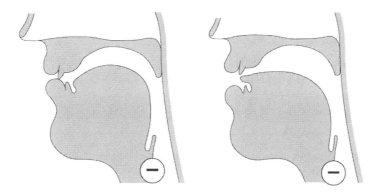

Figure 4.9 Left: English /f/; right: English /θ/

perform at the theater festival on Thursday. (5) Keith threw the pamphlet on the floor and left the office in a huff. (6) There's a wealth of wildlife in the rainforest, from elephants to panthers. (7) His frame was thick-set and athletic, but his physical strength was failing. (8) My nephew's going through a health food phase and refuses to eat fast food. (9) Kenneth felt the author was thoroughly confused about the definition of faith. (10) Edith's stiff, arthritic fingers made it difficult for her to hold her knife and fork.

4.10 Voiced labio-dental fricative /v/ vs. voiced dental fricative /ð/

4.10.1 Minimal pairs with /v/ and /ð/

vale/they'll, van/than, vat/that, clove/clothe, loaves/loathes, fervor/further

4.10.2 Words with /v/ and /ð/

nevertheless, themselves, weathervane

4.10.3 Phrases with /v/ and /ð/

breathe heavily, a loving father, develop a rhythm, relatively smooth, whatever the weather, rather clever, a smooth curve, leather gloves, further investment, soothe your nerves, a smooth shave, a worthy victory, protective clothing

4.10.4 Sentences with /v/ and /ð/

(1) Heather has a very overbearing father. (2) My mother's mauve velvet clothes are lovely. (3) Vera advised us to invest in breathable clothes. (4) My brother ventures out whatever the weather. (5) Victoria's smooth voice was soothing and forgiving. (6) Oliver's intervention saved them the bother of having to leave Nevada. (7) My beloved half-brother won a decisive victory over his seething rival. (8) They were envious of Steven's move to a southern province in the Netherlands. (9) It was evident that the volunteers loathed the novice's

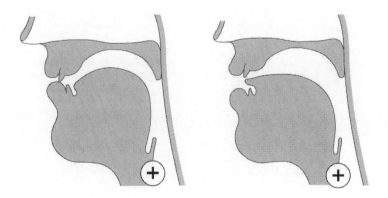

Figure 4.10 Left: English /v/; right: English /ð/

holier-than-thou behavior. (10) They were very relieved when they discovered that their father had survived unscathed.

4.11 Voiceless alveolar fricative /s/ vs. voiceless dental fricative /θ/

4.11.1 Minimal pairs with /s/ and /θ/

a) Word-initial

sank/thank, saw/thaw, seam/theme, sick/thick, sigh/thigh, sink/think, sin/thin, song/thong, sought/thought, sum/thumb, symbol/thimble

b) Word-final

eights/eighth, face/faith, force/forth, frost/frothed, gross/growth, miss/myth, moss/moth, mouse/mouth, pass/path, tense/tenth, truce/truth, worse/worth

c) Word-medial

ensues/enthuse, unsinkable/unthinkable

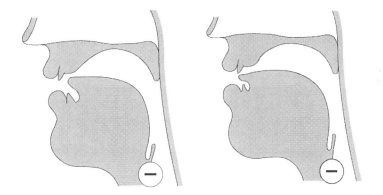

Figure 4.11 Left: English /s/; right: English /θ/

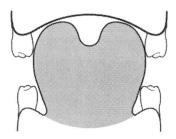

Figure 4.12 Mouth viewed from front showing grooved tongue shape for /s/

4.11.2 Words with /s/ and /θ/

absinthe, amethyst, anthrax, arthritis, atheist, birthplace, breathless, enthusiastic, faithless, henceforth, hyacinth, hypothesis, locksmith, mathematics, orthodox, pathos, psychopath, seventh, south, stealth, stethoscope, strength, sympathy, thanks, thesaurus, thesis, thirsty, thrust

4.11.3 Phrases with /s/ and /θ/

an assessment method, thrown off balance, birthday celebrations, a death certificate, the thrill of the chase, a thick crust, a lengthy description, a thin face, a thick mist, nothing to say, scared to death, a thin slice, a theme song, speech therapy, a faithful servant, slow growth, a solemn oath, the tenth century, a central theme, stop a thief, a thorough search, a school of thought, a serious threat, a sore throat, suck your thumb, speak the truth, lost youth, a thick sauce

4.11.4 Sentences with /s/ and /θ/

(1) Sue gave birth to a healthy son last Saturday. (2) Beth was threatened with expulsion by the principal. (3) The cathedral's famous for its seventh-century ceiling. (4) Psychologists now think there is such a thing as a sixth sense. (5) The discipline of mathematics develops at a breathtaking pace. (6) The circus got an enthusiastic reception in Plymouth yesterday. (7) Matthew has produced an in-depth study of the symptoms of apathy. (8) I'm sick to death of listening to his hypotheses and unsound theories. (9) The authors stress that this is the least expensive method of assessment. (10) For the past six months, I've been seeing a speech therapist who specializes in stammering.

4.12 Voiced alveolar fricative /z/ vs. voiced dental fricative /ð/

4.12.1 Minimal pairs with /z/ and /ð/

Zen/then, bays/bathe, breeze/breathe, tease/teethe, wizard/withered

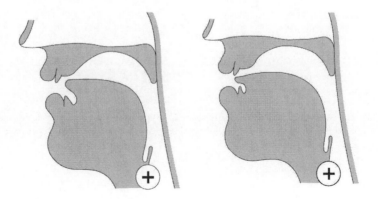

Figure 4.13 Left: English /z/; right: English /ð/

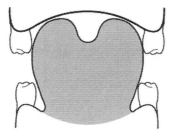

Figure 4.14 Mouth viewed from front showing grooved tongue shape for /z/

4.12.2 Words with /z/ and /ð/

bothers, brothers, dithers, feathers, mothers, newsworthy, others, otherwise, praiseworthy, Southerners, theirs, these, those

4.12.3 Phrases with /z/ and /ð/

a worthy cause, rather busy, breathe easily, resemble your father, a further reason, rather bizarre

4.12.4 Sentences with /z/ and /ð/

(1) My mother always wears designer clothes and shoes. (2) I loathe his jeans, turquoise jersey, and leather blazer. (3) Although he pretends otherwise, he finds her irresistible. (4) He believes rhythmic breathing's a means of minimizing anxiety. (5) Alexander raises funds from many sources to further worthy causes. (6) His stepfather's a rhythm and blues and jazz musician from Louisiana. (7) The weather has hitherto been pleasant for the season, but now it's freezing. (8) Heather resembles her mother physically with her hazel eyes and frizzy curls. (9) There was a reasonable breeze, but nevertheless, the northern horizon was hazy. (10) Mr. Kenworthy's transition from Kansas to southern Arizona caused a lot of misery.

4.13 Voiceless alveolar fricative /s/ vs. voiceless palato-alveolar fricative /ʃ/

4.13.1 Minimal pairs with /s/ and /ʃ/

a) Word-initial

said/shed, sake/shake, same/shame, save/shave, sealed/shield, seat/sheet, self/shelf, sell/shell, sigh/shy, sign/shine, sin/shin, single/shingle, sip/ship, sock/shock, sort/short, sour/shower, sun/shun

b) Word-final

ass/ash, fist/fished, gas/gash, lease/leash, mass/mash, mess/mesh, Paris/parish, rust/rushed

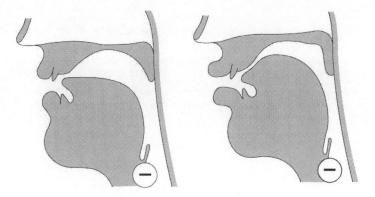

Figure 4.15 Left: English /s/; right: English /ʃ/

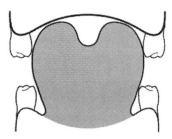

Figure 4.16 Mouth viewed from front showing grooved tongue shape for /s/ and /ʃ/

4.13.2 Words with /s/ and /ʃ/

ambitious, anxious, assurance, astonish, atrocious, cautious, celebration, censorship, circulation, concession, conscious, conversation, deception, delicious, discretion, discussion, disruption, distinguish, essential, establish, expression, gracious, horseradish, infectious, malicious, patience, precious, seashell, seashore, section, session, shameless, shoelace, slash, social, spacious, Spanish, special, splash, squash, superstition, sushi, tenacious, vicious

4.13.3 Phrases with /s/ and /ʃ/

a modest ambition, absolutely astonished, a stiff brush, spare cash, a glass of champagne, a personality clash, a serious crash, from start to finish, fish soup, nice and fresh, cast a shadow, a sense of shame, a distinctive shape, a silk sheet, seek shelter, a nasty shock, sensible shoes, show business, a secret wish

4.13.4 Sentences with /s/ and /ʃ/

(1) Tracy's voice sounded so shrill and sharp. (2) The ship sailed extremely close to the shore. (3) Susan was shivering in her short-sleeved shirt. (4) She pushed and shoved to get the best possible seat. (5) There wasn't a shred of evidence for this assumption. (6) There's a shuttle bus from the station to the city center. (7) The ice fashion show was fabulous from start to finish. (8) Sharon's life's ambition was to be financially successful. (9) Sheila slipped

between the sheets and was asleep in an instant. (10) The nurse must respect the patient's wish for confidentiality should this be requested.

4.14 Voiced alveolar fricative /z/ vs. voiced palato-alveolar fricative /ʒ/

4.14.1 Minimal pairs with /z/ and /ʒ/

baize/beige, rues/rouge, Caesar/seizure, composer/composure

4.14.2 Phrases with /z/ and /ʒ/

a barrage of criticism, cause a collision, lose your composure, cause confusion, a pleasure cruise, a wise decision, an organized excursion, resist an invasion, easy to measure, a casual observer, rise to the occasion, use persuasion, business as usual

4.14.3 Sentences with /z/ and /ʒ/

(1) Our treasurer has amazing powers of persuasion. (2) It's wise to minimize your children's exposure to television. (3) It was by no means unusual for James to lose his composure. (4) He was imprisoned for espionage activities against the regime. (5) The shows,

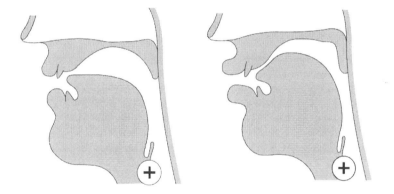

Figure 4.17 Left: English /z/; right: English /ʒ/

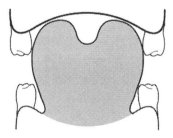

Figure 4.18 Mouth viewed from front showing grooved tongue shape for /z/ and /ʒ/

films, and television series are categorized by genre. (6) Elizabeth resented her husband's intrusion into her leisure activities. (7) The explosion was caused by soldiers disguised in desert camouflage. (8) The decision to close the business was met with a barrage of criticism. (9) Alexander hides his treasured beige Suzuki in the garage, refusing to let me use it. (10) The excursion to the museums of Rio de Janeiro was a pleasant conclusion to their cruise to Brazil.

4.15 Voiced alveolar nasal /n/ vs. voiced velar nasal /ŋ/

4.15.1 Minimal pairs with /n/ and /ŋ/

a) Word-final

ban/bang, bun/bung, clan/clang, done/dung, fan/fang, kin/king, pan/pang, pin/ping, ran/rang, run/rung, sin/sing, son/sung, tan/tang, thin/thing, ton/tongue, win/wing

b) Word-medial

hand/hanged, wind/winged

4.15.2 Words with /n/ and /ŋ/

anything, beginning, cunning, delinquent, England, evening, fascinating, gardening, handwriting, interesting, landing, lengthen, lightning, morning, nothing, penguin, warning, wingspan, yearning

4.15.3 Phrases with /n/ and /ŋ/

pain and anguish, a broken ankle, a bank account, financial backing, an enormous bang, a new beginning, uneven breathing, winter clothing, a newspaper cutting, an emergency landing, thunder and lightning, earn a living, a sunny morning, an opening ceremony, singing

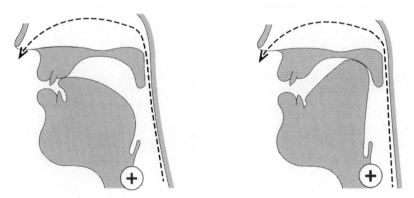

Figure 4.19 Left: English /n/; right: English /ŋ/; the arrow indicates the escape of the airstream through the nose

lessons, a sense of timing, a wedding present, the animal kingdom, a marching band, a strong bond, a growing demand, a young man, a fleeting moment, a throbbing pain, a frying pan, boiling point, hunting season, a long sentence, spring cleaning, sparkling wine, the kitchen sink, many thanks

4.15.4 Sentences with /n/ and /ŋ/

(1) My son Norman earns a living giving singing lessons. (2) Are your parents going to attend the meeting tonight? (3) It's been raining torrentially with distant thunder and lightning. (4) He's been working morning, noon, and night on his writing assignment. (5) Joanna has a charming collection of pen and ink drawings of town scenes. (6) His children are in a stimulating environment where learning's fun and exciting. (7) Wendy was waiting for her dancing partner at the main entrance of the building. (8) John and his girlfriend from Arlington are making preparations for their wedding. (9) I've been reading an intensely moving and thought-provoking novel about a lonely teenager. (10) I recommend this exhibition to anyone looking for an inspiring introduction to nineteenth-century painting.

4.16 Voiced post-alveolar approximant /r/ vs. voiced labial-velar approximant /w/

4.16.1 Minimal pairs with /r/ and /w/

rage/wage, raid/wade, rail/wail, raise/ways, rake/wake, rare/wear, rate/wait, ray/way, reel/wheel, rent/went, rest/west, rich/which, ride/wide, right/white, rinse/wince, rip/whip, ripe/wipe, roar/war, room/womb, run/one, write/white, array/away

4.16.2 Words with /r/ and /w/

aquarium, brainwave, breadwinner, brickwork, crossword, driveway, everyone, framework, inquiry, mouthwatering, quarrel, quarry, query, railway, request, require, reward, runway, squirrel, warrant, wary, weary, withdraw, worry

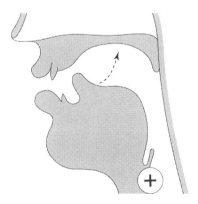

Figure 4.20 English /r/ (post-alveolar approximant); arrow indicates raising of sides of tongue toward back teeth

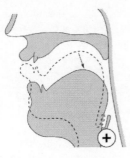 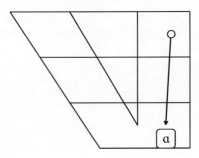

Figure 4.21 English /w/; diagram shows approximate change in tongue shape; note that English /w/ is a semi-vowel and can therefore be indicated on a vowel diagram. Here the sequence /wɑ/ in *wasp* is shown

4.16.3 Phrases with /r/ and /w/

choir practice, a farewell appearance, routine paperwork, the correct password, a rhetorical question, a generous reward, sworn to secrecy, a narrow waist, a war hero, the wrong way, arrange a wedding, a rich widow, received wisdom, rotten wood, the right word

4.16.4 Sentences with /r/ and /w/

(1) Wendy broke down and wept uncontrollably. (2) The three workmen were stripped to the waist. (3) Walter received a serious wound during the war. (4) Wild waves crashed relentlessly against the rocks. (5) Rebecca always pronounces this word incorrectly. (6) Robert wants to go for a quick swim before breakfast. (7) The weather grew progressively worse and unpredictable. (8) The runners were dripping with sweat and screaming for water. (9) Edward broke off a dry twig from the tree and threw it into the well. (10) They carried out the fieldwork in whatever language was natural to the respondents.

4.17 Voiced alveolar lateral approximant /l/ vs. voiced post-alveolar approximant /r/

4.17.1 Minimal pairs with /l/ and /r/

a) Word-initial

bland/brand, blink/brink, bloom/broom, blush/brush, clamp/cramp, clash/crash, climb/crime, cloud/crowd, clown/crown, clue/crew, flame/frame, flea/free, flesh/fresh, flight/fright, flute/fruit, fly/fry, glass/grass, glow/grow, lace/race, lack/rack, lake/rake, lamb/ram, lamp/ramp, lane/rain, late/rate, law/raw, light/right, list/wrist, liver/river, load/road, lock/rock, long/wrong, loot/root, lot/rot

b) Word-medial

alive/arrive, belated/berated, believe/bereave, belly/berry, collect/correct, collection/correction, pilot/pirate

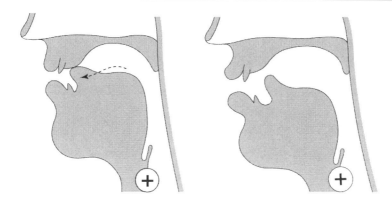

Figure 4.22 Left: dark /l/ showing velarized tongue shape; arrow indicates airstream escapes over lowered sides of tongue; right: English /r/ (post-alveolar approximant)

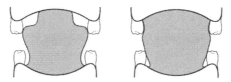

Figure 4.23 Mouth viewed from front; left: tongue sides lowered for lateral /l/; right: tongue sides raised for /r/

c) Word-final

bell/bear, fell/fair, hell/hair, shell/share, spell/spare, swell/swear, well/wear, deal/dear, feel/fear, heel/here, meal/mere, kneel/near, peel/peer, steal/steer

4.17.2 Words with /l/ and /r/

airplane, agriculture, alert, approval, arrival, barrel, brawl, brilliant, brutal, calorie, carol, celebrity, salary, cereal, chlorine, clarify, clear, control, coral, crawl, crocodile, cruel, crystal, early, floor, florist, formal, frail, fragile, friendly, gallery, glamorous, glory, glossary, gorilla, grill, growl, hilarious, large, larynx, laundry, lord, lurid, luxury, lyric, material, military, parallel, plural, problem, profile, purple, rail, really, relative, relax, relic, relief, relish, rival, roll, rule, tolerate, welfare

4.17.3 Phrases with /l/ and /r/

a legal agreement, the last to arrive, below average, wild berries, brain cells, garlic bread, buried alive, black cherries, a life of crime, split the difference, a look of disapproval, a lifelong dream, old and frail, a self-help group, hold a grudge, a look of horror, a loveless marriage, a price list, problem solving, lose a race, a railroad car, ready and willing, follow a recipe, a silly remark, a lack of respect, early retirement, the last straw, crystal clear, fear of failure, green fields, a cry for help, pilot error, friends and relations, a regular supply

4.17.4 Sentences with /l/ and /r/

(1) The pitcher tried to throw the ball toward the plate. (2) Fresh barrels of ale were brought up from the cellar. (3) Brian's closing remarks were greeted with wild applause. (4) Carol's worries proved completely and utterly groundless. (5) The primary stress falls on the last syllable in *kangaroo* and *referee*. (6) Harry held up his shorts with suspenders and a cracked leather belt. (7) Unfortunately, we ran up a very large hotel bill on our brief trip to London. (8) They had to drive slowly, as the road was partially blocked by fallen logs. (9) The overall responsibility lies with the authorities of the individual countries. (10) The program was broadcast live on national television on Friday the 11th of April.

4.18 Voiceless alveolar plosive /t/ vs. voiceless palato-alveolar affricate /ʧ/

4.18.1 Minimal pairs with /t/ and /ʧ/

a) Word-initial

talk/chalk, tart/chart, tatty/chatty, tease/cheese, test/chest, tick/chick, till/chill, tin/chin, tip/chip, toes/chose, top/chop, tore/chore, two/chew

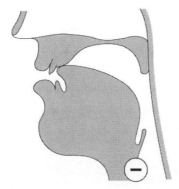

Figure 4.24 English /t/ (hold stage)

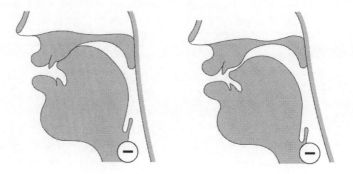

Figure 4.25 English /ʧ/; left: hold stage; right: release with homorganic friction; note trumpet-shaped lip-rounding

b) Word-final

art/arch, bat/batch, beat/beach, belt/belch, bent/bench, cat/catch, coat/coach, eat/each, hat/hatch, hit/hitch, hut/hutch, it/itch, knot/notch, mat/match, pat/patch, pit/pitch, port/porch, rent/wrench, start/starch

c) Word-medial

jester/gesture

4.18.2 Words with /t/ and /tʃ/

attach, chant, chapter, chariot, chart, chat, cheat, chest, futuristic, merchant, ratchet, statue, stitch, stench, teacher, torch, torture, touch, twitch

4.18.3 Phrases with /t/ and /tʃ/

a kitchen table, a chilling tale, Chinese tea, a tennis coach, watch your tongue, a beach towel, a change of heart, market research, pitch a tent, a gift voucher, a witch hunt, a safety catch, a chain of events, cheese on toast, hot chocolate, an irritating itch, attend a lecture, a nasty scratch, a satirical sketch

4.18.4 Sentences with /t/ and /tʃ/

(1) Ted can't stop scratching that irritating itch on his chest. (2) We got tickets to watch a championship match last March. (3) If you've got any questions, don't hesitate to get in touch with Rachel. (4) Charles was appointed as a research assistant at Wichita State University. (5) Archie got two bottles of water to quench his thirst in the scorching heat. (6) Unfortunately, the chief of staff didn't understand the gravity of the situation. (7) The team coach stressed the importance of a culture based on mutual respect. (8) The concepts and facts from each chapter were checked in a multiple choice test. (9) Richard's lecture entitled "Climate Challenges in the Twenty-first Century" was fascinating. (10) The teacher watched the children snatching my daughter's toys without reproaching them.

4.19 Voiced alveolar plosive /d/ vs. voiced palato-alveolar affricate /dʒ/

4.19.1 Minimal pairs with /d/ and /dʒ/

a) Word-initial

dab/jab, dam/jam, day/jay, dear/jeer, debt/jet, dental/gentle, din/gin, dog/jog, dot/jot, dug/jug, dump/jump, dust/just

b) Word-final

aid/age, bad/badge, buddy/budgie, head/hedge, lard/large, paid/page, raid/rage, rid/ridge, wade/wage

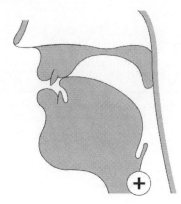

Figure 4.26 English /d/ (hold stage)

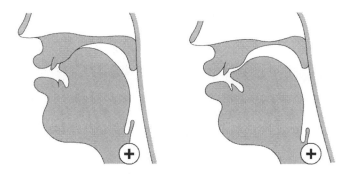

Figure 4.27 English /ʤ/; left: hold stage; right: release with homorganic friction; note trumpet-shaped lip-rounding

c) Word-medial

murder/merger

4.19.2 Words with /d/ and /ʤ/

advantage, agenda, bandage, damage, danger, dejected, detergent, digest (n.), digit, diligent, dirge, discourage, diverge, dodge, dungeon, frigid, gingerbread, indulge, jade, jeopardy, judo, legend, prodigy, rigid, tragedy

4.19.3 Phrases with /d/ and /ʤ/

a tragic accident, an adoption agency, a huge advantage, a prestigious award, a ginger beard, board and lodging, body language, in this day and age, encourage debate, a voyage of discovery, flood damage, food shortage, a country cottage, a change of mood, a range of products, old age, a hidden agenda, a food allergy, build a bridge, change your mind, a vivid image, bread and jam, traditional jazz, a dirty job, a dead language, a sudden urge

4.19.4 Sentences with /d/ and /dʒ/

(1) The older generation finds it hard to adapt to major changes. (2) The offender managed to avoid jail by pleading self-defense. (3) Jess denied all knowledge of what had happened to her lodger. (4) We stayed in a delightful cottage in a seaside village in Jersey. (5) David's engineering project turned out to be a voyage of discovery. (6) Jill's daughter's studying modern languages at a college in Georgia. (7) Joe just couldn't understand the difference between adjectives and adverbs. (8) The original budget was exceeded by an average of a hundred dollars a day. (9) Dozens of passengers were stranded after floods damaged the roads and bridges. (10) My friend Jenny was injured in a tragic road accident when she was a teenager.

4.20 Voiceless palato-alveolar affricate /tʃ/ vs. voiceless palato-alveolar fricative /ʃ/

4.20.1 Minimal pairs with /tʃ/ and /ʃ/

a) Word-initial

chair/share, chatter/shatter, cheat/sheet, cheer/sheer, cherry/sherry, chew/shoe, chin/shin, chip/ship, chop/shop, chore/shore

b) Word-final

batch/bash, butch/bush, catch/cash, crutch/crush, ditch/dish, hutch/hush, latch/lash, leech/ leash, march/marsh, match/mash, much/mush, watch/wash, witch/wish

4.20.2 Words with /tʃ/ and /ʃ/

archbishop, championship, cherish, childish, situation

4.20.3 Phrases with /tʃ/ and /ʃ/

boyish charm, a butcher's shop, a chain reaction, a chat show, a crucial match, culture shock, a delicious lunch, a distinguishing feature, a fresh approach, a short chat, a special feature,

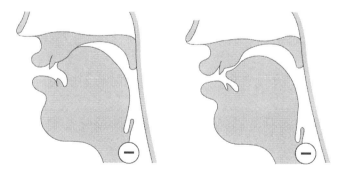

Figure 4.28 Left: hold stage of English /tʃ/; right: release of English /tʃ/ (with homorganic friction), identical to English /ʃ/; note trumpet-shaped lip-rounding

an English teacher, cheap champagne, fish and chips, the finishing touch, catch a fish, launch a ship, watch a show, a refreshing change

4.20.4 Sentences with /ʧ/ and /ʃ/

(1) Sean's childhood shaped his future. (2) They wished to establish a branch in China. (3) The lunch special seemed suspiciously cheap. (4) The fisherman watched anxiously as the shark approached. (5) Charlie's donations to the charity shop were much appreciated. (6) The national squash championships were held in Massachusetts. (7) In March, they established an association for the teaching of Dutch. (8) The situation in Massachusetts had changed beyond all recognition. (9) There was a short discussion on the relationship between nature and nurture. (10) Rachel put the finishing touches on her translation of the brochure into Czech.

4.21 Voiced palato-alveolar affricate /ʤ/ vs. voiced palato-alveolar fricative /ʒ/

4.21.1 Minimal pairs with /ʤ/ and /ʒ/

lesion/legion

4.21.2 Phrases with /ʤ/ and /ʒ/

an unusual arrangement, the logical conclusion, a majority decision, a dangerous delusion, a rigid division, a huge explosion, a gentle massage, a visual image, an emergency measure, a joyous occasion, precision engineering, a major revision

4.21.3 Sentences with /ʤ/ and /ʒ/

(1) John was injured in the explosion in June. (2) Jessica's graduation was a joyous occasion. (3) Add a generous measure of gin to the ginger ale. (4) The possessions were split with surgical precision. (5) I was overjoyed when a logical conclusion emerged. (6) Joe challenged the judge's decision to end supervision. (7) Jill's most treasured possession is her engagement ring. (8) A strategy was needed for the diffusion of digital television. (9) Major changes

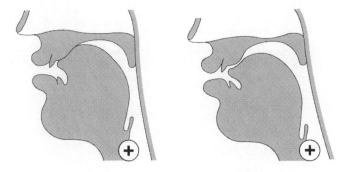

Figure 4.29 Left: hold stage of English /ʤ/; right: release of English /ʤ/ (with homorganic friction), identical to English /ʒ/; note trumpet-shaped lip-rounding

generally have to start with gentle persuasion. (10) The archaeologists salvaged some of the religious treasures of Egypt.

4.22 Voiceless bilabial plosive /p/ vs. voiceless labio-dental fricative /f/

4.22.1 Minimal pairs with /p/ and /f/

a) Word-initial

pad/fad, paid/fade, paint/faint, pair/fair, pan/fan, past/fast, pat/fat, pour/four, pea/fee, peel/feel, peer/fear, pierce/fierce, pig/fig, pile/file, pill/fill, pine/fine, pit/fit, poke/folk, pond/fond, pool/fool, pork/fork, port/fort, pound/found, prose/froze, pull/full, pun/fun, purr/fir, put/foot

b) Word-final

cheap/chief, clip/cliff, cup/cuff, leap/leaf, ripe/rife, sheep/sheaf, snip/sniff, whip/whiff, wipe/wife

c) Word-medial

depend/defend, puppy/puffy, supper/suffer

4.22.2 Words with /p/ and /f/

amplify, apostrophe, campfire, coffeepot, fingerprint, fishpond, flap, flipper, grapefruit, helpful, leapfrog, painful, pamphlet, paraffin, paragraph, penknife, perform, platform, powerful, prefer, profession, professor, profile, profit, proof, self-pity, shoplift, specify

4.22.3 Phrases with /p/ and /f/

a different approach, fitted carpet, a famous composer, fetch help, hopes and fears, a leap forward, the front page, pain relief, fresh paint, a fountain pen, a pillow fight, a gift shop, pure

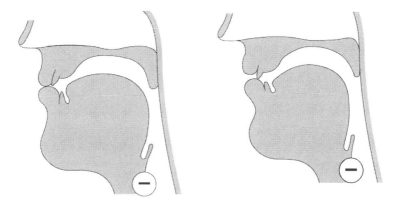

Figure 4.30 Left: English /p/ (hold stage); right: English /f/

fantasy, a pig farm, deep fear, a feather pillow, an important feature, plain flour, pet food, a tropical forest, a picture frame, a special friend, a pension fund, a passport photo, a petty thief, a proper breakfast, a cup of coffee, a difference of opinion

4.22.4 Sentences with /p/ and /f/

(1) Please don't forget to pay the full membership fee. (2) For lunch, Fred typically has fried potatoes and a piece of fruit. (3) An atmosphere of defeat and hopelessness pervaded the office. (4) It's difficult to compare and interpret the findings in these reports. (5) Pete's a super sportsman and in fact a former professional golf player. (6) My friends planned a surprise farewell party when I left the department. (7) After a bumpy flight over the Alps, we flew safely into one of the Paris airports. (8) He suffers from an inferiority complex, which explains his fear of public speaking. (9) We'd be happy to clarify any points of confusion before you make an appointment. (10) Providing positive feedback to your staff's a simple procedure but surprisingly effective.

4.23 Voiced bilabial plosive /b/ vs. voiced labio-dental fricative /v/

4.23.1 Minimal pairs with /b/ and /v/

a) Word-initial

bail/veil, banish/vanish, bat/vat, beer/veer, bent/vent, best/vest, bet/vet, bigger/vigor, boat/vote, bolt/volt, bowel/vowel, bury/very

b) Word-final

curb/curve

c) Word-medial

cupboard/covered, dribble/drivel, fiber/fiver, marble/marvel, saber/savor

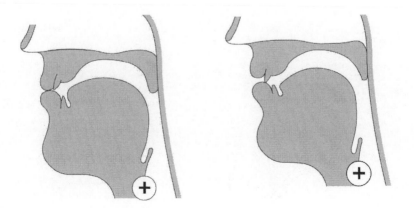

Figure 4.31 Left: English /b/ (hold stage); right: English /v/

4.23.2 Words with /b/ and /v/

available, abbreviation, above, abusive, beaver, beehive, behavior, believe, beverage, brainwave, brave, everybody, invisible, lovable, lovebird, November, objective, observe, obvious, proverb, riverbank, riverboat, subjective, variable, verb, vibrant

4.23.3 Phrases with /b/ and /v/

a big advantage, a bit of advice, public approval, above average, best behavior, a book cover, a bitter divorce, a bus driver, rubber gloves, a brief interval, a job interview, double vision, a booming voice, navy blue, a book review, a favorite hobby, reserve a table

4.23.4 Sentences with /b/ and /v/

(1) This bird has a distinctive curved beak. (2) The book covers the subject comprehensively. (3) The boat'll leave the harbor at seven this evening. (4) Bill and Violet had breakfast at their favorite bar. (5) Toby has a reliable passive vocabulary in Bulgarian. (6) These baked beans are suitable for vegetarians and vegans. (7) A number of villages were evacuated after the river burst its banks. (8) In November, we celebrated the seventh anniversary of the rugby club. (9) He made an invaluable contribution to the development of the university. (10) Elizabeth's feedback provided a basis for improvements in our environment.

4.24 Voiceless alveolar plosive /t/ vs. voiceless dental fricative /θ/

4.24.1 Minimal pairs with /t/ and /θ/

a) Word-initial

tank/thank, taught/thought, team/theme, tie/thigh, tick/thick, torn/thorn, trash/thrash, tread/thread, tree/three, true/threw, trust/thrust, tug/thug

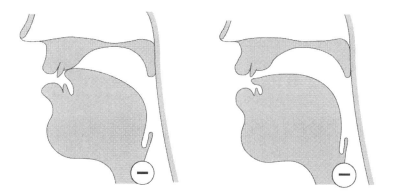

Figure 4.32 Left: English /t/ (hold stage); right: English /θ/

b) Word-final

boat/both, debt/death, fate/faith, fort/fourth, heart/hearth, heat/heath, oat/oath, tent/tenth

4.24.2 Words with /t/ and /θ/

afterbirth, aftermath, afterthought, amethyst, antipathy, antithesis, apathetic, arithmetic, arthritis, atheist, athlete, authentic, authority, bathtub, birthrate, breathtaking, mathematics, pathetic, sympathetic, theater, theft, thicket, thirsty, thirty, threat, throat, thrust, tooth, truth, stealthy, stethoscope, telepathic

4.24.3 Phrases with /t/ and /θ/

a bath tub, a tax threshold, a sympathetic teacher, healthy teeth, a bath towel, thigh-length boots, a thin coat of paint, date of birth, eat healthily, a fate worse than death, fit and healthy, a thank-you note, a breathtaking sight, a death threat, a thick blanket, a mythical monster, a thing of the past, test a hypothesis, the tenth time, tell the truth, a test of strength

4.24.4 Sentences with /t/ and /θ/

(1) I don't think it'll fit, but it's worth a try. (2) The city's Gothic cathedral's a breathtaking sight. (3) Ruth bought me a guitar as a thirtieth birthday present. (4) Arthur should do the decent thing and tell her the truth. (5) Edith gave birth to twins at two thirty yesterday afternoon. (6) Matthew sent a heartfelt thank-you letter to his math teacher. (7) Thelma wrote a thorough report containing a wealth of detail. (8) Agatha tried to determine the birth and death dates of her earliest ancestors. (9) Elizabeth spent the entire month of August in Gareth's beautiful thatched-roof cottage. (10) They co-authored an article on the monophthongs and diphthongs of Estonian in 2013.

4.25 Voiced alveolar plosive /d/ vs. voiced dental fricative /ð/

4.25.1 Minimal pairs with /d/ and /ð/

breed/breathe, dale/they'll, dare/there, day/they, den/then, dough/though, doze/those, header/heather, udder/other, wordy/worthy

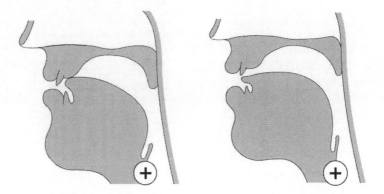

Figure 4.33 Left: English /d/ (hold stage); right: English /ð/

4.25.2 Words with /d/ and /ð/

bothered, brotherhood, creditworthy, dither, fatherhood, gathered, motherhood, roadworthy, smothered, tethered, weathered, withered

4.25.3 Phrases with /d/ and /ð/

abandon altogether, a feather bed, a motherless child, gathering clouds, weather conditions, a rhythmic dance, gather data, a southern dialect, gathering dust, other ideas, a blithering idiot, pretend otherwise, a smooth ride, gather speed, breathe deeply, blood brothers, a devoted father, a doting mother, rather difficult

4.25.4 Sentences with /d/ and /ð/

(1) Without further delay, they headed in a northerly direction. (2) Judy's older brother's definitely worthy of our admiration. (3) Blend these dry ingredients together, and then add the liquid. (4) Don's stupid featherbrained mother needs her head examined. (5) They were blood brothers bound together by shared hardship. (6) David's a blithering idiot, and it's absurd to pretend otherwise. (7) The data for the second study was gathered in the Netherlands. (8) Heather's wonderful idea either failed or was abandoned altogether. (9) Within days, his godfather had developed a delightful Southern drawl. (10) Her grandfather was seated behind an old-fashioned leather-topped desk.

4.26 Voiced labio-dental fricative /v/ vs. voiced labial-velar approximant /w/

4.26.1 Minimal pairs with /v/ and /w/

vale/wail, vary/wary, veal/wheel, veered/weird, vein/wane, vent/went, verse/worse, vest/west, vet/wet, vine/whine, viper/wiper, vow/wow

4.26.2 Words with /v/ and /w/

driveway, equivalent, everyone, heavyweight, overqualified, overweight, overwork, persuasive, quiver, reservoir, swerve, twelve, vanquish, wave, weave, whatever, wives

4.26.3 Phrases with /v/ and /w/

an award for bravery, a lavish banquet, a male-voice choir, solve a crossword, a private dwelling, vital equipment, wave farewell, at frequent intervals, a valid password, a violent quarrel, covered in sweat, the average wage, an evening walk, a civil war, river water, heavy weapons, wedding vows, vintage wine, a word of advice, alive and well, a worldview, well worth a visit, a live wire

4.26.4 Sentences with /v/ and /w/

(1) Victor wants to divorce his wife. (2) Oliver quickly recovered his wits. (3) Vera is wondering what the work will involve. (4) They served an expensive wine at the wedding. (5) We couldn't quite work out the value of the investment. (6) David invited Vanessa for a walk

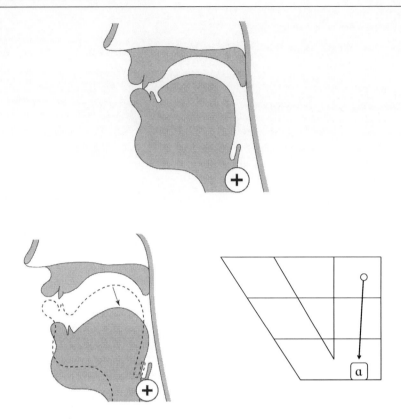

Figure 4.34 Top: English /v/; bottom: English /w/; note that English /w/ is a semi-vowel and can therefore be indicated on a vowel diagram; here the sequence /wɑ/ in *wasp* is shown

along the river on that warm evening. (7) My Welsh acquaintance was visibly moved by his visit to the war graves. (8) Walter and Gwen traveled to Cornwall on their seventeenth anniversary. (9) Sweden won the silver in women's volleyball in Venezuela on Wednesday. (10) The women became involved in a quarrel with their supervisor at the workshop.

4.27 Voiced palato-alveolar affricate /ʤ/ vs. voiced palatal approximant /j/

4.27.1 Minimal pairs with /ʤ/ and /j/

gel/yell, Jew/you, jot/yacht, jeer/year, jet/yet

4.27.2 Words with /ʤ/ and /j/

fugitive, genuine, huge, jocular, jugular, junkyard, musicology, refuge, usage

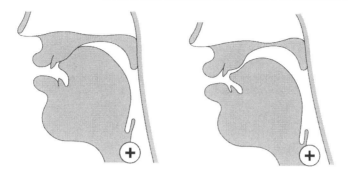

Figure 4.35 English /ʤ/; left: hold stage; right: release with homorganic friction; note trumpet-shaped lip-rounding

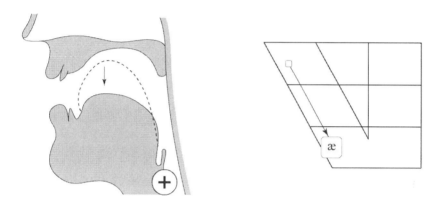

Figure 4.36 English /j/: sequence /jæ/ in *yak*; diagram shows approximate change in tongue shape; since /j/ is a semi-vowel, it can be indicated on a vowel diagram

4.27.3 Phrases with /ʤ/ and /j/

the younger generation, jet fuel, gentle humor, a jazz musician, job security, an emergency unit, a university graduate, gentle yoga, youthful energy, a young age, a storage unit

4.27.4 Sentences with /ʤ/ and /j/

(1) Geoffrey's a popular jazz musician. (2) The US has a huge Jewish community. (3) Muriel used any excuse to indulge in orange juice. (4) Matthew's suggestions are outrageous and ridiculous. (5) The juniors had divergent views on gene manipulation. (6) Jack was evacuated from the emergency unit yesterday. (7) Judith's an insecure, belligerent, and rebellious teenager. (8) Jenny graduated from Jacksonville State University in June. (9) Our journal reviewers usually provide objective opinions and views. (10) Eugene managed to enlarge his vocabulary at the engineering college in Houston.

4.28 Voiceless glottal fricative /h/ vs. zero

4.28.1 Minimal pairs with /h/ vs. zero

had/add, hair/air, hall/all, harm/arm, heal/eel, hear/ear, heart/art, heat/eat, hedge/edge, high/eye, hill/ill, hit/it, hold/old, hotter/otter, hurl/earl

4.28.2 Phrases with /h/ vs. zero

an unhappy childhood, an annoying habit, auburn hair, an abrupt halt, easy to handle, irreparable harm, in absolute harmony, a head injury, intense heat, afraid of heights, expert help, ancient history, ice hockey, home address, an empty house

4.28.3 Sentences with /h/ vs. zero

(1) Ellen heard an audible hiss through the headphones. (2) Henry's eaten all the oranges because he was hungry. (3) Here are eight helpful hints if you're afraid of heights. (4) The hedgehog emerged from hibernation in early April. (5) All hospitals have been equipped to handle emergencies. (6) I'm indebted to Hamish Hamilton for his invaluable help. (7) We hope we'll have an abundant harvest of apples in our home orchard. (8) He helped in the areas that had been hit especially hard by the earthquake. (9) Hilary's husband happened to be in the house when the explosion occurred. (10) I was happy I'd insisted on an air-conditioned hotel, as Huntsville was oppressively hot in August.

4.29 Voiced velar nasal + velar plosive /ŋk/ or /ŋg/ vs. voiced velar nasal /ŋ/

In many languages, the velar nasal [ŋ] only occurs before the velar plosives /k/ or /g/. In English, however, /ŋ/ can occur with or without a following velar plosive. Word-medially, /ŋ/ contrasts with both /ŋk/ and /ŋg/, but word-finally, only /ŋ/ and /ŋk/ are possible.

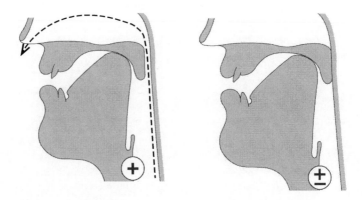

Figure 4.37 English /ŋ/ (left); note that the soft palate is lowered; if /ŋ/ is followed by a homorganic plosive (/k/ or /g/), the soft palate rises to form a velic closure (right)

4.29.1 Minimal pairs with /ŋ/ and /ŋk/

bang/bank, bung/bunk, bring/brink, cling/clink, ping/pink, ring/rink, sing/sink, sling/slink, sting/stink, tang/tank, thing/think, wing/wink; hanger/hanker, singer/sinker, stinger/stinker

4.29.2 Words with /ŋ/ and /ŋk/ or /ŋg/

angling, gangplank, inkling, ranking, scaremongering, tingling, sprinkling, Thanksgiving, twinkling, blinking, warmongering

4.29.3 Phrases with /ŋ/ and /ŋk/ vs. /ŋg/

increasingly angry, a wedding banquet, a strong drink, surprisingly frank, the missing link, shocking pink, a long think, swimming trunks, a knowing wink, mounting anger, my ring finger, matching fingerprints, hunger pangs

4.29.4 Sentences with /ŋ/ and /ŋk/ vs. /ŋg/

(1) We're buying a bungalow in Yonkers. (2) I'm growing increasingly angry with my uncle. (3) Angus will be traveling to Helsinki in the spring. (4) It was amusing to see the chattering monkeys in the jungle. (5) Frank's developing a programming language for linguistics. (6) Bianca's no longer wearing an engagement ring on her finger. (7) Duncan and Ingrid are holding their wedding banquet in Hong Kong. (8) Her handwriting's appalling and her spelling and punctuation incorrect. (9) Mr. Jenkins is working on strengthening the link between planning and budgeting. (10) Why does Hank think pink flamingos and king penguins are on the brink of extinction?

Chapter 5

Vowel theory

5.1 Describing vowels

We saw in Chapter 2 that a consonant is a speech sound that involves an obstruction to the airstream on its way through the vocal tract. So what then is a vowel? A vowel is the opposite of a consonant: a sound made with *no* obstruction in the vocal tract to the air as it passes through it.

Say a long /ɑ/, the sound doctors ask us to make when they want to look into our mouths, and feel how the air flows out through your mouth without any obstruction. Try the same for /i/, the <ee> of *tree*, and /æ/, the <a> of *cat*. You will notice that the lips and tongue take different positions for these different vowels, but in each case, there's no obstruction or blockage of the kind that we find in consonants.

If consonants are analyzed in terms of the kind of obstruction involved and where it is in the vocal tract, how can we analyze vowels, which have no such obstruction? Although the tongue and lips assume a wide range of complex shapes for the articulation of different vowels, a relatively simple system has been developed to describe them. Figure 5.1 shows the vowel diagram from the chart of the International Phonetic Association, which is based on this system of vowel description.

5.1.1 Tongue shape

In order to understand the system behind the diagram, the first step is to explore the limits of the range of tongue positions used to make vowels, known as the **vowel space**. There are two fixed articulatory reference points to the system. To find the first, you make a vowel with the front of the body of your tongue pushed as far forward and as far up toward the hard palate as possible. This is the position for the [i] vowel (see Figure 5.2). If you move your tongue any further forward or up, audible friction would result between the tongue and the hard palate, and the sound would no longer be a vowel. The second reference point is found by doing the opposite – opening your mouth and pulling your tongue as far down and back as possible without causing friction between the root of the tongue and the back wall of the pharynx (see Figure 5.3). This is the [ɑ] vowel. A further two positions can be identified by pushing the tongue as far up and back as possible (see Figure 5.4), which gives us the [u] vowel, and by pushing the tongue as far forward and down as possible (see Figure 5.5), which gives us the [a] vowel. Note that during the production of all these vowels, the tongue tip and blade (see Figure 5.6) remain low in the mouth. They are not involved in vowel production, and this is why the front of the tongue as a technical term is not where non-phoneticians usually expect it to be. The front of the tongue is actually the front of the part used in vowel articulations and is what laypeople would think of as the center or middle of the tongue.

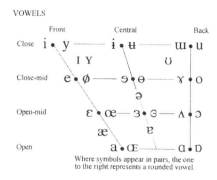

VOWELS

Figure 5.1 Vowel diagram from the IPA chart

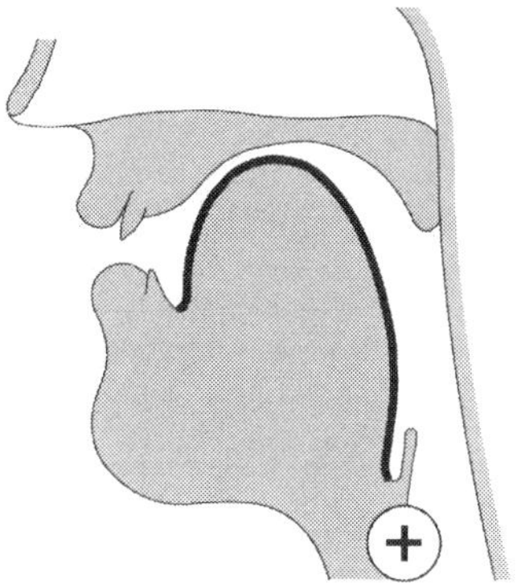

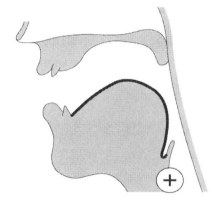

Figure 5.3 Tongue shape for [ɑ]

Figure 5.2 Tongue shape for [i]

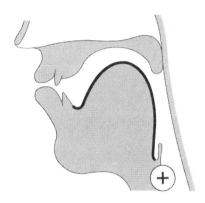

Figure 5.4 Tongue shape for [u]

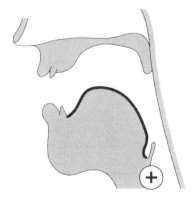

Figure 5.5 Tongue shape for [a]

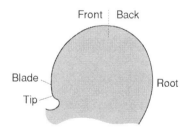

Figure 5.6 Tongue body raised and tip and blade lowered, as for vowel articulations

Now spend some time exploring the limits of the vowel space. Paradoxical as it may seem, it's best to do this silently. If you voice the vowels as you articulate them, it makes you less able to appreciate the sensations of touch, movement, and position you receive from your articulators. Start at the [i] position; then silently and slowly glide to the [u] position while keeping your tongue as close as possible to the palate without turning the sound into a consonant. Next, slowly glide to [ɑ], making sure to pull your tongue back to the lower back limit

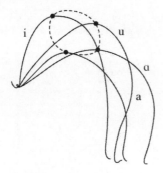

Figure 5.7 Tongue shapes for [i, u, a, ɑ] superimposed; black dots indicate highest points of the tongue for each of the vowels; dashed line shows limits of the vowel area

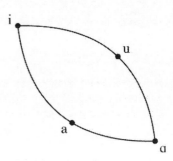

Figure 5.8 Vowel area

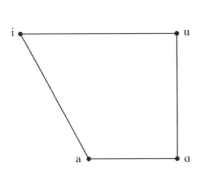

Figure 5.9 Vowel quadrilateral

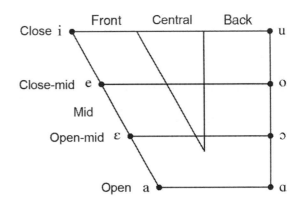

Figure 5.10 The eight basic reference vowels

of the vowel space. Do the same from the [i] position to [a] and then to [ɑ], moving your tongue along the front limit of the vowel space. You will feel that your tongue is moving in an oval shape like that shown in Figures 5.7 and 5.8.

The oval is too awkward a shape for practical purposes, and so in a schematic representation, its sides are straightened to give it the basic shape of the vowel quadrilateral (see Figure 5.9) that we are familiar with from the IPA chart.

The shape isn't a perfect square, which reflects the fact that there's greater distance between [i] and [u] than between [a] and [ɑ] and also more space between [i] and [a] than between [u] and [ɑ]. The vowel diagram is further elaborated on by providing symbols for four further positions equally spaced on the left [e ɛ] and right sides [o ɔ]. Finally, lines are added to divide the vowel space into manageable vertical and horizontal areas (see Figure 5.10).

Vertically, the positions are called **close**, **mid**, and **open**, with mid being further divided into **close-mid** and **open-mid**. Horizontally, they are **front**, **central**, and **back**.

5.1.2 Lip shape

So far, we've only considered the position of the tongue, but the shape of the lips is also important. Since the tongue and lips can move independently of each other, every vowel position can be accompanied by either **unrounded** or **rounded** lips. This is why the symbols on the IPA vowel diagram mostly come in pairs, the left symbol having unrounded lips and the right symbol having rounded lips.

5.1.3 Vowel labels

Serendipitously, it turns out that as in the case of consonants, the basics of vowel description can be summarized in terms of three factors: vertical tongue position, horizontal tongue position, and lip shape. The peripheral vowels (see Figure 5.1), for example, are described thus:

[i]	close front unrounded		[ɯ]	close back unrounded
[y]	close front rounded		[u]	close back rounded
[e]	close-mid front unrounded		[ɤ]	close-mid back unrounded
[ø]	close-mid front rounded		[o]	close-mid back rounded
[ɛ]	open-mid front unrounded		[ʌ]	open-mid back unrounded
[œ]	open-mid front rounded		[ɔ]	open-mid back rounded
[a]	open front unrounded		[ɑ]	open back unrounded
[ɶ]	open front rounded		[ɒ]	open back rounded

5.2 English vowels

In its simplest form, the GA vowel system consists of thirteen vowel phonemes. Here, we list them with their phonemic symbol, a keyword, and a selection of examples demonstrating a range of spellings used for them. The keywords (written in small capitals) will be used throughout this work and are based on those established by Wells (1982) and now widely used in English phonetics. The schwa vowel /ə/ needs no keyword because the name "schwa" is so well established, but note that the word *schwa* /ʃwɑ/ doesn't actually contain the schwa vowel /ə/.

/ɪ/	KIT	gym, busy, pretty, build, sieve, women
/ʊ/	FOOT	book, put, would, woman
/ɛ/	DRESS	bread, friend, leopard, bury, rare, carry, pair, heir, aerial
/æ/	TRAP	cat, meringue
/ə/	schwa	above, murder, circus, concern, mustard
/i/	FLEECE	pea, bee, key, even, pizza, field, weird, baby, acne, taxi, coffee, money
/u/	GOOSE	food, blue, fruit, move, tour, flew
/ɑ/	PALM	job, father, heart, knowledge
/eɪ/	FACE	pay, mail, take, break, vein, prey, gauge
/aɪ/	PRICE	pie, dry, dye, pi, high, aisle
/ɔɪ/	CHOICE	toy, foil
/aʊ/	MOUTH	now, loud
/oʊ/	GOAT	blow, hero, nose, hoax, soul

5.2.1 The THOUGHT /ɔ/ vowel

Speakers from the east of the US can also have an additional vowel phoneme, THOUGHT /ɔ/, in certain words, where speakers from other parts of the country (and Canada) have the PALM /ɑ/ vowel. The THOUGHT words are typically spelled:

<a> before <l>:	also, always, false, salt, always, tall, fall, walk
<au>:	author, launch, cause, daughter, caught, taught
<aw>:	law, straw, dawn, awkward, awful
various:	brought, ought, thought, broad, water

The THOUGHT /ɔ/ vowel also occurs in a set of words known as the CLOTH words. These are usually spelled with the letter <o> and followed by a voiceless fricative or voiced velar consonant:

/f θ s ʃ/:	off, soft, cloth, moth, loss, cost, gosh
/g ŋ/:	long, wrong, song, dog, fog, log
various:	sausage, wash, cough, wasp

For GA speakers who don't have the THOUGHT /ɔ/ vowel in their accent, the pairs *cot/caught*, *wok/walk*, *tot/taught*, *Don/dawn*, *odd/awed* are homophones: /kɑt wɑk tɑt dɑn ɑd/. For those who do have a THOUGHT /ɔ/ vowel, they are minimal pairs that demonstrate the contrast between the two vowels: /kɑt kɔt/, /wɑk wɔk/, /tɑt tɔt/, /dɑn dɔn/, and /ɑd ɔd/. Similarly, for speakers with no THOUGHT /ɔ/ vowel, the two vowels in *hot dog* and *long shot* are the same, /ˈhɑt dɑg/ and /ˈlɑŋ ʃɑt/, while for those with a THOUGHT /ɔ/ vowel, they have two different vowels: /ˈhɑt dɔg/ and /ˈlɔŋ ʃɑt/. We use the terms THOUGHT-less and THOUGHT-ful to refer to the two kinds of vowel system, speaker, and accent.

Both THOUGHT-ful and THOUGHT-less GA accents are suitable models for foreign learners, but we will take the THOUGHT-less form of GA as the norm in this work because a thirteen-vowel accent is easier for learners than a fourteen-vowel accent and because the phonetic similarity of THOUGHT /ɔ/ and PALM /ɑ/ (see Figure 5.12) makes THOUGHT /ɔ/ a difficult vowel to learn. A further important factor is that the THOUGHT-ful pronunciation of GA is in decline, as THOUGHT /ɔ/ is increasingly merged with PALM /ɑ/ (as is already the case in Canada). It seems likely that eventually the THOUGHT vowel /ɔ/ will be restricted to certain regional accents and will no longer be considered a feature of GA.

5.2.2 The SPORT [o] vowel

One consequence of there being two possible GA vowel systems, THOUGHT-less and THOUGHT-ful, is that it complicates the analysis of what we will refer to as the SPORT vowel, [o]. The vowel [o] occurs before /r/ in words spelled in the following ways:

<or>	north, force, sort, sword, born, cork, form, lord, pork, normal, forty, organ
<ore>	more, score, sore, store, shore, core, bore, chore, gore, before
<our>	four, pour, court, mourn, course, source
<oar>	oar, boar, soar, roar, board, hoard
<oor>	door, floor
<ar> after /w/	war, warm, ward, quartz, quart, quartet

When the /r/ following the SPORT [o] vowel is followed by another vowel, the pronunciation is more variable. The following words can have only the SPORT [o] vowel:

[o]:	story, glory, gory, choral, chorus, forum, floral, storage, porous, memorial, notorious, tutorial, victorious, mandatory, category, territory

Other words vary between having either the SPORT [o] vowel or PALM /ɑ/, depending on the habits of the individual speaker:

[o] or /ɑ/:	borrow, orange, forest, authority, quarrel, warrior, coroner, categorical, correlate, correspondent, Florida, florist, historic, horrible, majority, Oregon, origin, foreign, torrent, historian, corridor, priority

The PALM /ɑ/ pronunciation is particularly common in the words *sorry* and *tomorrow*.

In THOUGHT-ful GA accents, the SPORT [o] vowel can be analyzed as belonging to the THOUGHT /ɔ/ phoneme on the basis of phonetic similarity and the intuitions of speakers of such accents, i.e., SPORT [o] sounds much like THOUGHT, and THOUGHT-ful speakers instinctively feel that SPORT [o] is a variant of THOUGHT /ɔ/. For speakers with a THOUGHT-less GA accent, the SPORT [o] vowel is best analyzed as a variant of the GOAT /oʊ/ vowel though there is less phonetic similarity between [o] and other realizations of the GOAT /oʊ/ phoneme.

Although the transcriptions in this work are of THOUGHT-less GA, we use the [o] symbol for the SPORT vowel, not /oʊ/, in order to emphasize the strikingly different allophone of GOAT in this context and as a reminder of the alternative analysis for THOUGHT-ful accents. As a consequence, our transcriptions will be non-phonemic in this respect, but for the sake of simplicity, we will continue to use slanted phonemic brackets and not constantly switch between different types of brackets. For example:

[o]   *north* /norθ/, *more* /mor/, *course* /kors/, *board* /bord/, *door* /dor/, *foreign* /ˈforən/

5.3 Strong and weak vowels

When describing English vowels, a distinction can be made between the vowels that typically occur in stressed syllables and those that typically occur in unstressed syllables. The former are said to belong to the **strong vowel** system and the latter to the **weak vowel** system. There's a striking difference between the sets of vowels that are usually found in these two types of syllable, a distinction that isn't found in most other languages. All vowels are found in stressed syllables, but in unstressed syllables, a much smaller set of vowels predominates – schwa (including schwar, see Section 5.7.2), FLEECE, KIT, GOOSE, and FOOT (see Chapter 8). This isn't to say that the strong vowels cannot occur in unstressed syllables but rather that they are unusual in this context.

A number of works on English phonetics use different symbols for the same GA vowel phonemes depending on whether they appear in stressed syllables as strong vowels or in unstressed syllables as weak vowels.

Some writers use the symbol [ʌ] when the schwa phoneme is stressed and [ə] when it is unstressed:

Strong/weak: *above* /əˈbʌv/, *London* /ˈlʌndən/, *ultra* /ˈʌltrə/, *gunman* /ˈgʌnmən/
Phonemic: *above* /əˈbəv/, *London* /ˈləndən/, *ultra* /ˈəltrə/, *gunman* /ˈgənmən/

Some writers use the symbol [ɝ] when schwar (see Section 5.7.2) is stressed and [ɚ] when it is unstressed:

Strong/weak: *burger* /ˈbɝgɚ/, *murmur* /ˈmɝmɚ/, *perturb* /pɚˈtɝb/, *burglar* /ˈbɝglɚ/
Phonemic: *burger* /ˈbərgər/, *murmur* /ˈmərmər/, *perturb* /pərˈtərb/, *burglar* /ˈbərglər/

Some works, notably the *Cambridge English Pronouncing Dictionary* and the *Longman Pronunciation Dictionary*, use the symbols [iː] and [uː] for FLEECE and GOOSE as strong vowels and [i] and [u] for them as weak vowels:

Strong/weak: *easy* /ˈiːzi/, *devious* /ˈdiːviəs/, *mutual* /ˈmjuːtʃuəl/
Phonemic: *easy* /ˈizi/, *devious* /ˈdiviəs/, *mutual* /ˈmjutʃuəl/

The strong/weak style of transcription is not phonemic, and we haven't adopted it because learners (and many native speakers!) find it confusing. For students of phonetics and English pronunciation, the concept of phonemic transcription usually poses little or no difficulty. Transcription systems based on a strong/weak analysis of English vowels, however, require more than one symbol for a single phoneme, and this often appears arbitrary and unnecessarily complicated to learners, especially when the differences between the strong/stressed and the weak/unstressed variants of the phoneme are not very noticeable, as is the case with FLEECE, GOOSE, and schwar. The difference, however, between stressed and unstressed schwa is more obvious, stressed schwa being more open than unstressed schwa (for example, the two vowels in *custom* /ˈkəstəm/); see Figures 6.5 and 6.6.

5.4 Checked and free vowels

The strong vowels fall into two groups: **checked vowels** (Figure 5.11) and **free vowels** (Figures 5.12–5.14).

Checked: KIT /ɪ/, FOOT /ʊ/, DRESS /ɛ/, TRAP /æ/, **schwa** /ə/
Free: FLEECE /i/, GOOSE /u/, PALM /ɑ/, (THOUGHT /ɔ/), FACE /eɪ/, PRICE /aɪ/, CHOICE /ɔɪ/, MOUTH /aʊ/, GOAT /oʊ/

Note that the shape of the lips is shown as follows on the vowel diagrams: a square ☐ for an unrounded vowel and a circle ◯ for a rounded vowel. If the lip shape changes from unrounded to rounded, we show this by means of a square that becomes a circle, and if the lips change from rounded to unrounded, we show it as a circle that becomes a square.

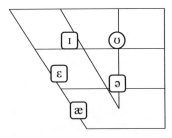

Figure 5.11 Checked vowels

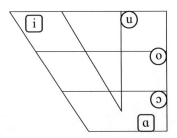

Figure 5.12 Free vowels: monophthongs

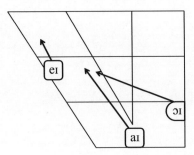

Figure 5.13 Free vowels: closing fronting diphthongs

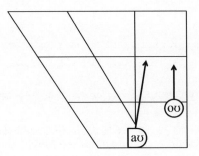

Figure 5.14 Free vowels: closing backing diphthongs

The checked/free categorization is based on the types of syllable the strong vowels occur in. A **closed syllable** is one that has a coda (i.e., one or more consonants after the vowel), while an **open syllable** is one that does not have a coda. Free vowels are "free" to occur in both closed and open syllables. Checked vowels are "checked" in the sense that their distribution is restricted because they can only occur in closed syllables, or in the sense that the vowel is "blocked" by a following consonant.

The following examples demonstrate the free vowels in closed and open syllables:

FLEECE **(closed):**	*seed* /sid/, *team* /tim/, *cheer* /ʧir/, *meat* /mit/
FLEECE **(open):**	*see* /si/, *tea* /ti/, *free* /fri/, *knee* /ni/
GOOSE **(closed):**	*lose* /luz/, *moon* /mun/, *nude* /nud/, *suit* /sut/, *tour* /tur/
GOOSE **(open):**	*two* /tu/, *few* /fju/, *do* /du/, *clue* /klu/
PALM **(closed):**	*nod* /nɑd/, *car* /kɑr/, *yacht* /jɑt/, *shop* /ʃɑp/
PALM **(open):**	*spa* /spɑ/, *ma* /mɑ/, *schwa* /ʃwɑ/, *bra* /brɑ/
(THOUGHT **(closed):**	*yawn* /jɔn/, *caught* /kɔt/, *four* /fɔr/, *crawl* /krɔl/)
(THOUGHT **(open):**	*paw* /pɔ/, *saw* /sɔ/, *thaw* /θɔ/, *jaw* /ʤɔ/)
FACE **(closed):**	*haze* /heɪz/, *maize* /meɪz/, *late* /leɪt/, *chase* /ʧeɪs/
FACE **(open):**	*pay* /peɪ/, *stay* /steɪ/, *weigh* /weɪ/, *may* /meɪ/
PRICE **(closed):**	*size* /saɪz/, *tight* /taɪt/, *time* /taɪm/, *nice* /naɪs/
PRICE **(open):**	*try* /traɪ/, *high* /haɪ/, *buy* /baɪ/, *fly* /flaɪ/
CHOICE **(closed):**	*point* /pɔɪnt/, *voice* /vɔɪs/, *moist* /mɔɪst/, *join* /ʤɔɪn/
CHOICE **(open):**	*toy* /tɔɪ/, *ploy* /plɔɪ/, *boy* /bɔɪ/, *joy* /ʤɔɪ/
MOUTH **(closed):**	*town* /taʊn/, *loud* /laʊd/, *shout* /ʃaʊt/, *crowd* /kraʊd/
MOUTH **(open):**	*how* /haʊ/, *cow* /kaʊ/, *brow* /braʊ/, *now* /naʊ/
GOAT **(closed):**	*load* /loʊd/, *smoke* /smoʊk/, *host* /hoʊst/, *grown* /groʊn/
GOAT **(open):**	*low* /loʊ/, *go* /goʊ/, *owe* /oʊ/, *flow* /floʊ/

Since the checked vowels do not occur in open syllables, there are no English words of the type */nɪ/, */ʧʊ/, */dɛ/, or */fæ/. There are, however, words like *comma* /ˈkɑmə/, *extra* /ˈɛkstrə/, *panda* /ˈpændə/, *pizza* /ˈpitsə/, and *zebra* /ˈzibrə/ in which schwa /ə/ appears in open syllables. The explanation for this is that the checked/free distinction applies only to the strong vowel system (i.e., only to vowels in stressed syllables). In unstressed syllables, the distribution of vowels in open/closed syllables is not the same as in stressed syllables (which demonstrates another way in which the weak and strong vowel systems differ from each other).

The following examples demonstrate the checked vowels in closed syllables:

KIT:	*sit* /sɪt/, *tin* /tɪn/, *sick* /sɪk/, *itch* /ɪʧ/
FOOT:	*put* /pʊt/, *pull* /pʊl/, *push* /pʊʃ/, *look* /lʊk/
DRESS:	*head* /hɛd/, *mess* /mɛs/, *hair* /hɛr/, *hen* /hɛn/
TRAP:	*sad* /sæd/, *match* /mæʧ/, *sang* /sæŋ/, *has* /hæz/
schwa:	*luck* /lək/, *thumb* /θəm/, *tough* /təf/, *bird* /bərd/

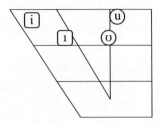

Figure 5.15 The different qualities of the pairs FLEECE/KIT and GOOSE/FOOT

The checked/free distinction has also been described as one of length. The checked vowels have been called the "short" vowels, and the free vowels have been called the "long" vowels. There's some truth in this generalization because it's a fact that in the same phonetic context, the free vowels are consistently longer than the checked vowels. However, there are many factors that affect vowel duration in English speech (see Section 5.6), meaning that the "short" checked vowels can sometimes be lengthened and, in particular, the "long" free vowels are often shortened. Furthermore, the TRAP vowel doesn't easily fit into the long/short categorization since it's often as long as the "long" free vowels despite being a "short" checked vowel. It's better, therefore, to categorize the strong vowels according to the fixed, unchanging fact of their distribution in different types of syllables and not in terms of their variable duration.

There is a common misconception that FLEECE and KIT, and GOOSE and FOOT form long/short vowel pairs distinguished by length alone. As Figure 5.15 demonstrates, this isn't true. The pairs FLEECE/KIT and GOOSE/FOOT differ in vowel quality (resulting from different tongue positions), and this is the most important feature that distinguishes them, their lengths being variable. It's simply not true that, as some learners believe, shortened FLEECE and GOOSE become KIT and FOOT or that lengthened KIT and FOOT become FLEECE and GOOSE.

5.5 Monophthongs and diphthongs

Vowels can be further divided into **diphthongs**, which involve a glide from one vowel position toward another during their production, and **monophthongs**, during which there's no change of vowel position. The checked vowels are all monophthongs. The free vowel category contains both monophthongs and diphthongs (see Figures 5.12–5.14):

Free monophthongs: FLEECE /i/, GOOSE /u/, PALM /ɑ/, (THOUGHT /ɔ/)
Free diphthongs: FACE /eɪ/, PRICE /aɪ/, CHOICE /ɔɪ/, MOUTH /aʊ/, GOAT /oʊ/

Monophthongs are written with a single vowel symbol, while the diphthongs have two symbols. The first symbol represents the starting position of the diphthong, and the second gives the direction of the glide.

The diphthongs can be categorized according to the direction of the glide. All the GA diphthongs are **closing diphthongs**, where the tongue moves toward the top of the vowel space as they are pronounced. Closing diphthongs can be divided into the **fronting** diphthongs – FACE /eɪ/, PRICE /aɪ/, and CHOICE /ɔɪ/ – which glide toward the front of the vowel space (Figure 5.13), and the **backing** diphthongs – MOUTH /aʊ/ and GOAT /oʊ/ – which glide toward the back of the vowel space (Figure 5.14). The GA diphthongs are all **falling diphthongs**, which means that the first element is longer while the second gliding element is shorter and weaker. Consequently, the closing diphthongs only glide *toward* the close front and close back areas but rarely reach them. [ɪ] and [ʊ] are used in the phonemic symbols for the closing diphthongs to represent the general close front and close back areas; it's not meant that [ɪ] and [ʊ] are their actual targets or that they represent the KIT and FOOT phonemes. On our vowel diagrams, we identify the starting point of a diphthong and represent the glide with an arrow.

An alternative way of categorizing the diphthongs is according to the extent of the gliding element. Accordingly, PRICE /aɪ/, MOUTH /aʊ/, and CHOICE /ɔɪ/ are **wide diphthongs**, involving a relatively long glide, while FACE /eɪ/ and GOAT /oʊ/ are **narrow diphthongs**, involving a rather short glide. FLEECE /i/ and GOOSE /u/ can have slightly diphthongal realizations, especially when they have their full length, making them a kind of narrow diphthong in such cases.

5.6 Pre-fortis clipping

Numerous factors affect vowel duration besides the inherent length of checked and free vowels, and many of these factors, such as speech rate, are not unique to English. One universal tendency, however, that is notably exaggerated in English is the shortening of vowels (and other sonorants) when immediately followed by a voiceless consonant in the same syllable. This phenomenon is called **pre-fortis clipping**, "fortis" being an alternative term for "voiceless," and "clipping" meaning "shortening." This shortening is most noticeable in the free vowels, since they are inherently rather long to begin with:

FLEECE	full length:	*seed* /sid/	shortened:	*seat* /sit/
GOOSE		*lose* /luz/		*loose* /lus/
PALM		*nod* /nɑd/		*not* /nɑt/
(THOUGHT		*thawed* /θɔd/		*thought* /θɔt/)
FACE	full length:	*save* /seɪv/	shortened:	*safe* /seɪf/
PRICE		*side* /saɪd/		*site* /saɪt/
CHOICE		*void* /vɔɪd/		*voice* /vɔɪs/
GOAT		*code* /koʊd/		*coat* /koʊt/
MOUTH		*loud* /laʊd/		*lout* /laʊt/

When diphthongs are clipped, it's the first part, not the glide, which is shortened, making them less obviously falling diphthongs.

The checked vowels are already inherently short, and therefore, the extent of the shortening they undergo is rather slight but nevertheless still present.

KIT	full length:	*his* /hɪz/	shortened:	*hiss* /hɪs/
FOOT		*hood* /hʊd/		*hook* /hʊk/
DRESS		*bed* /bɛd/		*bet* /bɛt/
TRAP		*rag* /ræg/		*rack* /ræk/
schwa		*mug* /məg/		*muck* /mək/

Pre-fortis clipping affects all sonorants, not just vowels, which means that the approximants /l r/ and the nasals /m n ŋ/ are shortened together with the vowel that precedes them (see Section 2.4.1). It's typically checked vowels that can be followed by a sonorant and an obstruent, in which case the combined clipping of both the sonorant and the vowel is much more striking than when a checked vowel alone is clipped.

Examples of vowel + /l/:

full length:		shortened:	
	shelve /ʃɛlv/		*shelf* /ʃɛlf/
	build /bɪld/		*built* /bɪlt/
	falls /fɑlz/		*false* /fɑls/
	bowled /boʊld/		*bolt* /boʊlt/
	culled /kəld/		*cult* /kəlt/

Examples of vowel + /r/:

full length:		shortened:	
	fears /firz/		*fierce* /firs/
	card /kɑrd/		*cart* /kɑrt/
	ford /ford/		*fort* /fort/
	hard /hɑrd/		*heart* /hɑrt/
	scares /skɛrz/		*scarce* /skɛrs/
	heard /hərd/		*hurt* /hərt/

Examples of vowel + nasal:

full length:		shortened:	
	hummed /həmd/		*hump* /həmp/
	rammed /ræmd/		*ramp* /ræmp/
	lend /lɛnd/		*lent* /lɛnt/
	wins /wɪnz/		*wince* /wɪns/
	banged /bæŋd/		*bank* /bæŋk/

Pre-fortis clipping is important not only for the correct pronunciation and recognition of vowels but also as a cue to the identity of consonants. As we saw in Section 2.4.2, English voiced obstruents (plosives, affricates, and fricatives) are actually only potentially fully voiced – they are often only partially voiced or may even be fully devoiced. In such cases, the length of the preceding sonorant (vowels, nasals, and approximants) is an important indicator for distinguishing between voiced and voiceless obstruents.

5.7 Rhoticity

GA is a **rhotic** accent, which means that the phoneme /r/ occurs not only before vowels but also before consonants and at the end of words:

Before vowels:	*reach* /riʧ/, *rude* /rud/, *rat* /ræt/, *bright* /braɪt/
Intervocalic:	*story* /ˈstori/, *very* /ˈvɛri/, *sorry* /ˈsɑri/, *hurry* /ˈhəri/
Before consonants:	*heart* /hɑrt/, *form* /form/, *church* /ʧərʧ/, *course* /kors/
Word-final:	*fur* /fər/, *more* /mor/, *near* /nir/, *scare* /skɛr/

In **non-rhotic** accents, such as General British (GB), /r/ has been lost historically before consonants and word finally and so only occurs before vowels (including intervocalically).

5.7.1 Vowels before /r/

Whether /r/ is articulated with the tongue tip or as bunched /r/, it involves considerable movement and shaping of the tongue. For tongue-tip /r/, the blade and front of the tongue form
a cupped, hollow shape as the tongue tip approaches the alveolar ridge, while for bunched
/r/, the body of the tongue is bunched up as the center of the tongue approaches the area
where the hard and soft palate meet. This influences the articulation of immediately preceding vowels, particularly those in the same syllable, making them less precise and blurring the
distinctions between vowels in the same vowel area. As a consequence, over time, vowels
tend to merge in this context, and the number of distinct vowel phonemes is reduced. So, just
as we can say that there is a separate subsystem of GA vowels in unstressed syllables (the
weak vowel system, see Section 5.3), we can say that there is a subsystem of GA vowels in
the pre-/r/ context.

The vowels that occur before /r/ are:

FLEECE:	*near* /nir/, *fear* /fir/, *pierce* /pirs/, *mirror* /ˈmirər/
GOOSE:	*cure* /kjur/, *allure* /əˈlur/, *boor* /bur/, *tourist* /ˈturɪst/
SPORT:	*north* /norθ/, *force* /fors/, *more* /mor/, *story* /ˈstori/
PALM:	*start* /stɑrt/, *car* /kɑr/, *hard* /hɑrd/, *starry* /ˈstɑri/
DRESS:	*square* /skwɛr/, *scarce* /skɛrs/, *berry* /ˈbɛri/, *carry* /ˈkɛri/
schwa:	*nurse* /nərs/, *stir* /stər/, *worm* /wərm/, *current* /ˈkərənt/

There is no contrast between the two close front vowels FLEECE /i/ and KIT /ɪ/ before
/r/. Historically, there was such a distinction, and it can still exist in other accents but
not in GA. Traditional descriptions of GA (still reflected in many dictionaries) have
classified the merged FLEECE/KIT vowel before /r/ as KIT and transcribed words like
near as /nɪr/. Nowadays, however, this vowel is usually more like FLEECE than KIT and
speakers feel that it belongs phonemically with FLEECE and should be transcribed /ir/
rather than /ɪr/. This is especially true when the following /r/ is word-final (e.g., *here*)
or pre-consonantal (e.g., *fierce*), while more variation can be heard before intervocalic
/r/ (e.g., *spirit*).

The situation as regards the two close back vowels GOOSE /u/ and FOOT /ʊ/ before /r/ is
almost parallel to that of FLEECE /i/ and KIT /ɪ/ before /r/. The distinction between them is neutralized, and the merged vowel that occurs before /r/ has traditionally been analyzed as FOOT
and transcribed with /ʊ/ in words like *cure* /kjʊr/, but present-day GA speakers feel that the
merged vowel is GOOSE, not FOOT, and should be transcribed that way (i.e., *cure* /kjur/). The
situation is further complicated by the tendency for /ur/ to be replaced by /or/ in some words
(e.g., *poor*) or by /ər/ in most others (e.g., *sure*, *cure*). These changes are so far advanced that
/ur/ is now the less common variant in such words.

In the mid back vowel area, the contrast between GOAT /oʊ/ and THOUGHT /ɔ/ has been lost
before /r/ (e.g., *hoarse/horse*). The resulting vowel, SPORT [o], can be interpreted differently
depending on the speaker. For those with THOUGHT-less accents (i.e., those where THOUGHT
has been replaced by PALM), the SPORT [o] vowel is a monophthongal pre-/r/ allophone of the
GOAT /oʊ/ phoneme, while for speakers of THOUGHT-ful accents, the SPORT [o] vowel is the
pre-/r/ allophone of the THOUGHT /ɔ/ phoneme. Before intervocalic /r/, the pronunciation of
such words is variable. Some (e.g., *story*) must have the SPORT [o] vowel, while others have
an alternative pronunciation with the PALM /ɑ/ vowel, which may be more (e.g., *tomorrow*)
or less (e.g., *forest*) common depending on the word; see Section 5.2.2.

In the mid front vowel area, the FACE /eɪ/ vowel has historically merged with the DRESS /ɛ/ vowel before pre-consonantal and word-final /r/, resulting in /ɛr/ (e.g., *fairy/ferry*). During the twentieth century, it became increasingly common to also merge TRAP /æ/ with DRESS /ɛ/ before intervocalic /r/, making *marry* homophonous with *merry* /'mɛri/, so that in contemporary GA, /ɛr/ is now the most usual variant in words like *carrot, arrow, charity, narrow*, and so on.

Although there is only one mid central vowel phoneme, schwa /ə/, in GA and therefore no loss of contrast between vowels before /r/ in /ər/, it is interesting to note the range of spellings in schwa + /r/ words: *stir, dirt, turn, fur, term, herb*. These are relics of an earlier wave of mergers before /r/ that took place before the English language arrived in North America.

5.7.2 R-coloring

When a vowel occurs before /r/ in GA, especially when there is no syllable boundary between the vowel and /r/, the articulation of the /r/ tends to begin during the articulation of the vowel, giving the vowel an /r/-like quality known as **r-coloring**. Typically, it is the latter part of the vowel that becomes r-colored, but in the case of schwa /ə/, the vowel is usually r-colored throughout. In other words, the two phonemes /ə/ and /r/ are realized as a single r-colored vowel, the IPA symbol for which is [ɚ]. The realization of /ər/ as [ɚ] is so common in GA, both in stressed and unstressed syllables, and so characteristic of the accent that it has been given its own name, "schwar." Compare schwar transcribed phonemically and phonetically:

Phonemic: *curve* /kərv/, *ever* /'ɛvər/, *perceive* /pər'siv/, *merger* /'mərdʒər/
Phonetic: *curve* [kɚv], *ever* ['ɛvɚ], *perceive* [pɚ'siv], *merger* ['mɚdʒɚ]

In some works, a non-phonemic approach to transcription is combined with a strong/weak analysis (see Section 5.3), resulting in two different symbols for schwar, [ɚ] in unstressed syllables and [ɝ] in stressed syllables:

/ər/:   *nurture* ['nɝtʃɚ], *further* ['fɝðɚ], *worker* ['wɝkɚ], *burger* ['bɝgɚ]
          nurture /'nərtʃər/, *further* /'fərðər/, *worker* /'wərkər/, *burger* ['bərgər]

When schwa and the following /r/ are not in the same syllable, they do not merge completely to form schwar:

/ə/ + /r/:   *peruse* /pə'ruz/, *interrupt* /ɪntə'rəpt/, *around* /ə'raʊnd/, *marine* /mə'rin/
               peruse [pə'ruz], *interrupt* [ɪntə'rəpt], *around* [ə'raʊnd], *marine* [mə'rin]

5.8 Influence of dark /l/

The raising of the back of the tongue, i.e., velarization, for **dark /l/** (see Section 2.25) has the effect of making a preceding vowel more retracted (i.e., causing it to be articulated as a backer vowel than in other contexts). This effect is greater with front and central vowels, such as KIT /ɪ/, DRESS /ɛ/, TRAP /æ/, FOOT /ʊ/, and schwa /ə/ than with back vowels, such as PALM /ɑ/ and GOAT /oʊ/, which are already articulated in the back area of the vowel space.

5.9 Breaking

Articulating a dark/velarized /l/ after a close vowel tends to take the center of the tongue through the position for a mid central vowel, i.e., schwa [ə], as the tongue tip and back rise. Particularly when a consonant or word boundary follows, this process leads to a schwa /ə/ developing before the dark/velarized /l/, a phenomenon known as **breaking**. Breaking occurs not only after the two close vowels – FLEECE /i/ and GOOSE /u/ – but also after the diphthongs FACE /eɪ/, PRICE /aɪ/, CHOICE /ɔɪ/, MOUTH /aʊ/:

FLEECE:	*deal* [diəɫ], *field* [fiəɫd], *peeled* [piəɫd], *steals* [stiəɫz]
GOOSE:	*tool* [tuəɫ], *school* [skuəɫ], *ruled* [ruəɫd], *fools* [fuəɫz]
FACE:	*pale* [peɪəɫ], *Wales* [weɪəɫz], *failed* [feɪəɫd], *sales* [seɪəɫz]
PRICE:	*mile* [maɪəɫ], *child* [ʧaɪəɫd], *smiled* [smaɪəɫd], *files* [faɪəɫz]
CHOICE:	*oil* [ɔɪəɫ], *soil* [sɔɪəɫ], *spoiled* [spɔɪəɫd], *boils* [bɔɪəɫz]
MOUTH:	*owl* [aʊəɫ], *foul* [faʊəɫ], *howled* [haʊəɫd], *scowls* [skaʊəɫz]

Because breaking is more usual when /l/ is word-final than when a vowel follows, speakers may alternate between pronouncing the same word with and without breaking depending on whether a word-final /l/ is followed by by a pause or by a vowel (in a suffix or an immediately following word), for example:

FLEECE:	*feel* [fiəɫ] vs. *feeling* [ˈfiɫɪŋ] or *feel it* [ˈfiɫ ɪt]
GOOSE:	*fool* [fuəɫ] vs. *foolish* [ˈfuɫɪʃ] or *fool him* [ˈfuɫ ɪm]
FACE:	*sail* [seɪəɫ] vs. *sailing* [ˈseɪɫɪŋ] or *sail along* [seɪɫ əˈɫɑŋ]
PRICE:	*smile* [smaɪəɫ] vs. *smiling* [ˈsmaɪɫɪŋ] or *smile at* [ˈsmaɪɫ ət]
CHOICE:	*toil* [tɔɪəɫ] vs. *toiling* [ˈtɔɪɫɪŋ] or *toil away* [ˈtɔɪɫ əˈweɪ]
MOUTH:	*prowl* [praʊəɫ] vs. *prowling* [ˈpraʊɫɪŋ] or *prowl around* [ˈpraʊɫ əˈraʊnd]

Breaking can also occur with FLEECE and GOOSE before /r/:

FLEECE:	*beer* [biər], *dear* [diər], *steer* [stiər], *rear* [riər]
GOOSE:	*poor* [puər], *tour* [tuər], *moor* [muər]

Chapter 6

Practice

Individual vowels

This chapter provides practice in pronouncing the vowels of GA and their various allophones. The exercise material includes the target sounds in different phonetic contexts, in words and phrases where they occur multiple times, in sentences, and in dialogues.

6.1 Checked monophthongs: summary of key features

The five checked monophthongs are KIT /ɪ/, FOOT /ʊ/, DRESS /ɛ/, TRAP /æ/, and schwa /ə/. Strictly speaking, the checked vs. free distinction applies only to vowels in stressed syllables. Here for convenience, however, we treat the unstressed variants of vowels together with their stressed variants.

The key features of the checked monophthongs are:

1   As checked vowels, they must be followed in stressed syllables by a syllable-final consonant (i.e., by one or more consonants; see Section 5.4).
2   They are of relatively short duration when compared with the free vowels (and therefore are sometimes referred to as "short" vowels). TRAP /æ/ is an exception. For most speakers, it's rather long (see Section 5.4).
3   They are shortened when followed by a voiceless consonant in the same syllable (pre-fortis clipping); see Section 5.6.

    a)   The shortening is slight in the case of the checked vowels, as they are already inherently rather short.
    b)   The shortening is more noticeable when combined with the shortening of another sonorant (nasal or approximant).
    c)   Shortening of vowels is an important cue for identifying whether a following obstruent is voiced or voiceless.

4   KIT /ɪ/ and FOOT /ʊ/ aren't merely short versions of FLEECE /i/ and GOOSE /u/ (see Section 5.4).
5   Besides its occurrence as a stressed vowel, schwa /ə/ also very frequently occurs as an unstressed vowel (see Sections 5.3 and 8.1).
6   Stressed schwa tends to be opener (open-mid) than unstressed schwa (mid); see Section 5.3.
7   When schwa is followed in the same syllable by /r/, the two phonemes are realized as a single r-colored vowel – schwar [ɚ] (see Section 5.7.2).
8   When TRAP /æ/ is followed by /r/, most speakers now replace it with DRESS /ɛ/, making such pairs as "marry" and "merry" homophones (see Section 5.7.1).

6.2 KIT /ɪ/

6.2.1 Description

Just above close-mid, front-central, unrounded.

6.2.2 Spelling

<i> big, lid, bill
<y> typical, myth, symbol

Unusual spellings

English, pretty, sieve, busy, business, build, guilt, women

6.2.3 Full length before voiced consonants

big, bin, bridge, fin, fridge, give, grin, king, lid, pig, pin, quiz, ring, sing, skin, slim, spin, spring, sting, string, swim, swing, thin, thing, tin, twig, twin, wig, win, wing

6.2.4 Clipped before voiceless consonants

brick, chip, dip, dish, drip, fish, fist, fit, fix, gift, hip, kick, knit, lift, lip, list, miss, mist, mix, quick, risk, shift, ship, sick, sit, six, slip, stick, switch, this, trick, trip, twist, which, wish, wrist

6.2.5 Full length vs. clipped

nib/nip, rib/rip; bid/bit, grid/grit, hid/hit, kid/kit, lid/lit, slid/slit; pig/pick, wig/wick; ridge/rich; his/hiss

6.2.6 Before /l/

bill, chill, drill, fill, grill, hill, ill, kill, mill, pill, skill, spill, will; build, film; guilt, milk, silk

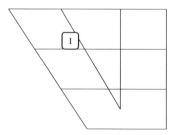

Figure 6.1 The KIT /ɪ/ vowel

6.2.7 Multiple

fingerprints, thick-skinned, individual, dipstick, bigwig, skinflint, hillbilly, silverfish, insufficient, inconsistent, intermittent, inapplicable, inconsiderate, inefficient

6.2.8 Additional words

begin, bitter, busy, city, chicken, different, difficult, dinner, figure, guilty, idiot, injure, innocent, insect, interesting, kitchen, kitten, little, middle, opinion, picture, pillow, pity, pretty, river, scissors, silly, sister, sticky, tickle, tricky, typical, window, winter

6.2.9 Phrases

big business, binge drinking, a bitter wind, a brick building, silicon chips, the inner city, living conditions, a film critic, a difficult decision, an English dictionary, Christmas dinner, a fizzy drink, written English, a film script, physically fit, a quick fix, flip a switch, a giggling fit, the village idiot, an innocent victim, a kiss on the lips, little children, skim milk, the missing link, a bitter pill, a sinking ship, a stiff drink, a business trip, a wicked witch, a wish list, a big difference, English literature, as fit as a fiddle, sink or swim

6.2.10 Sentences I

(1) Sit still! (2) Liz lives in Italy. (3) Phil's as fit as a fiddle. (4) Isabelle drinks skim milk. (5) Did Dylan win the competition? (6) This put him in a difficult position. (7) Fish and chips is originally a British dish. (8) Bridget's kids are sick of chicken for dinner. (9) Christopher and Imogen are in their mid-fifties. (10) The living conditions in the inner city are abysmal.

Sentences 2

(1) Jill didn't stick to the script but instead improvised. (2) Lydia lives in a little village in the middle of England. (3) Melissa's interested in the history of English literature. (4) It's fulfilled his ambition of becoming a physical therapist. (5) Will Patricia give me her recipe for ginger and garlic chicken wings? (6) My dictionary of English idioms disappeared within fifteen minutes. (7) In my opinion, Jim's quick-thinking, but I think Sid's pretty dim-witted. (8) Who was commissioned to build the bridge across the Mississippi River? (9) My little sister's a bitter cynic and my big sister an interfering busybody. (10) We established a statistically significant difference between British and Finnish children.

6.2.11 Dialogues

A: He can mix six drinks in a minute.
B: Six is very quick.
A: He does it for a living.
B: Six isn't quick if he does it for a living.

A: This is ridiculous!
B: It's silly!

A: Nearly fifty different symbols!
B: For nearly fifty different English sounds!

A: Give me a sip of your drink.
B: Only if you give me one of your fish sticks.
A: Are you swindling me?
B: Business is business . . .

6.3 FOOT /ʊ/

6.3.1 Description

Just above close-mid, back-central, weakly rounded.

6.3.2 Spelling

<ook> = /ʊk/ book, cook, look, took (exceptions: spooky, snooker) + certain other words containing <oo> foot, good, hood, childhood, stood, wool
<oul> could, should, would
<o> woman, wolf, wolves, bosom
<ul, ull> = /ʊl/ full, pull, bullet, fulfill
<ush> = /ʊʃ/ bush, push
Certain other words with <u>, sugar, put, pudding, butcher, cuckoo

6.3.3 Full length before voiced consonants

could, good, hood, should, stood, wood

6.3.4 Clipped before voiceless consonants

foot, put, soot; book, brook, cook, crook, hook, look, nook, rook, shook, took; woof; bush, push

6.3.5 Before /l/

bull, full, pull, wool; wolf

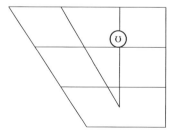

Figure 6.2 The FOOT /ʊ/ vowel

6.3.6 Additional words

ambush, bosom, bullet, bully, bushel, bulletin, butcher, childhood, cookbook, crooked, cushion, cushy, fulfil, pudding, rookie, sugar, wooden, understood, woman

6.3.7 Phrases

a good look, by hook or by crook, fully booked, a good cook, push and pull, woof woof!

6.3.8 Sentences 1

(1) He couldn't put a foot wrong. (2) He was hooked on books. (3) Who took my wool cushions? (4) She stood barefoot in the brook. (5) The bully pushed him into the bush. (6) The crooks pulled down their hoods. (7) I would if I could, but it's just no good. (8) The bulldogs chased him into the woods. (9) The cooking courses are all fully booked.

Sentences 2

(1) He stood up when my queen took his rook. (2) The bullfight was held at the Acapulco bullring. (3) He played football before he became a butcher. (4) Could you cook pudding without putting sugar in? (5) He fully understood why she'd put her foot down. (6) It would be good if you could put the full text here. (7) He took a good look at her and then shook his head. (8) I didn't know whether to push him away or pull him closer. (9) The book looks at the bully's journey from childhood to manhood. (10) Brooke was the type who stood her ground and took the bull by the horns.

6.3.9 Dialogues

A: You shouldn't cook that pudding any more.
B: And *you* shouldn't bully the cook, should you?
A: I couldn't bully you, could I? You'd butcher me!
B: Good cooks have sharp knives!

A: Now look, how can I hook the heart of a good woman?
B: It took me a lot of looking to find a good woman.
A: How do I ambush the affections of a good woman?
B: Put your best foot forward, and by hook or by crook, you'll find a good woman.
A: Is there a good book on how to look for a good woman?

A: For a good pudding you shouldn't add much sugar.
B: A good cook wouldn't add more than a spoonful.
A: A tablespoonful of sugar or a teaspoonful of sugar?
B: I couldn't say. Let me have another look in the cookbook.
A: It wouldn't look good if we put too much sugar in the pudding, would it?
B: Goodness no! We'd look like a pair of rookie cooks!

6.4 DRESS /ɛ/

6.4.1 Description

Mid, front, unrounded.

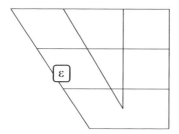

Figure 6.3 The DRESS /ɛ/ vowel

6.4.2 Spelling

\<e\> bed, beg, bell, there, where
\<ea\> bread, dead, pleasure, bear
\<a\> any, many, scarce
\<air\> = /ɛr/ air, chair, flair, questionnaire
\<are\> = /ɛr/ bare, care, share, parent
\<ary, arry\> = /ɛri/ scary, canary, marry, voluntary
\<aria\> = /ɛriə/ vegetarian, Hungarian, variable
\<arious\> = /ɛriəs/ various, hilarious, gregarious
\<eir\> = /ɛr/ their, heir, heiress

Unusual spellings

friend, aga*in*(st), said, says, l*eo*pard, G*eo*ffrey, j*eo*pardy, b*u*ry

6.4.3 Full length before voiced consonants

bread, egg, end, fed, friend, head, hedge, leg, lend, pen, red, send, shed, spend, spread, ten, when

6.4.4 Clipped before voiceless consonants

best, breath, check, chest, deaf, death, desk, dress, fetch, fresh, get, guess, left, less, mess, neck, nest, net, next, pet, rest, step, stretch, sweat, test, yes

6.4.5 Full length vs. clipped

bed/bet, led/let, dead/debt, said/set, wed/wet; peg/peck; edge/etch; rev/ref

6.4.6 Before /l/

bell, sell, fell, gel, hell, shell, smell, tell, well; weld, elm; self, shelf, help, else, belt, felt, melt

6.4.7 Before syllable-final /r/

air, bear, blare, cairn, care, chair, dare, fare, flare, glare, hair, pair, rare, share, spare, square, stare, swear, there, wear, affair, aware, beware, compare, declare, despair, millionaire, nightmare, prepare, questionnaire, repair, welfare; scarce

6.4.8 Before intervocalic /r/

America, bury, ceremony, cherry, error, heritage, heroine, herring, hysterical, imperative, inherit, merry, perish, terrible, therapy, verify, very; aerial, aquarium, area, barbarian, canary, dairy, fairy, hilarious, malaria, parent, prairie, various, vegetarian, wary; legendary, military, necessary, ordinary, secretary, temporary, voluntary; apparent, Arabic, arid, arrogant, arrow, barrel, barren, barrier, carol, carrot, carry, character, charity, clarity, embarrass, guarantee, marathon, marrow, marry, narrow, paradise, paragraph, paranoid, parrot, popularity, similarity, sparrow, transparent

6.4.9 Multiple

deathbed, eggshell, epilepsy, existential, extraterrestrial, headrest, nevertheless, recollect, egghead, recommend, redhead, referendum, represent, headset, retrospect, self-centered, self-defense, self-help, temperamental, trendsetter, well-fed, well-read, whenever, health care, elsewhere, anywhere, welfare, wherever, everywhere, farewell, menswear, airbed, daredevil, hairdresser, questionnaire, threadbare, vegetarian, parallel, airfare, hairnet

6.4.10 Additional words

adventure, airplane, any, belly, cellar, center, clever, collect, comment, context, correct, credit, defend, dentist, develop, echo, elephant, enemy, energy, engine, event, feather, healthy, heavy, index, jealous, leather, lemon, letter, many, measure, message, pleasant, plenty, question, ready, technique, weather, yellow

6.4.11 Phrases

a best friend, a dead end, a debt collector, a health center, a special event, a treasure chest, an electric fence, death threats, a sense of adventure, a defense mechanism, a desperate effort, dress sense, forensic tests, a French head chef, fresh eggs, gentle exercise, genuine leather, an intelligence test, lemon zest, a precious gem, red peppers, send a letter, a sense of adventure, a wedding dress, wet cement, deadly enemies

6.4.12 Sentences 1

(1) He left his heirs all his shares. (2) Beth has no sense of adventure. (3) Her boyfriend has a hairy chest. (4) The men were mending the nets. (5) The desert stretched out endlessly. (6) Claire and Emma were best friends. (7) How can I tell if the eggs are fresh? (8) Ken has no dress sense whatsoever! (9) The breathalyzer test proved negative. (10) Fred says he regularly gets death threats.

Sentences 2

(1) The hotel was excellent in every respect. (2) Derek wasn't ready to accept these tenets. (3) Dennis places a heavy emphasis on ethics. (4) Mary made several perceptive suggestions. (5) The empty desk suggested that Jeremy had left. (6) Megan's always one step ahead of everyone else. (7) I'll never forget the expression on Edward's face. (8) These sectors are heavily dependent on technology. (9) We had a very helpful attendant at the check-in desk. (10) The elections are scheduled for December the seventh.

6.4.13 Dialogues

A: Is this your best effort?
B: Yes, it's my very best attempt.
A: It's a terrible mess.
B: Well, I'm fairly certain that the rest aren't any better.

A: Fred, have you been sending scary death threats to Larry again?
B: I penned my ten best ever on Wednesday and sent them direct. A real treasure chest of devilish, hellish threats. A clever jest for my very best friend.
A: But your secretary neglected to append your name and address, Fred! He read your letter and more or less wet the bed!
B: Wet the bed? What a terrible defense mechanism.
A: I meant he drenched it in sweat. Now get ready to tell him you sent the letter in error, and you're terribly repentant.

A: Have you carefully prepared for your French test?
B: I scarcely need to prepare anything. French is my best subject. The test'll be an effortless success.
A: Have you kept abreast of the expected content of the test – the irregular present tense and the imperative?
B: My friends said to expect questions about the feminine gender and inflections.
A: Apparently, your friends aren't as friendly as you guessed!

6.4.14 Extra practice /ɛ/ before /r/

6.4.15 Phrases

wear and tear, a caring parent, fair hair, a marriage ceremony, a glaring error, the heir apparent, the American military, a fair share, a hairy chest, a leather armchair, a teddy bear, the depths of despair, a menacing glare, a terrible nightmare, an aircraft engine, elderly parents, a steady stare, a hairpin bend, a rare event, a fairweather friend, hairy legs, a sensitive area, essential repairs, a charity event, a temporary measure, an imaginary friend, a terrible headache, a therapy session, a red herring, a breath of fresh air, a wedding ceremony, red hair, scared to death, a spelling error, a spare bed

6.4.16 Sentences 1

(1) Sarah was scarcely ever there. (2) The hardware was beyond repair. (3) Mary was aware of all his affairs. (4) The chairman was a gregarious person. (5) I swear the pair of them looked hilarious. (6) Claire wouldn't share the airfare with him. (7) We prepared the questionnaire with great care. (8) I can scarcely bear to see her in that wheelchair. (9) We tasted the carefully prepared vegetarian fare. (10) We had dairy-free éclairs with caramelized pears.

Sentences 2

(1) Her visual awareness was impaired after the scare. (2) It's rare for it to be colder upstairs than downstairs. (3) Enter if you dare, and prepare yourselves for a scare! (4) Her nightmares

scared her, but her parents didn't care. (5) The Hungarian millionaire was wary of monetary schemes. (5) They made Harry aware of their despair. (6) Care must be taken to wear suitable footwear. (7) It's unfair to compare this area with the Canaries.

6.5 TRAP /æ/

6.5.1 Description

Between open-mid and fully open, front, unrounded. TRAP tends to be rather long.

6.5.2 Spelling

<a> bang, cab, bank, mat, taxi

Unusual spellings

plaid, meringue, timbre

6.5.3 Full length before voiced consonants

add, bad, badge, bag, band, bang, can, drag, fan, gang, glad, grand, hand, hang, have, jam, land, man, pan, plan, rag, sad, sand, stand, van

6.5.4 Clipped before voiceless consonants

ask, ax, back, bath, black, blast, brass, calf, cash, cast, cat, catch, chance, chat, dance, draft, fast, flash, flat, gap, gas, gasp, glance, glass, grant, graph, grasp, grass, last, laugh, map, mask, mat, match, pass, past, pat, path, plant, rat, shaft, snap, staff, task, tax, track, trap, vast, wrap

6.5.5 Full length vs. clipped

cab/cap, lab/lap, slab/slap, tab/tap; bad/bat, fad/fat, had/hat, pad/pat, sad/sat; bag/back, lag/lack, rag/rack, sag/sack, snag/snack, tag/tack; badge/batch; calve/calf, halve/half

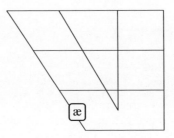

Figure 6.4 The TRAP /æ/ vowel

6.5.6 Before /l/

canal, pal, shall; scalp, talc

6.5.7 Multiple

abracadabra, acrobat, anagram, Anglo-Saxon, anthrax, anti-climax, backgammon, backlash, backscratcher, bandana, blackjack, cataract, catnap, claptrap, fantastic, flapjack, gangplank, granddad, handstand, haphazard, jackass, magnanimous, malpractice, mantrap, manufacture, mathematics, ransack, saddlebag, sandbag, satisfaction

6.5.8 Additional words

action, actor, advance, advantage, after, angry, animal, ankle, answer, apple, attack, attractive, balcony, banana, basket, battle, blanket, cabbage, camera, cancel, candle, capital, castle, channel, chapter, command, damage, demand, disaster, dragon, exam, example, fancy, fashion, gamble, giraffe, grammar, habit, imagine, manage, manners, massive, master, matter, nasty, packet, panic, plaster, plastic, practical, rabbit, rather, sample, shadow, slander, tablet, talent, taxi, travel, value, vanish

6.5.9 Phrases

a master class, demand an answer, a bad attitude, a balancing act, a bank manager, a plastic bag, a ham sandwich, a jazz band, half a chance, a dancing class, a matter of fact, natural talent, a panic attack, a bad back, a traffic jam, an asthma attack, an elastic band, as mad as a hatter, the last laugh, black magic, a gambling man, hand in hand, natural gas, pack your bags, a plan of action, a rat catcher, a relaxed attitude, a bad habit, a black cat, one last chance

6.5.10 Sentences 1

(1) Pack your bags. (2) Thanks for backing my plan. (3) Amanda was in absolute agony. (4) Andrew landed flat on his back. (5) Pat and Jack catch rabbits in traps. (6) My granddad was a past master of tact. (7) Anna has a natural talent for languages. (8) Annabel patted Janet on the back and ran. (9) Has Lance got an accurate map of Japan? (10) Can't you see the animal tracks in the sand?

Sentences 2

(1) Patrick's angry and demands a fast answer. (2) The manager valiantly tackled the challenge. (3) Alan has a rather callous attitude towards cats. (4) Alice is passionate about her dancing classes. (5) Matthew was very practical and matter of fact. (6) Alexandra understands how to handle the matter. (7) Catherine wore a black jacket and a matching hat. (8) Sebastian still has panic attacks after his accident. (9) The ham sandwiches were packed in a plastic bag. (10) Sandra had exams, so we had to cancel our plans to go camping.

6.5.11 Dialogues

A: Is that a fat black rat in your jacket?

B: Sally's a black rat, but she's not fat. Fancy calling her that! What bad manners!

A: Having a menagerie of angry animals jammed in your jacket pockets is bad manners and a very bad habit.

B: Don't exaggerate. A rabbit, a rat, and a cat aren't a menagerie. Here, pat Sally's back. She's saddened by your nasty, slanderous words.

A: Now that I'm engaged to Jan, I'm abandoning my bad habits.

B: Is Jan planning to abandon her bad habits too?

A: Jan's such a fantastic catch that I can't imagine she has any.

B: Can't you? There's a chance that even a fantastic catch like Jan has a bad habit or two.

6.6 Schwa /ə/

6.6.1 Stressed schwa

6.6.2 Description

Open-mid, central, unrounded.

6.6.3 Spelling

<u> sum, bus, butter
<o> love, money, nothing, color
<ou> cousin, trouble, enough, tough

Unusual spellings

blood, flood, does

6.6.4 Full length before voiced consonants

blood, bun, club, come, crumb, drug, drum, flood, fun, fund, gun, judge, jug, love, plug, rub, run, son, sponge, stuff, suck, thumb, tongue, young

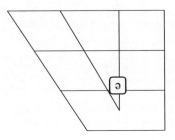

Figure 6.5 Stressed schwa /ə/

6.6.5 Clipped before voiceless consonants

blush, bust, crush, dust, hut, nut, rough, rush, shut, suck, touch, tough, trust

6.6.6 Full length vs. clipped

cub/cup, pub/pup; bud/but, cud/cut, mud/mutt; bug/buck, dug/duck, lug/luck, mug/muck, rug/ruck, tug/tuck; buzz/bus

6.6.7 Before /l/

cull, dull, gull, hull, lull, skull, bulb, bulge; bulk, sulk, gulp, pulse, culture, result

6.6.8 Multiple

bloodsucker, bubblegum, buttercup, dumbstruck, honeysuckle, multi-colored, mumbo-jumbo, stomach-pump, subculture, thunderstruck, unaccustomed, undercover, underdone, uninterrupted, uppercut

6.6.9 Additional words

brother, bubble, bucket, buckle, budget, bundle, butter, button, clumsy, color, country, couple, cousin, cover, cuddle, culture, cupboard, discover, double, dozen, enough, funny, glove, honey, hungry, lucky, money, monkey, mother, muscle, onion, oven, sudden, summer, trouble

6.6.10 Phrases

a dustpan and brush, a stomach bug, a double-decker bus, at the touch of a button, lovely colors, a young couple, the front cover, suddenly discover, a drug smuggler, a rubber duck, covered in dust, a sudden flood, just for fun, a trust fund, rubber gloves, runny honey, a loving husband, tough luck, a lump sum, run out of money, a couple of months, a young mother, a rumbling stomach, a wonder drug, the mother tongue, brotherly love

6.6.11 Sentences with stressed schwa 1

(1) Just my luck! (2) Justin was unintentionally funny. (3) Don't be upset. It was just for fun. (4) Douglas suffered the ultimate insult. (5) My son's truck got stuck in the mud. (6) The country was inundated by floods. (7) The young thug was covered in blood. (8) Russell finds lumpy custard disgusting. (9) One of her buttons had come undone. (10) My husband loves my oven-baked buns.

Sentences with stressed schwa 2

(1) The gunfire rumbled like distant thunder. (2) Russian and Dutch are my mother tongues. (3) Some of the customers had run out of money. (4) Button mushrooms are cultivated in Hungary. (5) We had a sumptuous lunch at my brother's. (6) There are dozens of cups and mugs in the cupboard. (7) My cousin has become reluctant to trust other adults.

(8) I subsequently discovered the company had gone bust. (9) For a month, the government was unable to run the country. (10) You can indulge in another cup of coffee at the touch of a button.

6.6.12 Dialogues

A: Cover the muffins and buns!
B: Is your son suddenly coming back?
A: Let's stuff them back in the oven. Pass me another dozen of the big ones.
B: But your mother and brother said he was running with your cousin . . .

A: Coming duck hunting on Monday?
B: I love the countryside, but hunting ducks sounds too bloody for my weak stomach.
A: It's rubber ducks we hunt. My mother covers a couple in mud and hides them in the garbage dump behind the pub near the country club.
B: Another one of your family's funny traditions? You really are a nutty bunch!

6.6.13 Unstressed schwa /ə/

6.6.14 Description

Mid, central, unrounded.

6.6.15 First syllable

about, across, address, adore, advance, advice, afford, afraid, agree, alarm, alive, allow, alone, amount, announce, appear, arrange, arrive, asleep, attack, avoid, awake, balloon, canal, career, collect, compare, complain, complete, concerned, conclude, confirm, confused, connect, contain, continue, convince, correct, machine, observe, occur, offend, parade, patrol, police, polite, possess, produce, promote, propose, protect, provide, success, suggest, supply, support, suppose

6.6.16 Word-medial syllable

acrobat, alcohol, alphabet, analyze, astronaut, atmosphere, autograph, caravan, compromise, crocodile, demonstrate, devastate, dinosaur, diplomat, dynamite, horoscope, kilogram,

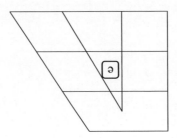

Figure 6.6 Unstressed schwa /ə/

microphone, microscope, nicotine, organize, parachute, paradise, paragraph, parallel, para-lyze, photograph, sympathize; contradict, guarantee, immature, introduce, kangaroo, lemon-ade, recommend, reproduce, volunteer

6.6.17 Final syllable

asthma, china, comma, drama, extra, panda, pasta, pizza, quota, sauna, sofa, zebra; cactus, campus, chorus, circus, citrus, fetus, focus, minus, virus; cautious, conscious, famous, gor-geous, gracious, jealous, spacious, precious, vicious, nervous; cheetah, atlas, August, ballot, barracks, bishop, breakfast, canvas, carrot, Christmas, compass, gallop, hammock, locust, mattress, method, parrot, pilot, purpose, salad, syrup, system, tortoise

6.6.18 Multiple unstressed schwas

adequate, algebra, ignorance, ignorant, impetus, syllabus, vigorous, agenda, arena, banana, cathedral, contagious, contentious, consensus, ferocious, gorilla, Jamaica, lasagna, Madonna, malicious, saliva, suspicious, vanilla, veranda, ballerina, agreement, appointment, European, acceptability, anonymous, asparagus, hippopotamus

6.6.19 Phrases with unstressed schwa

an asthma attack, a secret agenda, current affairs, an alleged assault, a police patrol, a con-sensus of opinion, a confirmed bachelor, a suspicious character, the focus of attention, an alternative method, a collector's item, a famous composer, the phonetic alphabet, a computer virus, suitable accommodation, a remarkable achievement, contradictory advice, unanimous agreement, continuous assessment, attract attention, a balanced diet, a brilliant success, a dramatic improvement, protect the environment, a substantial amount, thunderous applause, a lingua franca, abandon an attempt

6.6.20 Sentences with unstressed schwa

(1) Jonathan's afraid of being alone. (2) There are numerous recipes with pasta. (3) Rebecca had a tuna salad with asparagus. (4) Melissa's obsessed with dinosaurs and dragons. (5) Nich-olas observed a suspicious vehicle outside his residence. (6) Elizabeth was apparently a tre-mendous disappointment to her parents. (7) He's a terrific commentator – knowledgeable, articulate, and passionate. (8) My assistant's completely incapable of supplying solutions to the problems. (9) A woman was attacked by a ferocious gorilla in Central Africa in August. (10) I'm confused about commas and semi-colons and apostrophes in possessives and contractions.

6.6.21 Words with stressed and unstressed schwa

above, abundance, accompany, adjust, among, buffalo, company, compulsive, concussion, confront, construct, consult, corruption, custody, customer, fungus, hundred, husband, illus-trious, industrious, introduction, London, lullaby, luxury, obstruction, penultimate, produc-tion, publicity, Russia, stomach, succumb, suffocate, summary, vulnerable

6.6.22 Phrases with stressed and unstressed schwa

a touch of drama, consult a horoscope, a parachute jump, an introductory paragraph, a magazine cover, lucky to be alive, appear before a judge, a cinnamon bun, suppress a chuckle, gun control, add insult to injury, poisonous mushrooms, published anonymously, a solution to a puzzle, a humorous touch, trouble ahead, a position of trust, a color magazine

6.6.23 Sentences with stressed and unstressed schwa

(1) Brenda's stomach was pumped. (2) The old customs are very much alive. (3) Duncan jumped to the wrong conclusion. (4) He publishes a magazine on a monthly basis. (5) It was grudgingly tolerated by the government. (6) The woman was advised not to touch alcohol again. (7) The photograph was touched up to conceal her double chin. (8) My mother convinced me there was nothing to be afraid of. (9) Parents are welcome to come and have lunch with the children. (10) But that's nothing compared with the traumas suffered by others.

6.7 Schwar /ər/ [ɚ]

6.7.1 Description

Mid, central, unrounded, r-colored.

6.7.2 Spelling

<er> herd, determined, fertile
<ur> curry, fur, turn, occur, purpose, rural, sure, cure, mature
<ir> bird, girl, confirm, dirty
<ear> earth, rehearse, earnest
<our> adjourn, courage, courteous, journey, nourish
<yr> myrtle, myrrh
<wor> = /wər/ word, worthy, world, worry

Unusual spellings

colonel, attorney, entrepreneur, liqueur, neural

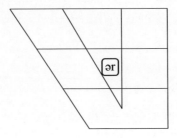

Figure 6.7 Stressed schwar /ər/

6.7.3 Full length

blur, cure, fur, pure, purr, sir, slur, spur, stir, sure; bird, burn, curb, curve, earn, fern, firm, germ, herb, learn, nerve, stern, term, third, turn, word, worm

6.7.4 Clipped before voiceless consonants

birth, church, dirt, earth, first, hurt, nurse, shirt, skirt, work, worse, worst, worth

6.7.5 Full length vs. clipped

curd/curt, heard/hurt, purred/pert; purge/perch; serve/surf; surge/search; curs/curse, purrs/purse

6.7.6 Before /l/

curl, earl, girl, hurl, pearl, twirl, whirl, world

6.7.7 Intervocalic

burrow, courage, current, currency, curry, encourage, flourish, flurry, hurricane, hurry, insurance, jury, luxurious, nourish, plural, rural, scurry, slurry, surrogate, thorough, turret, worry

6.7.8 Additional words

alert, allergic, burden, certain, circle, circuit, circus, commercial, concerned, confirm, curtain, deserve, dirty, early, emergency, eternal, expert, furniture, journal, merchant, observe, permanent, person, prefer, proverb, purple, purpose, refer, reserve, return, reverse, secure, servant, service, suburb, thirsty, turkey, version

6.7.9 Phrases

a first-class service, a bird reserve, a circular journey, a dirty word, an early bird, emergency first aid, an external observer, fertile earth, the First World War, an insurance firm, permanent work, a return journey, first-degree burns, serve a purpose, slurred words, search for a cure, virtually perfect, a turn for the worse, chirping birds, dirty work, emergency surgery, the first anniversary, a security alert, a permanent cure, a perfect world, a church service

6.7.10 Sentences I

(1) Herbert did the dirty work. (2) I'm allergic to certain animal furs. (3) She worked as a nurse in Serbia. (4) Ernest needed emergency surgery. (5) Earl's an expert on early furniture. (6) She worked like a whirling dervish. (7) Earl deserved to come first, not third. (8) The girls wore skirts that twirled. (9) The first version was virtually perfect. (10) How do you determine a pearl's worth?

Sentences 2

(1) The return journey from Berlin was murder. (2) Thursdays are the worst for service workers. (3) The girls were determined to learn Burmese. (4) Curse those chirping birds that disturb me so early! (5) Curtis and Gertie journeyed from Germany to Turkey. (6) It's my girlfriend's thirty-third birthday on the thirty-first. (7) She seemed unperturbed by Vernon's curt, hurtful words. (8) That murder reported in *The Mercury News* was certainly disturbing. (9) Shirley's journey to Burlington turned out to be nerve-racking. (10) Ferdinand was told in no uncertain terms not to disturb Gertrude.

6.7.11 Dialogues

A: Vernon's certainly nervous about burglars.
B: His work as a pearl and fur merchant means his house is perfect for burglars.
A: And his furniture's worth a fortune.
B: You're certain he's out on Thursday for his birthday party?
A: Burglary's dirty work, but the economy's taken a turn for the worse, and my girl's thirsty for pearls.

A: I'm concerned about Percy's thirst for Vernors.
B: It's worse than you know. The dental nurse told him to return for more work on the surfaces of his teeth.
A: He's impervious to the threat of emergency surgery. His perverted thirst for Vernors has given him scurvy.
B: I'm certain he'll never learn. He says it's worth it for his precious Vernors.

A: The first person he murdered was a burglar.
B: Did the burglar deserve it?
A: The burglar wasn't at work. He only learned later that burglary was that person's work.
B: Was the thirty-third murder victim also a burglar?
A: No, he murdered a colonel and then an earl.
B: This murderer went up in the world!

6.7.12 Unstressed schwar /ər/ [ɚ]

6.7.13 Description

Mid, central, unrounded, r-colored.

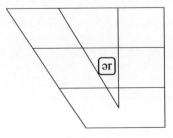

Figure 6.8 Unstressed schwar /ər/

6.7.14 *Final Syllable*

a) <-er>

anger, answer, border, brother, butter, center, chapter, clever, corner, cover, danger, daughter, dinner, eager, enter, father, feather, fever, fiber, filter, finger, folder, ginger, hammer, hunger, ladder, leather, letter, linger, liter, manner, matter, member, meter, monster, mother, number, offer, order, oyster, paper, partner, pepper, poster, powder, rather, river, shoulder, silver, sister, slender, snooker, sober, soldier, spider, stranger, summer, temper, tender, theater, thunder, tiger, timber, wander, water, weather, winter, wonder

b) Other spellings

actor, anchor, author, color, doctor, error, favor, flavor, harbor, honor, horror, humor, labor, major, minor, mirror, motor, neighbor, razor, rumor, sailor, terror, tractor, vapor; capture, creature, culture, failure, feature, figure, future, injure, lecture, leisure, measure, mixture, nature, picture, pleasure, pressure, structure, sulfur, treasure; beggar, cellar, collar, dollar, grammar, sugar, vulgar; awkward, backward, forward, orchard, standard, leopard, hazard, mustard, lizard, blizzard; comfort, effort; concert, cupboard, martyr, shepherd, yogurt

6.7.15 *First syllable*

ferment, forbid, forget, forgive, perceive, percent, perform, perhaps, persist, persuade, pursuit, surpass, survive

6.7.16 *Medial*

advertise, entertain, exercise, hibernate, interfere, interview, reservoir, Saturday, somersault, supervise, understand, yesterday

6.7.17 *Multiple*

afterwards, conqueror, emperor, governor, murderer, northerner, overture, undercover, undertaker, forever, performer, particular, survivor, vernacular, caterpillar, interloper, quartermaster, supertanker, supervisor

6.7.18 *Phrases*

forgive and forget, an underground reservoir, bitter anger, elder brothers and sisters, a pressure cooker, a father figure, a feather duster, a water heater, a painter and decorator, a character actor, a treasure hunter, a regular customer, a water container, a power generator, bigger and better, a future employer, river water, gather together, a former member, behavior patterns, a silver dollar, water vapor, never forget, winter hibernation, doctor's orders, gather information, a standard procedure, regular exercise, yesterday afternoon, weather patterns, powdered sugar, a visitor center, a better offer, sooner or later, a paper tiger, a modern painter, a spectacular performance, a water filter, a rubber hammer, a water meter

6.7.19 Sentences

(1) Better sooner than later. (2) My mother favors somber colors. (3) Peter works as a baker for his father. (4) I wonder if you could do me another favor. (5) The waiter offered to take a picture of us. (6) This is a standard feature on newer computers. (7) Winter brings colder temperatures and blizzards. (8) The youngster fell in the water but wasn't injured. (9) The editor spotted some minor grammatical errors. (10) He discovered, to his utter horror, that his neighbor had been murdered.

6.7.20 Words with stressed and unstressed schwar

berserk, burger, burglar, circular, cursor, deserter, determiner, fertilizer, fervor, further, furniture, impersonator, interpreter, learner, merger, murder, murmur, nurture, observer, overturn, surfer, undercurrent, undernourished, worker

6.7.21 Phrases with stressed and unstressed schwar

a registered nurse, in other words, offer an alternative, a silver anniversary, a birth certificate, forget a birthday, a member of a church, an inner circle, a matter of concern, an earth tremor, modern furniture, eager to learn, a collarless shirt, a customer survey, my word of honor, the pressure of work

6.7.22 Sentences with stressed and unstressed schwar

(1) Personally, I think Arthur deserves better. (2) That put a further burden on Pearl's shoulders. (3) "Birds of a feather flock together" is a proverb. (4) Herbert cursed himself for forgetting her birthday. (5) The weather turned for the worse in early December. (6) My sister formerly worked as a nurse and a journalist. (7) We heard that the circus performer had been murdered. (8) Thirty singers gathered for rehearsal on Thursday afternoon. (9) Security has been a major concern for Internet service providers. (10) My father urged me to return to university to get a master's in interpreting.

6.8 Free monophthongs: summary of key features

The three free monophthongs are FLEECE /i/, GOOSE /u/, and PALM /ɑ/. Their key features are:

1   As free vowels, they can appear in syllables with or without a coda (i.e., a following syllable-final consonant; see Section 5.4).
2   They are of relatively long duration when compared with the checked vowels (and are therefore sometimes referred to as "long" vowels); see Section 5.4.
3   They are shortened when followed by a voiceless consonant in the same syllable (pre-fortis clipping), which is an important cue for identifying whether a following obstruent is voiced or voiceless (see Section 5.6).
4   FLEECE /i/ and GOOSE /u/ aren't merely long versions of KIT /ɪ/ and FOOT /ʊ/ (see Section 5.4).
5   Both FLEECE /i/ and GOOSE /u/ have common slightly diphthongal variants consisting of a very narrow glide from a slightly opener position; see Section 5.5.

6   A schwa /ə/ is often inserted between FLEECE /i/ or GOOSE /u/ and a following /l/ or /r/ (breaking) (see Section 5.9).

7   Some speakers have an additional phoneme THOUGHT /ɔ/ (see Section 5.2.1).

8   The SPORT [o] vowel can be classified as the pre-/r/ allophone of GOAT or, for speakers who have a THOUGHT vowel, the pre-/r/ allophone of THOUGHT (see Section 5.2.2).

6.9   FLEECE /i/

6.9.1 Stressed FLEECE

6.9.2 Description

A little lower than close, a little backer than front, unrounded. Many speakers have a narrow diphthongal glide when the vowel has full length, notably in final positions (e.g., *free*). Before voiceless consonants, there's usually little or no glide (e.g., *feet*). Before /l/ and /r/, a centering glide can occur, a process known as breaking (e.g., *reel, beer*); see Section 5.9.

6.9.3 Spelling

<ee> bee, beer, see, glee, volunteer
<ea> sea, season, beard, reveal, clear
<ie> achieve, believe, grieve, niece, fierce, pier
<e> these, gene, scene, fetus, zero, atmosphere, bacteria
<ei> seize, receive, ceiling, weird, weir
<i> ski, magazine, pizza, technique, souvenir

Unusual spellings

people, Phoebe, Phoenix, key, quiche, mosquito, Portuguese, quay

6.9.4 Full length

a) Open syllables

bee, fee, flea, free, key, knee, pea, sea, ski, tea, tree, three

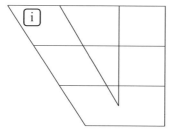

Figure 6.9 The FLEECE /i/ vowel

b) Closed syllables

bean, breeze, cheese, cream, dream, feed, freeze, gleam, green, jeans, keen, mean, need, please, queen, reed, scene, scream, screen, seem, sleeve, speed, squeeze, steam, stream, team, tease

6.9.5 Clipped before voiceless consonants

beach, beef, brief, cheap, cheat, cheek, deep, each, eat, feet, grease, keep, leak, meet, neat, peach, peak, reach, sheep, sheet, sleep, sneak, speak, speech, steep, street, sweet, teach, treat, week

6.9.6 Full length vs. clipped

bead/beat, greed/greet, heed/heat, seed/seat, tweed/tweet, weed/wheat; believe/belief, grieve/ grief, leave/leaf, thieve/thief; teethe/teeth; knees/niece, peas/peace, seize/cease

6.9.7 Pre-/l/ breaking

deal, feel, field, heel, kneel, meal, peel, shield, steal, wheel

6.9.8 Before syllable-final /r/

beer, cheer, clear, ear, dear, fear, gear, here, jeer, leer, mere, near, peer, queer, rear, sheer, smear, sneer, spear, sphere, steer, tier, veer, weir, year, appear, atmosphere, career, cashmere, disappear, engineer, interfere, persevere, severe, sincere, souvenir, volunteer; beard, weird; fierce, pierce

6.9.9 Before intervocalic /r/

appearance, clearance, coherent, hero, interference, series, zero; spirit, mirror, lyric, miracle, conspiracy, irritate, pyramid, syrup, myriad, irrigate, tyranny, virile, virulent

6.9.10 Multiple

peacekeeper, piecemeal, seaweed, TV

6.9.11 Additional words

agree, asleep, cathedral, ceiling, centipede, chlorine, colleague, complete, decent, defeat, delete, disease, eager, evening, extreme, feature, fever, freedom, hygiene, indeed, machine, people, police, protein, reason, release, repeat, secret

6.9.12 Phrases

green beans, a bleak scene, a deep-seated belief, a sea breeze, a brief meeting, a piece of cheese, a street cleaner, the deep blue sea, a feeling of relief, a devious scheme, complete disbelief, an elite athlete, an evening meal, an evil creature, a key feature, keep a secret, legal fees, a green field, free speech, a weak leader, lean meat, a weekly magazine, a secret meeting, a key ingredient, a peace treaty, a sneak preview, sea creatures, clean sheets, VIP treatment, extreme heat, deep grief, a reasonable fee, green tea, a secret ingredient, green leaves

6.9.13 Sentences 1

(1) Please leave me in peace! (2) The criteria seemed unclear. (3) We believe in freedom of speech. (4) These wheels are extremely cheap. (5) An elite athlete needs a lean physique. (6) Eat a piece of cheese after every meal. (7) Vera and Peter sealed the deal at 3:00 p.m. (8) Phoebe completed a degree in Swedish. (9) Eve seems reasonably easy to deal with. (10) Denise received treatment for the disease.

Sentences 2

(1) The sea breeze decreased the feeling of heat. (2) Reading tea leaves can reveal people's secrets. (3) We treated ourselves to a weekend at the beach. (4) I'll leave the green beans and peas in the freezer. (5) Keith has no redeeming features, but Sheila's sweet. (6) This is the first decent meal I've had in three weeks. (7) Pete speaks Greek, and Christina speaks Portuguese. (8) The bearded thief succeeded in deceiving the chief of police. (9) I have a feeling of deep grief, but his death's a relief. (10) The people of New Zealand are frequently called Kiwis.

6.9.14 Dialogues

A: You don't appear to be a keen reader.
B: Me? I read three magazines a week!
A: You need to read more signs. That one says, "Please keep feet off seats."
B: Oh! I see what you mean.

A: Steve's a keen beekeeper.
B: He keeps bees? So if I need any honey . . .
A: He's a vegan. He doesn't agree with stealing from bees.
B: Why does he keep the creatures?
A: He breeds three endangered species of honeybee.

A: How sweet of you to meet me this evening!
B: I need to see you to feel complete. Believe me!
A: I'm speechless. I can't feel the ground beneath my feet.
B: I mean it. I dream of leading an extremely genial life with you. Please be my queen!

6.9.15 Extra practice /i/ before /r/

6.9.16 Phrases

appear cheerful, peer into a mirror, clear the atmosphere, experience fear, steer clear, nearest and dearest, a mysterious disappearance, a dreary atmosphere, pierced ears, a coherent theory, sheer perseverance, a spiritual experience, the rearview mirror

6.9.17 Sentences 1

(1) Don't jeer and sneer. (2) The material's real cashmere. (3) He disappeared mysteriously: a miracle or a conspiracy? (4) There was an eerie atmosphere near the pyramids. (5) Keira had her ears pierced last year. (6) He's insincere, so steer clear of him. (7) He worked as a volunteer irrigation expert in Liberia. (8) I turned delirious with fear as we got nearer.

Sentences 2

(1) The early pioneers traveled to the frontier. (2) Superior mountaineering gear is available here. (3) A serious bacterial infection can cause delirium. (4) I saw that revered production of Shakespeare's *King Lear*. (5) Vera spent the early years of her career in Imperial College, London. (6) Our greatest experience in Siberia was seeing herds of reindeer. (7) Cheers! To many more years and many more beers with my peers!

6.9.18 Unstressed FLEECE

6.9.19 Description

This vowel has the same quality as stressed FLEECE.

6.9.20 Word-final

a) <-y>

angry, army, baby, body, bury, busy, carry, city, copy, country, dirty, dusty, duty, early, empty, entry, funny, fussy, guilty, happy, heavy, hungry, hurry, lady, lazy, lucky, many, naughty, party, pity, plenty, pretty, ready, silly, story, study, tidy, very, worry

b) Various other spellings <ie, ey, ee, i, e>

abbey, alley, barley, chimney, donkey, hockey, honey, jersey, jockey, journey, kidney, money, monkey, trolley, turkey, valley; khaki, muesli, taxi; coffee, toffee; cookie, movie; acne

6.9.21 Pre-vocalic

aerial, alien, aquarium, archaeology, area, audience, audio, barrier, comedian, create, curious, deodorant, embryo, enthusiastic, envious, furious, glorious, guardian, historian, idiom, idiot, librarian, malaria, material, meander, memorial, millennium, notorious, obvious, pedestrian, piano, radiator, radio, react, reality, stadium, studio, theatrical, trivial, various, vegetarian, video

6.9.22 Phrases

an area of difficulty, an enthusiastic audience, money worries, absolutely furious, a military historian, a silly idiot, a university librarian, a memorial ceremony, a movie studio, react badly, daily reality, a mighty army, a tiny baby, a healthy body, a juicy cherry, a friendly country, truly happy, an elderly lady, dirty laundry, a fancy-dress party, a conspiracy theory

6.9.23 Words with stressed and unstressed FLEECE

abbreviate, appreciate, bacteria, bleary, cafeteria, serial, cheery, criteria, delirious, dreary, easy, eerie, encyclopedia, experience, graffiti, imperial, inferior, ingredient, interior, material, media, mediocre, medium, mysterious, obedient, period, previous, query, series, serious, sleepy, superior, tedious, theory, weary

6.9.24 Phrases with stressed and unstressed FLEECE

an encyclopedia entry, previous experience, socially inferior, teaching materials, deadly serious, sleep peacefully, a steady beat, as sweet as honey, easy money, lean turkey, steaming coffee, an illegal alien, a legal guardian, receive money, extremely silly, a vicarious experience

6.9.25 Sentences with stressed and unstressed FLEECE

(1) The video's a real period piece. (2) We deeply appreciate your generosity. (3) His military experience was truly unique. (4) Amelia has a degree in industrial psychology. (5) The series received much publicity in the media. (6) I had a juicy kiwi and some sweetened strawberries. (7) Gillian's baby was teeny weeny but perfectly healthy. (8) Jamie recently volunteered as a DJ on university radio. (9) Olivia's an epidemiologist, and Celia's a meteorologist. (10) The encyclopedia features entries on the key themes of the twentieth century.

6.10 GOOSE /u/

6.10.1 Description

Close, back-central, weakly rounded. Many speakers use a diphthongal glide from a slightly opener position, especially word-finally (e.g., *blue, true, do*). Before /l/ and /r/, a centering glide can occur, a process known as breaking (e.g., *fool, tour*); see Section 5.9.

6.10.2 Spelling

\<oo\> boot, choose, food, poor
\<u\> duty, amusing, fury
\<u-e\> brute, cube, cute, lure

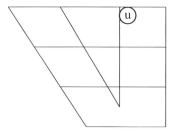

Figure 6.10 The GOOSE /u/ vowel

<o> do, to (strong form), two, tomb, who
<o-e> move, lose, prove, whose
<ou> group, through, youth, tour
<ui> bruise, fruit, juice, suit
<ue> blue, clue, true, venue
<eu> = /ju/ (/u/ following alveolar consonants) Europe, feud, maneuver, neutral, pseudo-
<ew> blew, chew, crew, interview

Unusual spellings

beauty, beautiful, shoe, mil<u>ieu</u> /mɪlˈju/

6.10.3 Full length

a) Open syllables

blue, chew, clue, crew, cue, do, drew, few, glue, grew, new, screw, shoe, through, true, two, view, who, you, zoo

b) Closed syllables

bruise, choose, food, huge, mood, move, smooth, moon, noon, room, soon, spoon, zoom

6.10.4 Clipped before voiceless consonants

flute, fruit, goose, hoot, juice, loop, roof, shoot, tooth

6.10.5 Full length vs. clipped

booed/boot, brewed/brute, cued/cute, rude/root, sued/suit; prove/proof; lose/loose

6.10.6 Before /l/

cool, fool, ghoul, pool, rule, school, stool, tool

6.10.7 Before syllable-final /r/

allure, assure, contour, demure, lure, mature, moor, poor, tour

6.10.8 Before intervocalic /r/

alluring, assurance, boorish, during, Europe, furious

6.10.9 Multiple

cock-a-doodle-do, foolproof, guru, supercomputer, superhuman, voodoo

6.10.10 Additional words

absolutely, afternoon, amusing, argue, balloon, beauty, bridegroom, computer, conclude, confusing, cuckoo, future, human, humor, improve, include, interview, issue, menu, movie, music, nephew, persecute, remove, rumor, student, stupid, substitute, superb, uniform, unit, volume

6.10.11 Unstressed

annual, constituency, continuous, evacuate, genuine, influence, manual, punctuate, situation, superfluous

6.10.12 Phrases

a soup spoon, a room with a view, absolutely true, fruit juice, doom and gloom, human communication, improve your mood, lose enthusiasm, move smoothly, a music school, nutritious food, conclusive proof, remove your shoes, room for maneuver, a useful clue, youthful enthusiasm, absolutely useless, lose a tooth, remove a tumor, a beautiful view

6.10.13 Sentences 1

(1) You stupid fool! (2) This view's too crude. (3) Fruit's a nutritious food. (4) Luke was confusing the issue. (5) Matthew was an astute student. (6) Ruth's suit is absolutely beautiful. (7) My tutor confused Judy with Lucy. (8) Drop your doom and gloom attitude. (9) Louis used it as an excuse to do it too. (10) Susan and Julie went to school together.

Sentences 2

(1) The room was filled with huge suitcases. (2) Fruit juice can boost your immune system. (3) My computer guru will be back on Tuesday. (4) Music was played throughout the afternoon. (5) They unanimously approved the constitution. (6) The shoes and boots in that boutique are cute. (7) Do you usually listen to music at full volume? (8) Hugh took the opportunity to interview some of the students. (9) Ruby knew that Andrew would soon lose his youthful enthusiasm. (10) A statue of Sir Isaac Newton can be found at one of the Oxford University museums.

6.10.14 Dialogues

A: There are too few serious issues in the news.
B: Who wants doom and gloom in June?
A: I assume you disapprove of truth in the news, you fool.
B: I knew you'd choose a gloomy mood instead of good humor and amusement.

A: Sue says she's through with Bruce.
B: The rumors are absolutely true. I knew they were doomed when I saw Bruce with Judy outside the music school on Tuesday.
A: You zoom in on all the clues!
B: The brute had on a new maroon two-piece suit and new blue shoes.
A: What a costume!

A: I don't know what to choose from the menu.
B: Do choose soon. I need food!
A: Don't be rude. I'll choose soon.
B: Just choose stew for you and goose for me.
A: No soup? No prune juice?
B: Choose soup and prune juice but soon! I'm drooling!

6.11 PALM /ɑ/

6.11.1 Description

Open, back-central, unrounded.

6.11.2 Spelling

<o> clock, stop, hot, rod, doll
<wa> = /wɑ/ swan, want, watt
<qua> = /kwɑ/ qualify, quality, quantity
<a> father, bra, façade, suave
<al> calm, palm /kɑ(l)m pɑ(l)m/
<ar> card, dark, remark, target
<oir> = /wɑr/ memoir, repertoire, reservoir

Unusual spellings

bourgeois, knowledge, yacht, sergeant, heart, hearth, Shah

THOUGHT *words*

<al> = /ɑl/ also, always, false, salt
<all> =/ɑl/ all, fall, hall, tall
<au, augh> author, launch, cause, daughter, caught
<aw> law, straw, dawn, awkward, awful

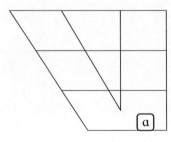

Figure 6.11 The PALM /ɑ/ vowel

Unusual spellings

walk, brought, ought, thought, broad, water

CLOTH *words*

<o> off, moth, loss, gosh, wrong, dog
<ou> cough, trough
<au> Austria, sausage

6.11.3 Full length

a) Open syllables (THOUGHT *words in italics*)

schwa, bra, spa, shah, Utah, grandma, grandpa, patois, bourgeois; *claw, jaw, law, saw, straw, thaw*

b) Closed syllables (THOUGHT *words in italics,* CLOTH *words in bold italics*)

blob, job, knob, lodge, odd, prod, rob, snob, sob, solve; façade, calm, kebab, palm; *cause, clause, fraud, pause, lawn, yawn*; ***bog, fog, log***

6.11.4 Clipped before voiceless consonants (THOUGHT *words in italics,* CLOTH *words in bold italics*)

block, box, crop, dot, drop, fox, hot, knock, lock, lot, mock, pop, rock, shock, shop, shot, sock, spot, top, want, watch, what, yacht; *caught, chalk, fought, talk, taught, walk*; ***off, soft, cough cloth, moth, boss, cost, cross, frost, loss, lost, moss, wasp, wash***

6.11.5 Full length vs. clipped (THOUGHT *words in italics,* CLOTH *words in bold italics*)

mob/mop, hob/hop; cod/cot, nod/not, plod/plot, pod/pot, rod/rot, trod/trot; *broad/brought, thawed/thought*; *saws/sauce*; ***clog***/clock, ***dog***/dock; ***flog***/flock, ***frog***/frock, ***log***/lock

6.11.6 Before /l/ (THOUGHT *words in italics*)

doll, golf, involve, solve; *all, appall, ball, brawl, call, drawl, fall, gall, hall, install, mall, recall, scrawl, shawl, small, sprawl, stall, tall, trawl, wall*

6.11.7 Before syllable-final /r/

bar, car, far, jar, scar, star, tar, arm, charm, farm, harm, barn, charge, barge, large, card, guard, hard, carve, starve; carp, sharp, bark, dark, mark, park, shark, spark, art, heart, cart, chart, part, start, smart, march, marsh, scarf; snarl, alarm, argue, artist, bargain, carpet, farmer, garden, garlic, guardian, guitar, harbor, harvest, market, parcel, pardon, partner, sergeant, target, memoir, rhubarb

6.11.8 Before intervocalic /r/

safari, guitarist, starry; sorry, tomorrow

6.11.9 Multiple (THOUGHT words in italics, CLOTH words in bold italics)

aardvark, archaeology, bodyguard, cardiology, chocoholic, farmyard, foxtrot, godfather, lollipop, monologue, monstrosity, oblong, shopaholic, stopwatch, barbershop, boxcar, hotspot, *daughter*-in-*law*, *waterfall*, *ball*park, **moth***ball*, **coffee**pot, watch**dog**

6.11.10 Additional words (THOUGHT words in italics, CLOTH words in bold italics)

accommodation, anonymous, apology, astonished, body, bomb, bottle, bottom, chocolate, collar, comedy, common, copy, cottage, doctor, follow, gossip, hobby, hollow, honest, honor, knowledge, modern, monster, pocket, popular, possible, profit, project, promise, proper, qualified, quality, rocket, solid, swallow, topic, trolley, wallet, October, alcohol; father, macho, mafia, pasta, salami, lasagna, latte; *abroad*, *author*, *naughty*, *water*, *audition*; **across**, **belong**, **coffee**, **coffin**, **donkey**, **office**, **sausage**

6.11.11 Phrases (THOUGHT words in italics, CLOTH words in bold italics)

a box of chocolates, common knowledge, a novel concept, a rock concert, rock solid, Mardi Gras, top quality, job prospects, an alarm clock, a logical argument, a model car, a rock garden, a heartfelt apology, a charming cottage, a sharp drop, a large profit margin, a guard of honor, heart problems, a golf *ball*, a **long-lost** *daughter*, a concert *hall*, a **long** *walk*, chocolate *sauce*, a *small* profit, a *daunting* prospect, an *awful* shock, a *bald* spot, a **coffee** shop, a hot *water* bottle, a **long** shot, **strong coffee**, a hot **dog**, a **long** scarf, **frog** *spawn*, **office** gossip, a **lost** cause, an awkward pause, small talk, a small **office**, a guard **dog**

6.11.12 Sentences 1

(1) Bob got a job in marketing. (2) They sell top-quality products. (3) They dropped an atomic bomb. (4) Tom's got a copy of the document. (5) Poverty's a complex phenomenon. (6) Molly got Roger a box of chocolates. (7) John's father is modest and charming. (8) Dominic's a highly qualified doctor. (9) The plot of the novel is hard to follow. (10) The economic prospects are promising.

Sentences 2 (CLOTH words in bold italics)

(1) Martha stopped the car to drop him **off**. (2) The problem was solved by a compromise. (3) It functions as an alarm clock and a stopwatch. (4) Charlie obviously favors quality over quantity. (5) Martin had a hot **dog** followed by some popcorn. (6) We want hot chocolate topped with marshmallows. (7) He was knocked unconscious and his heart stopped. (8) Oliver will have to drop his suave and confident façade. (9) How do we solve the problems of poverty and inequality? (10) Lots of Scots claim they've spotted the Loch Ness monster.

6.11.13 Sentences 3 (THOUGHT *words in italics*, CLOTH **words in bold italics**)

(1) *Pause* for *thought*. (2) He *caught all* the *balls*. (3) *Hawks* have **strong** *claws*. (4) *Maude* was *caught* for *fraud*. (5) It's a **long** *haul* and also **costly**. (6) Learn to *crawl* before you *walk*. (6) **Ross** *saw* that it was a **lost** *cause*. (7) *Claude* gave a *talk* on Jane *Austen*. (8) I *bought* this *drawing* at an *auction*. (9) *All* the *small talk* left me *exhausted*. (10) *All* I *recall* is that he is *tall* and *bald*.

6.11.14 Sentences 4 (THOUGHT *words in italics*, CLOTH **words in bold italics**)

(1) *Paul called* me to *withdraw* his **offer**. (2) My *daughter brought* a *small* catalog. (3) I'll just *walk* to the **office** and *talk* to *Claude*. (4) My *daughter-in-law* is going *abroad* in *August*. (5) We *saw* some *awesome waterfalls* in *Arkansas*. (6) How **often** do I need to add *salt* to the *water* **softener**? (7) The **song** *brought raucous applause* from the *audience*. (8) There was an *awkward pause* before *Walter walked* out. (9) The **washing** machine was *installed* next to the **dishwasher**.

6.11.15 Dialogues (THOUGHT *words in italics*, CLOTH **words in bold italics**)

A: Stop mocking John. It's **wrong** to sing such *awful* **songs**.
B: It's **wrong** to wear odd socks.
A: It's a common problem if you're not conscientious.
B: A common problem if you're a rotten slob!

A: A pot of **strong**, hot **coffee** will fix that **cough**.
B: The doctor said not to drink **coffee** until I've stopped **coughing**.
A: What a lot of nonsense! He's not a real doctor. It's common knowledge that **strong**, hot **coffee's** the best tonic for a **cough**.
B: Your *appalling* tonic makes me want to vomit.

A: It's so hot on this rotten yacht.
B: Get **off** if you want. I'm not stopping you.
A: You want me to drop in the *water*?
B: What an idiotic comment! We're in dock, you donkey. You can *walk* **off** this *awful* yacht whenever you want.

6.11.16 Extra practice /ɑ/ before /r/

6.11.17 Phrases

park a car, armed guards, a hard bargain, far apart, a jar of marmalade, a large part, a marketing department, a safari park, a car alarm, a star chart, an arms embargo, a farmers' market, car parts, a large margin, a dark mark, an artificial heart, a target market, a sarcastic remark, a backyard garden, rhubarb tart, an armored car, the hardest part, a large farm

6.11.18 Sentences 1

(1) Start the car. (2) It's far too large. (3) Martin's a hard bargainer. (4) We have garlic in our yard. (5) Let's have a barbecue party. (6) It broke my heart when we parted. (7) It's part and parcel of being an artist. (8) The sergeant was charged with arson. (9) Marsha kept to her part of the bargain. (10) Charlotte's a marvelous sparring partner.

Sentences 2 (THOUGHT *words in italics*, CLOTH *words in bold italics*)

(1) The larger the farm, the larger the harvest. (2) We put the jars of marmalade in the shopping cart. (3) Archie's a carpenter, and Mark's a pharmacist. (4) Martha started in the marketing department back in March. (5) We were charmed by the llamas and the aardvarks at the safari park. (6) Barbara had chronic **cough**. (7) The guard **dog** on the property barked non-stop. (8) We had garlic *sausages* followed by **coffee** and dark chocolate. (9) We submitted an electronic and a hard copy of the article. (10) Charlotte's a doctor, and Charles is an army **officer**. (11) He started a part-time job in March but **lost** it the following October.

6.12 The SPORT vowel [o]

6.12.1 Description

Close-mid, back, rounded. For speakers who have a THOUGHT vowel phoneme distinct from the PALM vowel, the SPORT [o] vowel can be considered an allophone of THOUGHT. For those who have no THOUGHT vowel, SPORT [o] can be considered an allophone of GOAT. Note that irrespective of how we classify the SPORT vowel, its pronunciation remains the same.

6.12.2 Spelling

<or> north, sort, force, sword /sord/
<ore> before, more, score
<oar> board, soar
<oor> door, floor
<our> four, pour
<quar> = /kwor/ quartet, quartz, quarter
<war> = /wor/ war, warm, reward

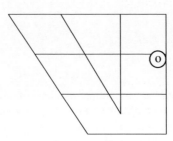

Figure 6.12 The SPORT [o] vowel

6.12.3 SPORT [o] before syllable-final /r/

chore, core, door, floor, four, more, pour, roar, score, sore, shore, snore, store, war; board, cord, hoard, lord, sword, born, corn, horn, mourn, thorn, form, storm, warm; cork, corpse, course, court, force, fork, horse, north, porch, pork, port, scorch, short, sort, source, sport, torch, warp; afford, award, before, divorce, enormous, important, ignore, normal, orchard, reward, order, platform, acorn, ordeal, tornado, organize, orchestra, formal, perform, corner, morning, portion, forty, mortal, torture

6.12.4 SPORT [o] before intervocalic /r/ (words in italics can also have PALM)

choral, chorus, story, storage, forum, floral, glory, porous, gory, memorial, notorious, tutorial, victorious, mandatory, category, territory; *sorry, tomorrow, borrow, sorrow, authority, orange, quarrel, quarry, warrant, warren, warrior, coral, coroner, categorical, correlate, Florida, florist, historic, horrible, majority, moral, Oregon, origin, porridge, rhetorical, foreign, torrent, oral, correspond, historian, corridor, priority, horizontal, forest*

6.12.5 Phrases

a court order, an important resource, a short course, a war memorial, a divorce court, more important, a short story, organized sport, a corner store, a foreign reporter, ignore a warning, moral authority, a foreign correspondent, moral norms, a short corridor, historically important, imports and exports, foreign origins, a court reporter, ignore an order, foreign imports

6.12.6 Sentences I

(1) Gloria adores horses. (2) Norma was born in Baltimore. (3) The floorboards were warped. (4) Everyone was bored or snoring. (5) He's an outdoor sports reporter. (6) Order was restored after the war. (7) It's on the fourth floor of the store. (8) It's a portrait of George the Fourth. (9) Reward them for doing their chores. (10) I can't afford my mortgage anymore.

Sentences 2

(1) Gordon served on four editorial boards. (2) Norman gave a course on the short story. (3) The orchestra and chorus were enormous. (4) Unfortunately, her warnings were ignored. (5) George Orwell's *1984* is more than just a story. (6) It's a Victorian fort restored to its former glory. (7) He is an important resource for our organization. (8) Forty corporations formally endorsed the report. (9) Explore the Norwegian fjords on board the *Queen Victoria*. (10) We were informed that a tornado would hit the northern shores.

6.12.7 Dialogues

A: It's not normal. You snore like a wild boar!
B: There's nothing boring about my glorious snoring.
A: It's neither glorious nor gorgeous. It's a horrible performance.
B: If you pour any more scorn on me, we'll be forced to divorce.

A: I finished my forty-fourth short story this morning.
B: You've amassed an enormous hoard since you took that short story course.

A: And I'm writing more and more – all sorts of stories.
B: That's why your hand's sore. It's worn out.

A: Is Norman short?
B: He's neither short nor enormous, just normal.
A: I heard his fortune is enormous.
B: His enormous fortune isn't important.
A: Of course, you adore Norman because he's normal.

6.13 Free diphthongs: summary of key features

The five diphthongs are FACE /eɪ/, PRICE /aɪ/, CHOICE /ɔɪ/, GOAT /oʊ/, and MOUTH /aʊ/. Their key features are:

1   They glide toward the close position at the top of the vowel space (see Section 5.5).

   a)   The fronting diphthongs, FACE /eɪ/, PRICE /aɪ/, and CHOICE /ɔɪ/, glide toward the close front position.
   b)   The backing diphthongs, GOAT /oʊ/ and MOUTH /aʊ/, glide toward the close back position.

2   They are falling diphthongs (see Section 5.5).

   a)   More time is spent at the start position than gliding.
   b)   The glides rarely reach the close position but finish around close-mid, hence the symbol for the second element.

3   Diphthongs can also be categorized according to the extent of the glide (see Section 5.5).

   a)   The narrow diphthongs, FACE /eɪ/ and GOAT /oʊ/, have short glides.
   b)   The wide diphthongs, PRICE /aɪ/, CHOICE /ɔɪ/, and MOUTH /aʊ/, have longer glides.

4   A schwa /ə/ is often inserted between the diphthongs and a following dark /l/ (pre-/l/ breaking) (see Section 5.9).
5   As free vowels, they can appear in syllables with or without a following syllable-final consonant (see Section 5.4).
6   They are of relatively long duration when compared with the checked vowels (and are therefore also "long" vowels) (see Section 5.4).
7   They are shortened when followed by a voiceless consonant in the same syllable (pre-fortis clipping), which is an important cue for identifying whether a following obstruent is voiced or voiceless (see Section 5.6).
8   The SPORT vowel [o] can be considered an allophone of GOAT /oʊ/ before /r/ (for speakers who have no THOUGHT /ɔ/ phoneme) (see Sections 5.2.2 and 5.7.1).

6.14 FACE /eɪ/

6.14.1 Description

Starts below close-mid front and moves toward close front, unrounded throughout.

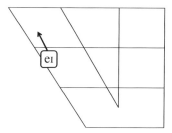

Figure 6.13 The FACE /eɪ/ vowel

6.14.2 Spelling

<a + consonant(s) + vowel> lady, change, amazing, nature, space
<ague> = /eɪg/ vague, plague
<ai(gh)> wait, contain, maintain, straight
<ay> gray, pay, stay, always
<ei> weigh, eight, beige
<ey> obey, they
Loanwords from French:
ballet, buffet, sachet, café, sauté, puree, foyer, dossier, décor, matinee, suede

Unusual spellings

steak, break, great, gauge, bass (but the fish is /bæs/)

6.14.3 Full length

a) Open syllables

clay, day, gray, hay, lay, may, pay, play, pray, ray say, spray, stay, they, tray, way

b) Closed syllables

age, aim, blame, brain, brave, cage, came, cave, chain, change, fame, flame, frame, game, gave, lane, main, maze, name, page, pain, rain, same, shame, shave, stage, train, vague, wage

6.14.4 Clipped before voiceless consonants

ache, bake, base, break, cake, case, chase, date, eight, gate, grape, hate, lake, place, plate, shake, snake, space, state, straight, take, tape, taste, waist

6.14.5 Full length vs. clipped

fade/fate, grade/great, laid/late, made/mate, raid/rate, trade/trait, wade/wait; save/safe; graze/grace, phase/face, raise/race, trays/trace

6.14.6 Pre-/l/ breaking

fail, gale, jail, mail, nail, pale, rail, sale, scale, snail, stale, tail, trail

6.14.7 Multiple

alienate, aviation, brainwave, database, maintain, mayonnaise, payday, radiator, wastepaper

6.14.8 Additional words

afraid, amazing, apron, arrange, ashamed, awake, baby, bacon, basic, cable, café, contain, cradle, danger, decorate, educate, escape, essay, favor, lady, lazy, major, mistake, nation, nature, paper, station, table

6.14.9 Phrases

a display case, aches and pains, a paper airplane, a real estate agent, stay awake, a naval base, a birthday cake, an isolated case, a state of chaos, a claim for compensation, grave danger, at a later date, major delays, a favorite destination, make a face, a claim to fame, play a game, hate mail, a safe haven, a middle-aged lady, a man-made lake, a fatal mistake, a change of pace, a waste of paper, a famous phrase, a safe place, a train station, a faint trace, radioactive waste, take a break, a radio station, bake a cake

6.14.10 Sentences 1

(1) Don't use spray paint near an open flame. (2) We were waiting for the plane to take off. (3) Wages are not keeping pace with inflation. (4) The patients complained of aches and pains. (5) "The rain in Spain stays mainly in the plain." (6) Amy hates changing lanes on the highway. (7) The waiter laid eight place settings at the table. (8) Caleb's place is amazingly tastefully decorated. (9) The translations were displayed on facing pages. (10) The stage swayed dangerously under their weight.

Sentences 2

(1) The tornado left a trail of devastation in its wake. (2) David's favorite meal is braised steak with gravy. (3) "See You Later, Alligator" was sung by Bill Haley. (4) James was shaking as he made his way to the stage. (5) The wage negotiations will take place later in April. (6) They escaped to a safe haven from a place of danger. (7) The waitress complained about the heavily laden tray. (8) Grace and Jason take their vacation in faraway places. (9) The train was late so we had to wait for ages at the station. (10) The age difference placed a great strain on their relationship.

6.14.11 Dialogues

A: Jane, take a break from saying hateful things for just one day!
B: It's my nature to be straight and to paint things the way they are.
A: But it's plainly a fatal mistake not to refrain from stating to Kate's face that you hate the way she bakes her favorite cake.

B: Is that what made her take the tray of pastries and throw them in my face in that painful way?

A: It may have some relation to the case . . .

A: These cave paintings are in a shameful state.

B: I'm afraid to say *we* may be to blame.

A: We're making the paint fade and flake away?

B: Eighty-eight groups of vacationers like us pay to circulate through the caves every day and say what a shame it is that they're obliterating all trace of the famous ancient cave paintings . . .

A: This place makes my favorite gravy.

B: Isn't it strange to rate a café on the taste of their gravy?

A: Wait till you taste the gravy. You'll be grateful we came.

B: If you claim this gravy will amaze me and awaken strange cravings in me, you may be exaggerating.

6.15 PRICE /aɪ/

6.15.1 Description

Starts open central and moves toward close front; unrounded throughout.

6.15.2 Spelling

<i> climb, kind, find, child, pilot
<i-e> side, time, wise
<ie> die, lie, lies
<igh> high, slight, tight
<ign> = /aɪn/ align, sign, design
<y> cry, try, why, apply
<ye> eye, bye, dye
<y-e> type, style
<ei> height, feisty
<ui> guide, quite
<uy> buy, guy

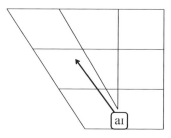

Figure 6.14 The PRICE /aɪ/ vowel

Unusual spellings

aisle, isle, island, maestro

6.15.3 Full length

a) Open syllables

buy, cry, die, dry, eye, fly, fry, high, pie, shy, sigh, sky, spy, tie, try, why

b) Closed syllables

blind, bribe, climb, crime, dive, drive, find, five, guide, kind, line, mind, mine, nine, shine, sign, size, spine, time, wine, wise

6.15.4 Clipped before voiceless consonants

bike, bite, fight, fright, hike, knife, life, like, mice, might, nice, night, pipe, quite, ripe, slice, spike, strike, stripe, twice, type, wife, wipe, write

6.15.5 Full length vs. clipped

tribe/tripe; bride/bright, hide/height, lied/light, ride/right, side/sight, slide/slight, tide/tight, tried/trite, wide/white; strive/strife; advise/advice, dies/dice, eyes/ice, lies/lice, prize/price, rise/rice

6.15.6 Pre-/l/ breaking

aisle, child, file, mild, mile, pile, smile, style, tile, while, wild

6.15.7 Multiple

acclimatize, childlike, cyanide, dynamite, eyeliner, eyesight, finalize, firefighter, firefly, highlight, hindsight, identify, lifelike, lifestyle, lifetime, likewise, limelight, nightlight, pipeline, sideline, skyline, twilight, wildlife

6.15.8 Additional words

appetite, apply, archive, arrive, behind, beside, crisis, cycle, decide, deny, describe, design, despite, exciting, exercise, final, idea, inside, multiply, occupy, pilot, polite, private, provide, qualify, realize, recognize, remind, reply, silence, slice, spider, survive, tidy, tiny

6.15.9 Phrases

a private archive, ride a bike, a bright child, a mild climate, a minor crime, the life cycle, a tight deadline, try to decide, a slight decline, a stylish design idea, a ninety-nine-mile drive, an exciting enterprise, light exercise, a high-fiber diet, a fight for survival, an exciting find, a nice guy, a five-mile hike, a worthwhile idea, a knight in shining armor, a driver's license, a lightning strike, a slice of lime, a fine line, white mice, an inquiring mind, a diamond mine, a slice of pie, an airline pilot, white rice, dry white wine, an exercise bike, a crime fighter

6.15.10 Sentences 1

(1) How time flies! (2) I find my life quite exciting. (3) Heidi's blind in her right eye. (4) Ryan was dying to ride my bike. (5) It's a ninety-mile drive to Miami. (6) He couldn't find Levi's in his size. (7) The flight arrival time is five past nine. (8) The tiny child didn't survive childhood. (9) The miners organized a strike in 1999. (10) It reminds me of the time I was in China.

Sentences 2

(1) It took Isaac quite a while to find his style. (2) I'd like to try a slice of your Key Lime pie. (3) I'm not trying to deprive you of your rights. (4) Pineapple with ice cream is delightful. (5) Right click on the icon, and select "Hide icon." (6) I can't specify the time of the crime precisely. (7) My Chinese wife likes to fry white rice with spices. (8) For the first time in my life, I realized I was worthwhile. (9) My wife and I were invited to dine at nine but declined. (10) Why did you buy that unsightly tie with those wide white stripes?

6.15.11 Dialogues

A: It's a kind of time-traveling device. It flies through time.
B: That's nice, Mike. It must be quite a ride.
A: I spy on knights as they fight crime.
B: That's frightfully exciting. Shall we fly the kite once you've finished fighting crime through time?

A: It's not right for Mike to ride his motorbike without a license.
B: You're quite right. He says riding a motorbike is nothing for a fighter pilot like him.
A: I'd never fly with a pilot like Mike. He rides his motorbike like a suicidal psychopath.
B: He's not quite right in the head. I think he's lying about being an airline pilot. And that diamond mine he acquired as a prize for saving the life of that VIP . . .
A: A qualified fighter pilot or a downright liar?

A: Brian's a nice, bright boy. Always smiling and so polite.
B: Nice? He's vile. I'd like to wipe that smile off his face.
A: Why are you so wildly riled by such a mild child?
B: That nice, bright, polite, mild child is a frighteningly sly, vile child.
A: Brian Price is a frighteningly sly, vile child?
B: Brian Price? No, Brian Price is a nice, bright, polite, mild child. Brian White's a frighteningly sly, vile child.

6.16 CHOICE /ɔɪ/

6.16.1 Description

Starts just below open-mid, back, and moves toward close front, starts rounded and ends unrounded.

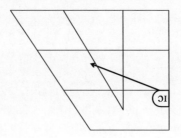

Figure 6.15 The CHOICE /ɔɪ/ vowel

6.16.2 Spelling

<oi> join, moisture, voice, Illinois
<oy> boy, toy, voyage

6.16.3 Full length

a) Open syllables

boy, coy, joy, ploy, toy

b) Closed syllables

coin, groin, join, loin, noise, poise, void

6.16.4 Clipped before voiceless consonants

choice, foist, hoist, joint, joist, moist, point, voice

6.16.5 Full length vs. clipped

boys/Boyce, joys/Joyce; joined/joint

6.16.6 Pre-/l/ breaking

boil, broil, coil, foil, oil, soil, spoil, toil

6.16.7 Additional words

alloy, android, annoy, appointment, avoid, convoy, decoy, deploy, destroy, devoid, disappointed, embroider, employ, enjoy, foible, invoice, loiter, moisture, noisy, ointment, oyster, paranoid, poison, sirloin, toilet, turmoil, typhoid, voyage

6.16.8 Phrases

anoint with oil, avoid disappointment, boiling point, a loyal employee, moist soil, voice your disappointment, boiled in oil

6.16.9 Sentences 1

(1) Cover the sirloin with foil. (2) Moira embroidered a doily. (3) That spoiled their enjoyment. (4) The cowboy was held at gunpoint. (5) It was a ploy to poison the playboy. (6) That was a very poignant rejoinder. (7) Our voyage to Hanoi was a real joy. (8) Royce was employed in Des Moines. (9) I had no choice but to pay the invoice. (10) Roy has an annoying adenoidal voice.

Sentences 2

(1) The hoity-toity try to avoid the hoi polloi. (2) I'm paranoid about catching typhoid fever. (3) We moved from Detroit to Troy in Illinois. (4) The employees voiced their disappointment. (5) Latoya and Joy are sweet without being coy. (6) Joyce bought the boys toys and the girls toiletries. (7) The original anointing oil was made from olive oil. (8) He toiled and toiled, which left his life devoid of any joy. (9) To roister means to enjoy oneself in a noisy or boisterous way. (10) He boiled with annoyance when his Rolls-Royce was destroyed.

6.16.10 Dialogues

A: I avoid Joyce out of choice.
B: Because she pointed out Roy's playboy ways?
A: It made me paranoid and spoiled our relationship.
B: What a poisonous ploy! The killjoy!

A: You've spoiled my oysters!
B: Olive oil doesn't spoil oysters.
A: Oh boy! You've really destroyed my lovely moist oysters.
B: So avoid the oysters and have the sirloin steak.
A: Have I any choice?

A: Moira's gotten a new boy toy.
B: What's the point of a boy toy?
A: It's just a foible of hers. She likes to loiter about with a convoy of boy toys.
B: Don't they exploit her and disappoint her?
A: *She* enjoys exploiting and disappointing *them*!

6.17 GOAT /oʊ/

6.17.1 Description

Starts mid back-central and moves toward close back, rounded – some speakers have an unrounded starting point.

6.17.2 Spelling

<o> no, hero, folio, don't, won't
<o-e> zone, those, smoke
<oe> toe, goes
<oa> moan, loan, road

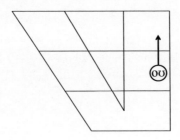

Figure 6.16 The GOAT /oʊ/ vowel

<ow> know, slow, narrow
<olk> = /oʊk/ folk, yolk
<ol, oul> = /oʊl/ gold, mold, boulder, shoulder
<ough> though, doughnut, thorough, Peterborough

Unusual spellings

brooch, yeoman

Words from French:
<au> or <eau> gauche, mauve, chauffeur, bureau, chateau, Rousseau, Bordeaux, plateau

6.17.3 Full length

a) Open syllables

blow, crow, flow, go, no, low, owe, show, slow, snow, so, though, toe

b) Closed syllables

bone, comb, drove, flown, foam, froze, groan, home, hose, load, loan, moan, nose, own, rose, stone, stove, those, throne, tone, zone

6.17.4 Clipped before voiceless consonants

both, choke, cloak, coach, coast, croak, don't, float, folk, ghost, goat, hope, host, joke, most, oak, poke, roast, slope, smoke, soak, soap, stroke, throat, toast, vote, woke, won't

6.17.5 Full length vs. clipped

robe/rope; code/coat, glowed/gloat, mode/moat, node/note, ode/oat, road/wrote; doze/dose, grows/gross, posed/post

6.17.6 Before /l/

bold, bowl, coal, cold, fold, goal, gold, hold, hole, mold, mole, old, patrol, pole, roll, sold, soul, stole, stroll, told, bolt

6.17.7 Multiple

cocoa, comatose, dodo, hobo, homeowner, kimono, logo, motorboat, oboe, overcoat, overdose, overgrown, overshadow, ozone, photo, polio, polo, portfolio, Romeo, slowpoke, soapstone, solo, towrope, yoyo

6.17.8 Additional words

approach, arrow, below, bonus, borrow, broken, comb, control, cozy, echo, elbow, emotion, folder, hero, hollow, local, mango, meadow, memo, moment, motto, narrow, ocean, open, over, phone, pillow, pony, potato, radio, shadow, shallow, social, soldier, suppose, swallow, tomato, tomorrow, total, vote, wardrobe, window, yellow, zero

6.17.9 Phrases

approach slowly, a bow and arrow, blow your nose, a bold stroke, bone marrow, a goldfish bowl, a flowing cloak, glowing coals, a coastal road, total control, a low dose, go with the flow, old folk, moan and groan, a local hero, a talk-show host, a low-interest loan, slow motion, open to negotiation, a broken nose, no smoking, a narrow road, a yellow rose, a row boat, stone-cold sober, a protest vote, a broken window, a bold approach, broken bones, a low profile, local radio

6.17.10 Sentences 1

(1) I don't know. (2) Lo and behold! (3) Go with the flow. (4) Don't moan and groan. (5) Growing old's no joke. (6) Show it in slow motion. (7) The coastal road is closed. (8) Joan was in total control. (9) Load the cargo on the boat. (10) Follow the Old Coach Road.

Sentences 2

(1) We don't hold out much hope. (2) Hold me close, and don't let go. (3) Zoe stood frozen for a moment. (4) The Rolling Stones stole the show. (5) Keep your nose to the grindstone! (6) The hotel is located in Coconut Grove. (7) The diagnosis was a broken collarbone. (8) He wrote both poetry and prose in Polish. (9) Note that there's no smoking in this zone. (10) Apollo is often shown with a bow and arrow.

6.17.11 Dialogues

A: Don't smoke in the old folks' home.
B: Is that a joke? You know the old blokes there smoke homegrown tobacco?
A: There's no hope for their croaky old throats, but it'd be most social if you quit tomorrow.
B: No, no, no. I don't think so. I won't be coaxed into lowering my dose by those gloating tones.

A: Don't moan. I'm only combing your ponytail.
B: You don't have to poke me with that old comb, you know!
A: Don't groan so much, you old goat. You're almost foaming at the mouth.
B: Since I broke my shoulder bone on that motorboat a week ago, you've grown cold, emotionless, and controlling.

A: Is it that I've grown cold, emotionless, and controlling, or is it that you've grown stone-cold sober?

A: I've chosen to focus on Polish heroes for my radio program.
B: Wasn't Chopin, the composer, a Pole?
A: Yes, he wrote mainly solo piano pieces but also two piano concertos.
B: And Yoko Ono, is she Polish? Or maybe Slovak?

6.18 MOUTH /aʊ/

6.18.1 Description

Starts open central and moves toward close back; unrounded, becoming slightly rounded.

6.18.2 Spelling

<ou> house, out, south, ground
<ow> howl, now, how, down

6.18.3 Full length

a) Open syllables

brow, cow, how, now, plow, prow

b) Closed syllables

brown, browse, cloud, clown, crowd, crown, down, drown, frown, gown, ground, loud, lounge, noun, pound, proud, round, sound, town

6.18.4 Clipped before voiceless consonants

crouch, doubt, drought, house, mouse, mouth, out, pouch, scout, shout, south, trout

6.18.5 Full length vs. clipped

bowed/bout, cloud/clout, mound/mount

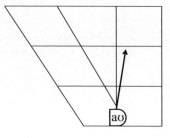

Figure 6.17 The MOUTH /aʊ/ vowel

6.18.6 Before /l/

cowl, foul, growl, howl, jowl, owl, prowl, scowl

6.18.7 Multiple

countdown, housebound, house-proud, loudmouth, powerhouse, sauerkraut, southbound

6.18.8 Additional words

about, account, amount, announce, discount, eyebrow, foundation, fountain, mountain, powder, pronounce, scoundrel, surround, trousers, thousand, voucher

6.18.9 Phrases

without foundation, proud to announce, bring down the house, a countable noun, crouch down, go 'round and 'round, a house mouse, a loud shout, a vowel sound, without a doubt

6.18.10 Sentences 1

(1) That blouse looks dowdy. (2) It sounds downright lousy. (3) What an astounding discount! (4) He was slouched on the couch. (5) She was bound to be found out. (6) His brows drew down in a scowl. (7) She crouched down beside the cow. (8) The pronoun "thou" is now outdated. (9) Mount Everest was shrouded in clouds. (10) Howard had no doubts about the outcome. (11) He has around about a thousand pounds in his bank account.

Sentences 2

(1) I found trout and flounder at the mouth of the river. (2) How do you pronounce the vowel sounds of Hausa? (3) I shouted out loud when I saw a mouse in the house. (4) I could hear the sounds of Strauss in the background. (5) Mr. Brown's pronouncements lack a sound foundation. (6) A thousand houses were built on the outskirts of town. (7) He's now an accountant in his hometown down south. (8) Her voice was drowned out by loud shouts from the crowd. (9) His bowing and kowtowing to the town council aroused outrage. (10) The hounds growled at the sound of a howling owl on the prowl.

6.18.11 Dialogues

A: I doubt that loudmouth clown owns the big town house he's so proud of.
B: That lout spouts a huge amount of nonsense without foundation.
A: The scoundrel belongs in a rundown house on the outskirts of town.
B: The louse should take his big mouth down south beyond the boundary of our proud county.

A: I'm proud to announce that I can pronounce all the English vowel sounds.
B: The MOUTH vowel too? Pronounce it out loud.
A: I'll shout it out right now, loudly and proudly: mouth, mouth, mouth!
B: That's without a doubt the loudest MOUTH vowel workout that's ever resounded throughout this town.

A: Is Brown still walking about town in his dressing gown?

B: He's very proud of his dressing gown and won't put it down.

A: How people in town must frown at that clown!

B: They shout, howl, and scowl at Brown the clown as he prowls around town in his gown and no trousers.

A: No *trousers*? I don't doubt he arouses shouts, howls, and scowls. The clown's out of his unsound mind!

Chapter 7

Practice
Vowel contrasts

This chapter provides practice in distinguishing between pairs of vowels that learners tend to confuse. The exercise material includes minimal pairs demonstrating the contrast in different phonetic contexts, and in words, phrases, and sentences containing both sounds. The numbers in the table refer to the sections dealing with the contrasts in question.

7.1 DRESS /ɛ/ vs. KIT /ɪ/
7.2 DRESS /ɛ/ vs. TRAP /æ/
7.3 schwa /ə/ vs. TRAP /æ/
7.4 DRESS /ɛ/ vs. schwa /ə/
7.5 PALM /ɑ/ vs. schwa /ə/
7.6 FLEECE /i/ vs. KIT /ɪ/
7.7 GOOSE /u/ vs. FOOT /ʊ/
7.8 TRAP /æ/ vs. PALM /ɑ/
7.9 PRICE /aɪ/ vs. FACE /eɪ/

7.10 PRICE /aɪ/ vs. CHOICE /ɔɪ/
7.11 MOUTH /aʊ/ vs. GOAT /oʊ/
7.12 DRESS /ɛ/ vs. FACE /eɪ/
7.13 /ir/ vs. /ɛr/
7.14 /ir/ vs. schwar /ər/ [ɚ]
7.15 /ɑr/ vs. schwar /ər/ [ɚ]
7.16 /ɛr/ vs. schwar /ər/ [ɚ]
7.17 [or] vs. schwar /ər/ [ɚ]

7.1 DRESS /ɛ/ vs. KIT /ɪ/

7.1.1 Minimal pairs with DRESS /ɛ/ and KIT /ɪ/

a) Full length

bed/bid, dead/did, head/hid, led/lid red/rid; beg/big, peg/pig; gem/gym; den/din, pen/pin, ten/tin; bell/bill, fell/fill, hell/hill, spell/spill, tell/till, well/will

b) Clipped

left/lift, bet/bit, crept/crypt, let/lit, meant/mint, net/knit, pet/pit, set/sit, wet/wit, belt/built; check/chick, neck/nick, peck/pick, trek/trick; etch/itch; bless/bliss, desk/disk, mess/miss, rest/wrist, sense/since

c) Longer words

lesson/listen, letter/litter, medal/middle, petty/pity, possession/position

7.1.2 Words with DRESS /ɛ/ and KIT /ɪ/

bridgehead, disrespect, gingerbread, index, influential, influenza, insect, Internet, sickbed, silhouette, incense, shipwreck, riverbed, figurehead, intellect, eccentricity, sensitivity

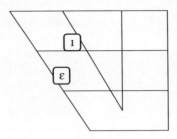

Figure 7.1 DRESS /ɛ/ and KIT /ɪ/

7.1.3 *Phrases with* DRESS /ɛ/ *and* KIT /ɪ/

red bricks, tender chicken breast, a cliff edge, a medical condition, a petty criminal, a sensible decision, a visitor center, a French dictionary, a special discount, a refreshing drink, a legendary figure, freshwater fishing, a clenched fist, a wedding gift, a gentle hint, a head injury, insect repellent, a tender kiss, a guest list, fresh milk, a mental picture, a steady rhythm, a terrible risk, sensitive skin, spring weather, a generous tip, a trick question, a pleasant trip, a regular visitor, a hidden agenda, a king-size bed, fringe benefits, a bread bin, a cement mixer, rigorous checks, energy bills, a difficult exercise, a hidden gem, a general principle, health issues, bitterly jealous, a stiff leg, a hidden message, a fishing net, a silly question, a split second, a big step, a fitness test, an expensive gift, a clever trick

7.1.4 *Sentences with* DRESS /ɛ/ *and* KIT /ɪ/

(1) Dennis is a healthy kid. (2) He paid the bill and left a generous tip. (3) I noticed Jim was limping on his left leg. (4) It wasn't difficult to get the general gist of it. (5) Neville felt a trickle of sweat drip down his neck. (6) There's definitely no such thing as a silly question. (7) Our best swimmer came in a split second before theirs. (8) We developed some simple exercises to assess his interests. (9) There are immense differences between printed and electronic texts. (10) Jenny has excellent organizational skills and a good head for business.

7.2 DRESS /ɛ/ VS. TRAP /æ/

7.2.1 *Minimal pairs with* DRESS /ɛ/ *and* TRAP /æ/

a) Full length

bed/bad, dead/dad, head/had, said/sad; beg/bag; gem/jam; bend/band, blend/bland, lend/land, men/man, pen/pan, send/sand, ten/tan

b) Clipped

bet/bat, met/mat, net/gnat, pet/pat, rent/rant, set/sat, vet/vat; neck/knack, peck/pack, trek/track, wreck/rack; wrench/ranch; deft/daft; dense/dance, guess/gas, lest/last, pest/past, vest/vast; flesh/flash

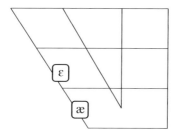

Figure 7.2 DRESS /ɛ/ and TRAP /æ/

c) Longer words

better/batter, commend/command, ember/amber, kettle/cattle, leather/lather, letter/latter, mention/mansion, celery/salary, slender/slander

7.2.2 *Words with* DRESS /ɛ/ *and* TRAP /æ/

academic, alphabet, access, accidental, ancestor, anorexia, antiseptic, apprehend, aspect, asset, backrest, bedpan, benefactor, blackhead, democratic, headband, melodramatic, rectangle, stepladder, telepathic, eggplant, reprimand

7.2.3 *Phrases with* DRESS /ɛ/ *and* TRAP /æ/

an American accent, a professional actor, the letters of the alphabet, a red apple, black pepper, an empty can, petty cash, excellent value, an aggressive attitude, a black belt, the best man, bad breath, a chemical reaction, black cherries, a delicate balance, a black dress, scrambled eggs, a family friend, a leather jacket, capital letters, a negative attitude, a black pen, a pet cat, plan ahead, a national treasure, bad weather, black leather, fancy dress, a pet rabbit, a weather forecast, an elderly aunt, wet grass, last forever, a member of staff

7.2.4 *Sentences with* DRESS /ɛ/ *and* TRAP /æ/

(1) Bury the hatchet. (2) Jack set a trap for Geoff. (3) Daniel banged his head again. (4) Get your act together, Alexander! (5) Fred acted as if it had never happened. (6) The best man can't wear a black leather jacket. (7) Bev's pet rabbit bit the hand of a family friend. (8) Frank said the letters of the alphabet backward. (9) Ben hadn't planned ahead and so met a bad end. (10) Ted has a negative attitude to American accents.

7.3 Schwa /ə/ vs. TRAP /æ/

7.3.1 *Minimal pairs with schwa* /ə/ *and* TRAP /æ/

a) Full length

cub/cab, dub/dab, grub/grab, stub/stab; bud/bad, dud/dad, mud/mad; bug/bag, drug/drag, hug/hag, rug/rag, tug/tag; budge/badge; crumb/cram, dumb/dam, hum/ham, rum/ram, slum/slam, swum/swam; fun/fan, pun/pan, spun/span; hung/hang, sprung/sprang

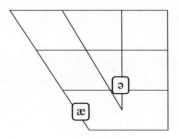

Figure 7.3 Schwa /ə/ and TRAP /æ/

b) Clipped

cup/cap, dump/damp, grunt/grant, lump/lamp; cut/cat, nut/gnat, putt/pat, rut/rat; buck/back, bunk/bank, drunk/drank, luck/lack, puck/pack, shrunk/shrank, stuck/stack, stunk/stank, truck/track; brunch/branch, hutch/hatch; cuff/calf, gruff/graph, huff/half, stuff/staff; dunce/dance, fussed/fast, lust/last, tusk/task; crush/crash, flush/flash, rush/rash, thrush/thrash, slush/slash

c) Longer words

begun/began, bubble/babble, butter/batter, compass/campus, double/dabble, flutter/flatter, mutter/matter, puddle/paddle, rubble/rabble, rumble/ramble, rupture/rapture, sudden/sadden, shutter/shatter, summon/salmon, uncle/ankle

7.3.2 Words with schwa /ə/ and TRAP /æ/

acupuncture, agriculture, aqueduct, bathtub, dustpan, grandmother, handcuffs, humpback, lumberjack, maladjusted, malfunction, manhunt, mustang, nutcracker, rucksack, stuntman, substandard, suntan, underpants, underclass, understand

7.3.3 Phrases with schwa /ə/ and TRAP /æ/

a blood bank, a plastic bucket, rancid butter, pineapple chunks, a fan club, matching colors, a country mansion, a drug addict, flood damage, hunger pangs, a panel of judges, bad luck, muscle spasms, a damp sponge, stomach cramps, a sun hat, a clap of thunder, an impulsive act, a splash of color, a struggling actor, a stuffed animal, apple crumble, front to back, a bloody battle, a rusty can, an introductory chapter, exam results, a compulsive gambler, a drug habit, hand luggage, plum jam, a panic button, a bundle of rags, a travel company, a flat stomach, an animal lover, a mud bath, half a dozen, a touch of class, colored glass

7.3.4 Sentences with schwa /ə/ and TRAP /æ/

(1) My mother's apple crumble is absolutely fantastic. (2) It was an impulsive act resulting from frustration and anxiety. (3) Dustin had a passion for jazz and ended up as a drummer in a jazz club. (4) Samantha's just come back from Southern California with a lovely suntan. (5) There were a dozen travel mugs and a stack of plastic cups in the cupboard. (6) The

Practice: vowel contrasts 185

company suffered massive cutbacks due to lack of government funding. (7) My husband wants a cat, but I'm reluctant to have one, as I'm not an animal lover. (8) She was upset about her financial troubles but said she'd overcome tougher challenges. (9) I don't understand why they've cancelled the plans for the construction of the new runway. (10) Your tagged luggage will be transferred automatically, so you just need to handle your hand luggage.

7.4 DRESS /ɛ/ vs. schwa /ə/

7.4.1 Minimal pairs with DRESS /ɛ/ and schwa /ə/

a) Full length

bed/bud, bled/blood, dead/dud, fled/flood; beg/bug, dregs/drugs, leg/lug, peg/pug; dredge/drudge; hem/hum; den/done, fend/fund, pen/pun, ten/ton, when/one; dell/dull, hell/hull

b) Clipped

hemp/hump; bet/but, get/gut, net/nut, pet/putt, rent/runt; check/chuck, deck/duck, flex/flux, peck/puck, trek/truck; bench/bunch; best/bust, crest/crust, dense/dunce, desk/dusk, guest/gust, rest/rust; flesh/flush, thresh/thrush

c) Longer words

better/butter, empire/umpire, fennel/funnel, many/money, medal/muddle, pedal/puddle, ready/ruddy, redder/rudder, section/suction, steady/study, tetchy/touchy, treble/trouble, wrestle/rustle

7.4.2 Words with DRESS /ɛ/ and schwa /ə/

anyone, bedbug, breadcrumb, checkup, chestnut, double-check, eggcup, everyone, fundamental, headhunt, kettledrum, moneylender, nonetheless, nutmeg, nutshell, pent-up, rough-and-ready, self-destructive, setup, stepbrother, stepmother, stepson, subset, sunbed, sunset, twenty-one, umbrella, undress

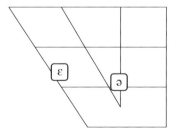

Figure 7.4 DRESS /ɛ/ and schwa /ə/

7.4.3 Phrases with DRESS /ɛ/ and schwa /ə/

a blood test, an empty bucket, a fresh bun, a bus shelter, fresh butter, press a button, an elderly couple, bread crumbs, a speck of dust, a sense of fun, a pension fund, leather gloves, a treasure hunt, a jealous husband, a healthy lunch, red onions, the general public, an empty stomach, a summer dress, a wonderful adventure, a double bed, a belt buckle, crusty bread, a cultural center, defense cuts, cutting edge, the end result, public enemy number one, engine trouble, a fundamental error, ruffled feathers, a lucky guess, summon help, a love letter, a blunt pencil, stuffed peppers, blood red, dusty shelves, a sunny spell, test results, bread and butter, blood pressure

7.4.4 Sentences with DRESS /ɛ/ and schwa /ə/

(1) Doug said it was just a lucky guess. (2) Dustin's belt was studded with gems. (3) I love your recipe for stuffed peppers. (4) My uncle plucked the dead hen's feathers. (5) In the end, their efforts will come to nothing. (6) My mother spread some honey on the bread. (7) She had a healthy lunch with a bunch of friends. (8) My husband was reluctant to accept their money. (9) I'm going to set up a treasure hunt for my son next weekend. (10) We request the pleasure of your company at my brother's wedding.

7.5 PALM /ɑ/ vs. schwa /ə/

7.5.1 Minimal pairs with PALM /ɑ/ and schwa /ə/ (THOUGHT words in italics, CLOTH words in bold italics)

a) Full length

hob/hub, rob/rub, snob/snub; cod/cud; fond/fund, wan/one; doll/dull; *daub*/dub; *flawed*/flood, *Maud*/mud, *thawed*/thud; *dawn*/done, *faun*/fun, *fawned*/fund, *pawn*/pun, *spawn*/spun; *call*/cull, *hall*/hull, *mall*/mull; ***bog***/bug, ***dog***/dug, ***hog***/hug, ***jog***/jug, ***smog***/smug; ***long***/lung, ***wrong***/rung, ***song***/sung

b) Clipped

cop/cup; cot/cut, got/gut, hot/hut, knot/nut, pot/putt, shot/shut; dock/duck, lock/luck, mock/muck, sock/suck, stock/stuck; golf/gulf; *bought*/but, *caught*/cut, *haunt*/hunt; *stalk*/stuck, *talk*/tuck; *haunch*/hunch, *launch*/lunch, *paunch*/punch; ***cough***/cuff; ***boss***/bus, ***lost***/lust

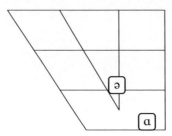

Figure 7.5 PALM /ɑ/ and schwa /ə/

c) Longer words

body/buddy, boggy/buggy, collar/color, dollar/duller, model/muddle, otter/utter, wander/wonder; *bauble*/bubble, *bawdy*/buddy, *caller*/color, *naughty*/nutty, *talker*/tucker

7.5.2 Words with PALM /ɑ/ and schwa /ə/ (THOUGHT *words in italics,* CLOTH *words in bold italics*)

blockbuster, bloodshot, butterscotch, godmother, gunshot, lunchbox, shotgun, shuttlecock, sunspot, sunblock, stardust, junkyard, sparkplug, unremarkable, mother-in-*law*, jugger*naut*, brother-in-*law*, son-in-*law*, under***dog***

7.5.3 Phrases with PALM /ɑ/ and schwa /ə/ (THOUGHT *words in italics,* CLOTH *words in bold italics*)

a humble apology, boxing gloves, a public concert, a troubled conscience, multiple copies, a country cottage, a bumper crop, a sudden drop, a golf club, chopped nuts, job cuts, money problems, a public monument, an odd number, an opera lover, bulging pockets, a muddy pond, a sudden shock, solve a puzzle, a luxury yacht, a drop of blood, mother and father, a mop and bucket, a bus stop, a tropical country, a shocking discovery, a pot of honey, a hot lunch, chopped onions, a hot summer, a public apology, government bonds, a duck pond, culture shock, a blood clot, a public *auction*, *chalk* dust, utterly *exhausted*, a sudden *fall*, lumpy *sauce*, an introductory *talk*, muddy *water*, an *awful* discovery, *raw* onions, ***strong*** colors, a ***dog*** lover, blood ***loss***, a ***long-lost*** brother, the ***long*** jump, a love ***song***, a ***strong*** cup of ***coffee***

7.5.4 Sentences with PALM /ɑ/ and schwa /ə/ (THOUGHT *words in italics,* CLOTH *words in bold italics*)

(1) The hot summer was tough on their crops. (2) A "hot***dog***" is a ***sausage*** shoved into a bun. (3) His drunken father had *caused* much trouble. (4) It'll comfortably accommodate a lot of stuff. (5) The ***song*** "Bus Stop" was sung by the Hollies. (6) She's not just a dumb blonde – she studies *law*. (7) My youngest *daughter* has a lot of money problems. (8) Top the chops with mushrooms and onions, and serve hot. (9) I wonder what country his *talkative* colleague comes from. (10) The *small* company suddenly claimed the documents were confidential.

7.6 FLEECE /i/ VS. KIT /ɪ/

7.6.1 Minimal pairs with FLEECE /i/ and KIT /ɪ/

a) Full length

bead/bid, deed/did, greed/grid, heed/hid, read/rid; ease/is, fees/fizz, freeze/frizz; bean/bin, gene/gin, green/grin, seen/sin, sheen/shin, teen/tin; eel/ill, feel/fill, heel/hill, kneel/nil, meal/mill, peel/pill, steal/still, wheel/will

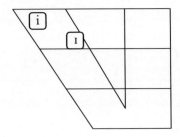

Figure 7.6 FLEECE /i/ and KIT /ɪ/

b) Clipped

bleep/blip, cheap/chip, deep/dip, heap/hip, leap/lip, sheep/ship, sleep/slip, weep/whip; beat/bit, eat/it, feet/fit, greet/grit, heat/hit, neat/knit, seat/sit, sleet/slit, wheat/wit; cheek/chick, leak/lick, peak/pick, seek/sick, weak/wick; each/itch, peach/pitch, reach/rich; feast/fist

c) Longer words

beaker/bicker, beater/bitter, liter/litter, peeler/pillar, reason/risen, scenic/cynic, sleeper/slipper, treacle/trickle, weaker/wicker

7.6.2 Words with FLEECE /i/ and KIT /ɪ/

bittersweet, chickpea, chimpanzee, disagree, fifteen, intermediate, intervene, millipede, millimeter, nicotine, reconsider, seasick, sixteen, windscreen, incomplete, reappear

7.6.3 Phrases with FLEECE /i/ and KIT /ɪ/

a key figure, a free gift, the grim reaper, grit your teeth, a guilty secret, a history teacher, a complete idiot, an interesting feature, kidney disease, a field trip, a window cleaner, a kiss on the cheek, a knitting needle, the speed limit, a complete list, liver disease, mixed feelings, a complete mystery, Greek myths, pins and needles, pink cheeks, pretty easy, sick leave, skin disease, a bee sting, a piece of string, deep sympathy, the legal system, a cheap thrill, a free ticket, an ego trip, twigs and leaves, a brief visit, a frequent visitor, Swiss cheese, a written agreement, quick and easy, a string of beads, a mythical beast, a brief history, a chilly breeze, spring cleaning, whipped cream, a business deal, a deep thinker, vivid dreams, an eager listener, greasy skin, a greedy pig, recent history, visibly relieved, a winning streak, a big deal, bits and pieces, an interesting feature, spill the beans

7.6.4 Sentences with FLEECE /i/ and KIT /ɪ/

(1) Jill eats kidney beans. (2) Steve didn't sleep a wink. (3) Keep it simple, quick, and brief. (4) A honey bee's sting kills the bee. (5) Edith refilled her beaker with gin. (6) Jean's a native speaker of Finnish. (7) Tim submitted his PhD thesis on the sixth. (8) How can we teach kids the skills they need? (9) There's a bit of spinach between Jim's teeth. (10) My English teacher makes a pretty decent living.

7.7 GOOSE /u/ vs. FOOT /ʊ/

7.7.1 Minimal pairs with GOOSE /u/ and FOOT /ʊ/

a) Full length

cooed/could, shooed/ should, who'd/ hood, wooed/wood; fool/full, pool/pull

b) Clipped

suit/soot; Luke/look

c) Longer words

lucre/looker

7.7.2 Words with GOOSE /u/ and FOOT /ʊ/

bulletproof, do-gooder, footstool, schoolbook

7.7.3 Phrases with GOOSE /u/ and FOOT /ʊ/

a book review, a cool new look, good news, a sugar cube, a good mood, a good view, good value, a good tune, a good loser, too good to be true, put two and two together, put down roots, book a room, a full moon, a crooked tooth, a wooden spoon, a bullet wound, the school bully, a beautiful woman

7.7.4 Sentences with GOOSE /u/ and FOOT /ʊ/

(1) Sue cooks good food. (2) Julian took a cruise to Acapulco. (3) Hugh looks like a real do-gooder! (4) The bully pushed Luke off his scooter. (5) Julie took a look through the new book. (6) The youth pulled out his crooked tooth. (7) It took some doing before she understood. (8) She took off her shoes and put on her boots. (9) The students put together a news bulletin on the issue. (10) Confused, Andrew shook his head; he knew it couldn't be true.

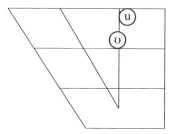

Figure 7.7 GOOSE /u/ and FOOT /ʊ/

7.8 TRAP /æ/ vs. PALM /ɑ/

7.8.1 Minimal pairs with TRAP /æ/ and PALM /ɑ/ (THOUGHT words in italics, CLOTH words in bold italics)

a) Full length

jab/job, lab/lob; add/odd, cad/cod; band/bond, bland/blond, can/con, fanned/fond, pad/pod, panned/pond, rang/**wrong**; fan/*fawn*, pan/*pawn*, sad/*sawed*; bag/**bog**, flag/**flog**, gang/**gong**, lag/**log**

b) Clipped

cap/cop, chap/chop, flap/flop, map/mop, ramp/romp, stamp/stomp, tap/top; cat/cot, gnat/knot, hat/hot, pat/pot, rat/rot; ax/ox, backs/box, black/block, knack/knock, lack/lock, rack/rock, sack/sock, shack/shock, smack/smock, stack/stock; bat/*bought*, cat/*caught*; hack/*hawk*, stack/*stalk*, wax/*walks*; crass/**cross**, mass/**moss**; calf/**cough**; cast/**cost**, glass/**gloss**, last/**lost**

c) Longer words

adapt/adopt, adder/odder, bandage/bondage, battle/bottle, packet/pocket, pander/ponder, patter/potter, racket/rocket, valley/volley, impassable/impossible, khaki/cocky, pasture/posture; action/*auction*, facet/*faucet*

7.8.2 Words with TRAP /æ/ and PALM /ɑ/ (THOUGHT words in italics, CLOTH words in bold italics)

alcohol, anthropology, combat, compact, contact, contract, contrast, copycat, grandfather, hospitality, jackpot, laptop, matchbox, padlock, *au*dacity, *au*tograph, *au*tomatic, basket**ball**, *draw*back, grand*daughter*, astro*naut*, alba**tross**, ana**log**, back**log**, cata**log**, lap**dog**

7.8.3 Phrases with TRAP /æ/ and PALM /ɑ/ (THOUGHT words in italics, CLOTH words in bold italics)

plant a bomb, a natural blonde, a family doctor, a classified document, a **dog** basket, a fashion model, a paperback novel, a natural phenomenon, a comedy act, modern agriculture,

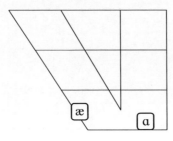

Figure 7.8 TRAP /æ/ and PALM /ɑ/

ankle socks, apple tart, a positive attitude, a marching band, chopped cabbage, a tom cat, a mock exam, an armed gang, a large gap, a noxious gas, a charming habit, a hat box, pots and pans, an attitude problem, catch a *ball*, answer a *call*, a nasty *fall*, a foot*ball* fan, *launch* a campaign, *call* a cab, a *watering* can, *straw*berry jam, a *water* rat, *caught* in a trap, a cannon *ball*, black ***coffee***, a sad ***loss***, a cramped ***office***, a ***strong*** accent, a hot***dog*** stand, travel ***costs***

7.8.4 Sentences with TRAP /æ/ and PALM /ɑ/ (THOUGHT *words in italics*, CLOTH *words in bold italics*)

(1) His answer *caused* me a lot of agony. (2) Chop the cabbage, and add to a hot pan. (3) You can't possibly imagine my gratitude. (4) He had the *audience* in the palm of his hand. (5) It doesn't *alter* the fact that Tom's analysis is ***wrong***. (6) We had a cocktail followed by sandwiches and a salad. (7) I *bought* a *small* plastic *watering* can for my potted plants. (8) This is the spot where my cat got *caught* in an animal trap. (9) There was a constant battle between my mom and my aunt. (10) The ***office*** manager was asked to *draw* up a plan to tackle the problem.

7.9 PRICE /aɪ/ VS. FACE /eɪ/

7.9.1 Minimal pairs with PRICE /aɪ/ and FACE /eɪ/

a) Full length

buy/bay, die/day, high/hay, lie/lay, my/may, pie/pay, sly/slay, sty/stay, try/tray, why/way; bride/braid, glide/glade, ride/raid, wide/wade; prize/praise, rise/raise; climb/claim, lime/lame, mime/maim, time/tame; brine/brain, line/lane, mine/main, pine/pain, spine/Spain; aisle/ale, file/fail, mile/mail, pile/pail, style/stale, tile/tail

b) Clipped

type/tape; bite/bait, fight/fate, height/hate, light/late, might/mate, pint/paint, right/rate, white/wait; bike/bake, like/lake; ice/ace, rice/race, spice/space

c) Longer words

reminder/remainder, viper/vapor

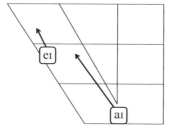

Figure 7.9 PRICE /aɪ/ and FACE /eɪ/

7.9.2 Words with PRICE /aɪ/ and FACE /eɪ/

brainchild, bridesmaid, canine, daylight, daytime, drainpipe, driveway, eyestrain, fireplace, fly-paper, Friday, grapevine, hibernate, highway, isolate, ladylike, lakeside, microwave, migrate, nationwide, playwright, primate, sideways, skyscraper, snakebite, timetable, vaporize, waistline

7.9.3 Phrases with PRICE /aɪ/ and FACE /eɪ/

retirement age, wide awake, a slice of bacon, brake lights, a cage fighter, a slice of cake, an iso-lated case, a bicycle chain, a high-speed chase, a lively debate, a delayed flight, a minor detail, a basic exercise, a bright flame, blind hatred, a winding lane, a divided nation, white paint, lined paper, a ray of light, a sliding scale, stage fright, a dining table, thriving trade, a train driver, a bridal veil, waist high, a tidal wave, a way of life, a late arrival, a major crisis, a failed enterprise, daily exercise, a brave fight, a layer of grime, a newspaper headline, a strange idea, day and night, a faint outline, a great prize, a grain of rice, a sleigh ride, a sacred shrine, failing eyesight, a range of sizes, a trail of slime, a waste of time, a famous writer, a hiding place, in plain sight

7.9.4 Sentences with PRICE /aɪ/ and FACE /eɪ/

(1) Iceland faced a major crisis. (2) James remained wide awake until daylight. (3) Ray's wife survived a dangerous snakebite. (4) They engaged in a lively debate on climate change. (5) They denied all accusations of inciting racial hatred. (6) It's a waste of time to try to get Amy to change her mind. (7) Jane regained her eyesight after going blind for five days. (8) I'm terrified of wide open spaces and not being able to escape. (9) We have motorbikes and racing bikes for sale at various prices. (10) A survey finds that the privately educated have higher rates of pay than the state-educated.

7.10 PRICE /aɪ/ vs. CHOICE /ɔɪ/

7.10.1 Minimal pairs with PRICE /aɪ/ and CHOICE /ɔɪ/

a) Full length

buy/boy, ply/ploy, tie/toy; pies/poise; kind/coined, line/loin; aisle/oil, bile/boil, file/foil, tile/toil

b) Clipped

vice/voice; pint/point

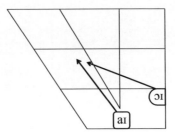

Figure 7.10 PRICE /aɪ/ and CHOICE /ɔɪ/

c) Longer words

ally/alloy, divide/devoid, imply/employ, lighter/loiter

7.10.2 Words with PRICE /aɪ/ and CHOICE /ɔɪ/

choirboy, joyride, moisturize, thyroid, viceroy

7.10.3 Phrases with PRICE /aɪ/ and CHOICE /ɔɪ/

find oil, appoint an adviser, a high voice, a wide choice, a spoiled child, a joint enterprise, lifetime employment, a mind in turmoil, an unspoiled paradise, boiled rice, mildly annoying, a bright boy, the right choice, an oil refinery, a full-time employee, a tired voice, a final invoice, wild joy, quite noisy, the high point, recoil slightly, oil prices, rheumatoid arthritis, a fine voice, a wise choice, quiet enjoyment, my pride and joy, emphasize a point, a point in time, dry soil, a joint exercise

7.10.4 Sentences with PRICE /aɪ/ and CHOICE /ɔɪ/

(1) Fry the spices in oil and add the rice. Enjoy! (2) He was diagnosed with rheumatoid arthritis of the joints. (3) The cowboys recoiled in surprise at the sight of the python. (4) I enjoy driving my Rolls-Royce along the winding coastline. (5) Five boys from Illinois were caught joyriding on motorbikes. (6) The key points were summarized concisely in his PowerPoint slides. (7) She declined point-blank to join him in his voyage to Paradise Island. (8) I was slightly disappointed when Clive decided to employ a full-time driver. (9) What makes one child coy, shy, and mild and another noisy and boisterous? (10) I was annoyed when he arrived late for his appointment without even apologizing.

7.11 MOUTH /aʊ/ VS. GOAT /oʊ/

7.11.1 Minimal pairs with MOUTH /aʊ/ and GOAT /oʊ/

a) Full length

how/hoe, now/know, sow/so; loud/load; clown/clone, crown/crone, drown/drone, town/tone; foul/foal, howl/hole

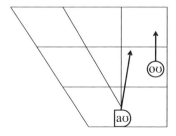

Figure 7.11 MOUTH /aʊ/ and GOAT /oʊ/

b) Clipped

flout/float, gout/goat, rout/wrote, stout/stoat; couch/coach, pouch/poach

c) Longer words

arouse/arose, devout/devote

7.11.2 Words with MOUTH /aʊ/ and GOAT /oʊ/

boathouse, lowbrow, merry-go-round, overcrowded, pronoun, snowplow, houseboat, household, outspoken, powerboat

7.11.3 Phrases with MOUTH /aʊ/ and GOAT /oʊ/

a blow-by-blow account, the total amount, a radio announcer, social background, low clouds, crowd control, growing doubts, a close encounter, a foundation stone, a hotel lounge, a snow-capped mountain, a social outcast, cocoa powder, a powerful antidote, a mouth-watering aroma, a loud explosion, a mountain goat, a loud groan, a ghost town, a proud moment, a foul odor, a proud owner, a snowbound road, a downward slope, the power of veto, a mountain road, a knock-out blow, a mountain slope, powdery snow

7.11.4 Sentences with MOUTH /aʊ/ and GOAT /oʊ/

(1) Noel is now the proud owner of a houseboat. (2) Joe's foul-mouthed outburst provoked the locals. (3) She sold her house in Youngstown, Ohio, in October. (4) I was dumbfounded at how my hometown had grown. (5) Joan found she couldn't cope with being a social outcast. (6) The bloodhound let out a low growl and pounced on him. (7) The snowplow was brought out to keep the town's roads open. (8) She told us there was a loud explosion, which had blown out the windows. (9) The remote outpost was surrounded by towering, snow-capped mountains. (10) The accountants had growing doubts about the outcome of the ongoing negotiations.

7.12   DRESS /ɛ/ vs. FACE /eɪ/

7.12.1 Minimal pairs with DRESS /ɛ/ and FACE /eɪ/

a) Full length

bread/braid, shed/shade; edge/age; men/main, pen/pain; fell/fail, gel/jail, sell/sail, tell/tail

b) Clipped

bet/bait, get/gate, sent/saint; chess/chase, chest/chased, less/lace, pest/paste, test/taste, west/waste

c) Longer words

letter/later, pepper/paper, cellar/sailor

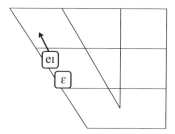

Figure 7.12 DRESS /ɛ/ and FACE /eɪ/

7.12.2 *Words with* DRESS /ɛ/ *and* FACE /eɪ/

accelerate, breathtaking, celebration, demonstration, education, essay, hesitation, investigate, lemonade, anyway, commemorate, decimate, decorate, dedicate, destination, devastate, entertain, generate, headache, meditate, penetrate, regulation, renovate, speculate

7.12.3 *Phrases with* DRESS /ɛ/ *and* FACE /eɪ/

a great adventure, a display of affection, a dangerous bend, a major benefit, make a bet, stale bread, save your breath, dangerous chemicals, a game of chess, a dreadful taste, a faint echo, the main entrance, a fatal error, a chain of events, a safe guess, a shake of the head, health and safety, weights and measures, a straight question, red in the face, fail a test, rented accommodation, aims and objectives, readily available, a healthy baby, an intense blaze, a wedding cake, a metal gate, wet paint, an empty plate, heavy rain, a deadly snake, an endless wait, freshly baked bread, a waste of energy

7.12.4 *Sentences with* DRESS /ɛ/ *and* FACE /eɪ/

(1) James went red in the face with rage. (2) State your name and address in your letter. (3) Making empty threats is a waste of energy. (4) What are the aims and objectives of Fred's paper? (5) We failed to make the deadline on September the eighth. (6) The wedding cake tasted great, but it was terribly expensive. (7) To save space, you can compress sentences into brief phrases. (8) With a shake of the head, he said, "I don't remember the date." (9) He held a reception for friends and acquaintances in the Croatian Embassy. (10) First, they played table tennis and then they settled down to a game of chess.

7.13 FLEECE + /r/ VS. DRESS + /r/: /ir/ VS. /ɛr/

7.13.1 *Minimal pairs with* /ir/ *and* /ɛr/

a) Full length

ear/air, beer/bear, cheer/chair, dear/dare, fear/fair, here/hair, leer/lair, pier/pair, rear/rare, sheer/share, sneer/snare, spear/spare, steer/stare, tear/tear; beard/bared

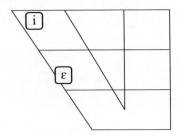

Figure 7.13 FLEECE + /r/ vs. DRESS + /r/: /ir/ vs. /ɛr/

b) Longer words

weary/wary

7.13.2 Phrases with /ir/ and /ɛr/

a fierce glare, years of wear, appear from nowhere, a rarefied atmosphere, a varied career, fairly cheerful, a shared experience, impaired hearing, fairly serious, a volunteer caregiver, clear the area, stare fiercely, a rare appearance, clear the air

7.13.3 Sentences with /ir/ and /ɛr/

(1) Claire's hearing was seriously impaired. (2) Keira scarcely ever interferes in my affairs. (3) He was the airline's chairman for nearly ten years. (4) Mary said getting her ears pierced was a nightmare. (5) He had a varied career in engineering and aircraft repair. (6) The millionaire made a rare appearance here in Delaware. (7) Take care shearing the mohair and cashmere goats this year. (8) Mr. Baird's fair-haired, so wearing a beard makes him look weird. (9) Nothing compares with experiencing Shakespeare in the open air. (10) The mountaineer was a fearless daredevil drawn to scary experiences.

7.14 FLEECE + /r/ vs. schwar: /ir/ vs. /ər/ [ɚ]

7.14.1 Minimal pairs with /ir/ and /ər/ [ɚ]

a) Full length

beer/burr, fear/fur, hear/her, mere/myrrh, peer/purr, spear/spur, steer/stir, weir/were; beard/bird, weird/word

b) Clipped

pierce/purse

7.14.2 Words with /ir/ and /ər/ [ɚ]

persevere, world-weary, tearjerker

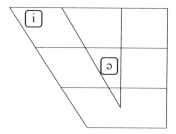

Figure 7.14 FLEECE + /r/ vs. schwar: /ir/ vs. /ər/ [ɚ]

7.14.3 Phrases with /ir/ and /ər/ [ɚ]

clearly absurd, a serious alternative, severe burns, a serious emergency, first-hand experience, period furniture, on the verge of tears, a word in your ear, the material world, a personal
appearance, a turbulent career, perfectly clear, seriously hurt, a nerve-racking experience,
burning tears, a volunteer worker, a serious concern, personal experience

7.14.4 Sentences with /ir/ and /ər/ [ɚ]

(1) It's his first personal appearance here. (2) We'll alert you if a serious emergency occurs.
(3) He nearly selected reverse instead of first gear. (4) It appears Gertrude's worst fears were
confirmed. (5) Pearl burst into tears when she heard that he'd disappeared. (6) The volunteers
clearly preferred turkey burgers to beef burgers. (7) The first turtles appeared on earth nearly
230 million years ago. (8) Vernon's had a turbulent career as a pioneer in nursing research.
(9) The girls with the pierced ears purchased sterling silver earrings. (10) They cheerfully
returned to work after a period of fearful uncertainty.

7.15 PALM + /r/ vs. schwar: /ɑr/ vs. /ər/ [ɚ]

7.15.1 Minimal pairs with /ɑr/ and /ər/ [ɚ]

a) Full length

bar/burr, car/cur, far/fur, par/purr, spar/spur, star/stir; bard/bird, card/curd, hard/heard; carve/
curve; farm/firm; barn/burn, yarn/yearn

b) Clipped

cart/curt, dart/dirt, heart/hurt, part/pert; lark/lurk, mark/murk, park/perk; parch/perch

c) Longer words

barley/burley, carnal/colonel, carton/curtain, farmer/firmer, parson/person

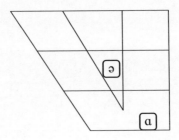

Figure 7.15 PALM + /r/ vs. schwar: /ɑr/ vs. /ər/ [ɚ]

7.15.2 Words with /ɑr/ and /ər/ [ɚ]

artwork, barperson, heartburn, churchyard, surcharge, birthmark

7.15.3 Phrases with /ɑr/ and /ər/ [ɚ]

hard work, a hurt arm, a commercial artist, a birthday card, worlds apart, a turkey farm, an herb garden, perfect harmony, a heart murmur, the worst part, a permanent scar, a perfect target, a birthday party, an impartial observer, dark purple, search far and wide, a commercial farm, heart surgery

7.15.4 Sentences with /ɑr/ and /ər/ [ɚ]

(1) Margaret hurt her arm at work. (2) Pearl looked smart in her tartan skirt. (3) First-degree burns leave permanent scars. (4) Charlotte planted parsley in her herb garden. (5) We worked hard to learn the words by heart. (6) The churchyard was dark and largely deserted. (7) Herman flirted with the charming girl behind the bar. (8) There are some remarkable birds in that part of the world. (9) The carpets were dirty, and the scarlet curtains looked absurd. (10) We searched far and wide for the perfect card for her birthday.

7.16 DRESS + /r/ vs. schwar: /ɛr/ vs. /ər/ [ɚ]

7.16.1 Minimal pairs with /ɛr/ and /ər/ [ɚ]

a) Full length

bare/burr, blare/blur, care/cur, fair/fur, hair/her, pair/purr, spare/spur, stare/stir, wear/were; cared/curd, haired/heard

b) Longer words

barely/burly, fairy/furry

7.16.2 Words with /ɛr/ and /ər/ [ɚ]

earthenware, airworthy, chairperson, swearword

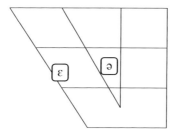

Figure 7.16 DRESS + /r/ vs. schwar: /ɛr/ vs. /ər/ [ɚ]

7.16.3 Phrases with /ɛr/ and /ər/ [ɚ]

a cesarean birth, urgent repairs, bear a burden, fairly certain, a nightmare journey, curly hair, a stern parent, germ warfare, a caring person, a careful search, a swear word, secretarial work, world affairs, a personal affair, an airport terminal, a research area, emergency care, perfectly fair, a recurring nightmare, working parents, emergency repairs, surface area, return fare

7.16.4 Sentences with /ɛr/ and /ər/ [ɚ]

(1) What's the fare for a return journey? (2) Karen permed her hair into girlish curls. (3) Mary preferred secretarial work to nursing. (4) Shirley's chairs are in urgent need of repair. (5) I'm preparing a workshop for health-care workers. (6) Claire says pairs of canaries are the perfect pet bird. (7) Harry said the airport terminal was virtually deserted. (8) Sarah swears she can draw perfect circles and squares. (9) He learned to swear in Hungarian with thirty new curses. (10) To the despair of his parents, he was only concerned with worldly affairs.

7.17 SPORT + /r/ vs. schwar: [or] vs. /ər/ [ɚ]

7.17.1 Minimal pairs [or] and /ər/ [ɚ]

a) Full length

four/fur, more/myrrh, sore/sir, store/stir; board/bird, hoard/heard, ward/word; form/firm, warm/worm; born/burn, torn/turn

b) Clipped

court/curt, short/shirt; pork/perk; porch/perch; course/curse

c) Longer words

conform/confirm, porpoise/purpose

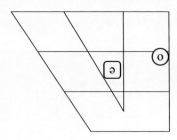

Figure 7.17 SPORT + /r/ vs. schwar: [or] vs. /ər/ [ɚ]

7.17.2 Words with |or| and /ər/ |ɚ|

furthermore, surfboard, workforce, coursework, foreword, sportsperson

7.17.3 Phrases with |or| and /ər/ |ɚ|

a personal fortune, a dirty floor, a first aid course, germ warfare, a gorgeous girl, a normal person, a memorial service, a short skirt, course work, a world war, an airport terminal, a border skirmish, an ordinary person, a reserve force, a reversal of fortunes, personal glory, the early morning, perfectly normal, a circular orbit, in reverse order, internal organs, earn a reward, the world of sport, a warm person, in normal circumstances, short term work

7.17.4 Sentences with |or| and /ər/ |ɚ|

(1) Laura's furniture's worth a fortune. (2) This is the worst sort of boring journalism. (3) The orchestra's first performance was superb. (4) The burglary was reported early in the morning. (5) Norman taught a first-aid course to orphanage workers. (6) Pearl learned to surf in California when she was fourteen. (7) She wore short skirts and shirts that showed off her curves. (8) She earned a reward for her extraordinary work as a nurse. (9) George turned up shortly before the first course was served. (10) What were the four most important causes of the First World War?

Chapter 8

Weak vowels and weak forms

8.1 Weak vowels

A small set of vowels (see Figure 8.1), known as the **weak vowels**, predominate in unstressed syllables:

- weak schwa /ə/: **a**rena, **a**nonymous, policeman, method
  weak schwar /ər/ [ɚ]: letter, actor, future, sugar, forget, percent
- weak FLEECE /i/: happy, money, coffee, area, react
- weak KIT /ɪ/: panic, message, college, finish, morning
- weak GOOSE /u/: continuous, musician
- weak FOOT /ʊ/: museum, superb

    Weak schwa, including its schwar /ər/ [ɚ] variant, is the most important weak vowel. It is more common than the other weak vowels and is much more frequent as a weak vowel in unstressed syllables than as a strong vowel in stressed syllables. In contrast, the remaining weak vowels range from being, like FLEECE /i/, roughly equally as common as their strong/ stressed equivalents to being, like FOOT /ʊ/, relatively rare in weak/unstressed syllables. Due to its predominance in weak syllables, schwa is the most common vowel and the most common phoneme in the language. Note that weak/unstressed schwa (and schwar) can be spelled with any vowel letter:

- *about* /əˈbaʊt/, *collar* /ˈkɑlər/, *system* /ˈsɪstəm/, *better* /ˈbɛtər/, *ability* /əˈbɪləti/, *Hampshire* /ˈhæmpʃər/, *pilot* /ˈpaɪlət/, *forget* /fərˈgɛt/, *bonus* /ˈboʊnəs/, *gesture* /ˈdʒɛstʃər/, *Pennsylvania* /pɛnsəlˈveɪnjə/, *martyr* /ˈmɑrtər/

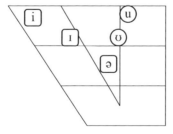

Figure 8.1 Weak vowels

Weak FLEECE occurs word-finally in numerous words:

- *any* /ˈɛni/, *monkey* /ˈməŋki/, *taxi* /ˈtæksi/, *cookie* /ˈkʊki/, *movie* /ˈmuvi/, *acne* /ˈækni/

word-medially before vowels:

- *alien* /ˈeɪliən/, *studio* /ˈstudioʊ/, *create* /kriˈeɪt/, *piano* /piˈænoʊ/, *beyond* /biˈɑnd/

and as an alternative to schwa in certain prefixes:

- *become* /biˈkəm/, *decide* /diˈsaɪd/, *repeat* /riˈpit/, *prevent* /priˈvɛnt/

The remaining weak vowels are rather marginal. Weak GOOSE mainly occurs word-medially before vowels (e.g., *duet* /duˈɛt/), weak FOOT occurs in very few words (e.g., *superior* /sʊˈpiriər/) and can usually be replaced by weak GOOSE. The status of KIT as a weak vowel is at present variable because for many people it is being supplanted by schwa. For those speakers who still distinguish KIT from schwa in unstressed syllables, KIT can occur before velar and palato-alveolar consonants and in certain suffixes:

- public /ˈpəblɪk/, exam /ɪgˈzæm/, expect /ɪkˈspɛkt/, punish /ˈpənɪʃ/, damage /ˈdæmɪdʒ/, artist /ˈɑɾ̯ɪst/, native /ˈneɪɾ̯ɪv/

Note that in some works, different symbols are used for weak vowels than for their strong equivalents, even though they represent the same phonemes (see Section 5.3).

8.2 Syllabic consonants

One notable characteristic of weak syllables is that in certain circumstances, they can have a consonant as their nucleus. Strong syllables, in contrast, must always center around a vowel. Syllabic consonants develop out of sequences of schwa and a sonorant, the more vowel-like type of consonant. When these sequences are preceded by particular consonants, the articulators can move directly from the consonant to the sonorant, skipping the schwa altogether. In such cases, the syllabicity (i.e., the syllable-forming capability) of the vowel is taken up by the sonorant, and the overall number of syllables in the word remains the same. Although syllabic consonant formation isn't completely obligatory, it's very common, and to never use syllabic consonants would be very unusual.

The most common syllabic consonants are /l/ and /n/. Syllabic /m/ is less usual because there are few words that provide the appropriate phonetic context, and syllabic /ŋ/ only occurs as a result of assimilation (see Section 12.3.1). In this work, we analyze the r-colored vowel [ɚ] as a realization of schwa /ə/ followed in the same syllable by /r/ because this agrees with the intuitions of native speakers. From a strictly phonetic point of view, however, the r-colored vowel [ɚ] is formed in the same way as [ɹ], and so we could analyze [ɚ] as syllabic /r/ and transcribe words like *murmur* as [ˈmɹ̩mɹ̩]. Note that such an approach would mean that syllabic consonants would have to be described as occurring in stressed syllables as well as in unstressed syllables (in the case of /r/, at least).

8.2.1 Syllabic /l/

Syllabic /l/ freely occurs after:

plosives: /p/ *apple*, /b/ *bubble*, /t/ *bottle*, /d/ *middle*, /k/ *tackle*, /ɡ/ *haggle*
affricates: /ʧ/ *satchel*, /ʤ/ *angel*
nasals: /m/ *normal*, /n/ *final*
fricatives: /f/ *trifle*, /v/ *devil*, /θ/ *lethal*, /ð/ *betrothal*, /s/ *parcel*, /z/ *nasal*, /ʃ/ *special*

but does not occur after:

approximants: /j/ *spaniel*, /w/ *equal*, /r/ *viral*, /l/ *school'll*

8.2.2 Syllabic /n/

There are more restrictions on syllabic /n/ than on syllabic /l/. Syllabic /n/ freely occurs after:

alveolar plosives: /t/ *button*, /d/ *sadden*
fricatives: /f/ *soften*, /v/ *oven*, /θ/ *python*, /ð/ *heathen*, /s/ *lesson*, /z/ *dozen*, /ʃ/ *mission*, /ʒ/ *vision*

and is less usual after:

non-alveolar plosives: /p/ *weapon*, /b/ *ribbon*, /k/ *token*, /ɡ/ *dragon*
affricates: /ʧ/ *question*, /ʤ/ *region*

and does not occur after:

nasals: /m/ *lemon*, /n/ *cannon*
approximants: /l/ *melon*, /r/ *barren*, /j/ *canyon*, /w/ *frequent*

There are further limitations on syllabic /n/ after alveolar plosives. Syllabic /n/ rarely occurs when /d/ is preceded by a nasal:

- *abandon, dependent, pendant, redundant, tendon, attendant, Camden*

when /t/ is preceded by a plosive or /s/ or by a bilabial or velar nasal:

- *disinfectant, expectant, reluctant, acceptance*
- *constant, instant, assistant, consistent, distance, insistent, persistent, resistance, substance*
- *Washington, Paddington, Hampton, Northampton*

or when /t/ or /d/ are preceded by an unstressed syllable:

- *accident, coincidence, confidence, confident, evidence, evident, incident, president, resident, skeleton, competent, impotent*

8.2.3 Syllabic /m/

Syllabic /m/ can be heard after fricatives in a small number of words, notably in the suffix **-ism**:

- *ransom, awesome, gruesome, handsome, blossom*
- *chasm, prism, sarcasm, spasm, communism, journalism, organism, tourism*
- *anthem*
- *fathom, algorithm, rhythm*

8.2.4 De-syllabification

When a suffix beginning with an unstressed vowel is added to a word ending in a syllabic consonant, the consonant can lose its syllabicity. This is termed **de-syllabification**. The more common the word is, the more likely this is to occur; for example:

bubbling may be /ˈbʌbəlɪŋ/ (three syllables), /ˈbʌbl̩ɪŋ/ (three syllables), or /ˈbʌblɪŋ/ (two syllables)
poisonous may be /ˈpɔɪzənəs/, /ˈpɔɪzn̩əs/, or /ˈpɔɪznəs/
ticklish may be /ˈtɪkəlɪʃ/, /ˈtɪkl̩ɪʃ/, or /ˈtɪklɪʃ/
gardener may be /ˈɡɑrdənər/, /ˈɡɑrdn̩ər/, or /ˈɡɑrdnər/

De-syllabification does not occur when the following vowel is strong:

vandalize may be /ˈvændəlaɪz/ or /ˈvændl̩aɪz/ but not */ˈvændlaɪz/
scrutinize may be /ˈskrutənaɪz/ or /ˈskrutn̩aɪz/ but not */ˈskrutnaɪz/

8.2.5 Sequences of syllabic consonants

Sequences of syllabic consonants are also possible but only in the order /n/ + /l/ because syllabic /n/ does not occur after /l/. Since syllabic /l/ is a variant of /əl/, and a syllabic consonant can lose its syllabicity when followed by a suffix beginning with a weak vowel, the syllabicity of /n/ can be lost in such sequences. The more common the word is, the more likely this is to happen:

national /ˈnæʃn̩l̩/ can become /ˈnæʃnl̩/
occasional /əˈkeɪʒn̩l̩/ can become /əˈkeɪʒnl̩/
personal /ˈpərsn̩l̩/ can become /ˈpərsnl̩/
professional /prəˈfɛʃn̩l̩/ can become /prəˈfɛʃnl̩/
rational /ˈræʃn̩l̩/ can become /ˈræʃnl̩/
traditional /trəˈdɪʃn̩l̩/ can become /trəˈdɪʃnl̩/

8.2.6 Transcription

As we have seen, the phonetic symbol used to show that a consonant is syllabic is a small vertical stroke under the consonant – [l̩], [n̩]. Strictly speaking, the syllabic consonant diacritic isn't a phonemic symbol because syllabic consonants are not separate phonemes but only a special way of realizing the sequence of schwa plus a consonant. In many cases, it's possible not to mark consonant syllabicity explicitly. When *juggle* and *garden* are transcribed /ˈdʒʌɡl/ and /ˈɡɑrdn/, for example, because of the structure of the English syllable, the final /l/ and /n/ could only be syllabic. However, when a vowel follows, as in *juggler* /ˈdʒɔglər/ or *gardening* /ˈgɑrdn̩ɪŋ/, it would be ambiguous not to use the syllabic consonant diacritic because the consonant could be either syllabic or non-syllabic.

For the sake of convenience and clarity, we will use phonemic bracketing with syllabic consonants in order to avoid constantly switching between slanted (phonemic) and square (phonetic) brackets, and we will always use the syllabic consonant diacritic whether the context is ambiguous or not.

8.3 Strong forms and weak forms

A number of high-frequency monosyllabic grammatical words (i.e., auxiliary verbs, prepositions, personal pronouns, conjunctions, and articles) have more than one pronunciation. The **strong form** is the pronunciation used when the word is stressed, as when citing it in isolation or giving it special emphasis in a sentence. The **weak form** is the pronunciation the word has when it's unstressed.

Although we are typically more conscious of the strong forms of words than the weak forms, the weak forms are actually more common because grammatical words are usually unstressed, in contrast to lexical words (i.e., nouns, main verbs, adjectives, and adverbs), which are typically stressed. (Grammatical words are sometimes termed *form* or *function* words, and lexical words may also be called *content* words.) Note that a number of grammatical words do not regularly take a weak form (e.g., *mine, those, on, they*).

The most important weak form words (shown below with both their strong and weak forms) are:

am	/ˈæm/	/əm/	*at*	/ˈæt/	/ət/
are	/ˈɑr/	/ər/	*for*	/ˈfor/	/fər/
have	/ˈhæv/	/əv həv/	*to*	/ˈtu/	/tə/
has	/ˈhæz/	/əz həz/	*he*	/ˈhi/	/i/
had	/ˈhæd/	/əd həd/	*him*	/ˈhɪm/	/ɪm/
do	/ˈdu/	/də/	*his*	/ˈhɪz/	/ɪz/
would	/ˈwʊd/	/əd wəd/	*them*	/ˈðɛm/	/ðəm/
will	/ˈwɪl/	/əl/	*her*	/ˈhər/	/ər/
can	/ˈkæn/	/kən/	*a*	/ˈeɪ/	/ə/
an	/ˈæn/	/ən/	*as*	/ˈæz/	/əz/
the	/ˈði/	/ðə/	*than*	/ˈðæn/	/ðən/
and	/ˈænd/	/ən ənd/	*that*	/ˈðæt/	/ðət/

For speakers who pronounce *was, of,* and *from* with PALM /ɑ/ (i.e., /wɑz/, /ɑv/, /frɑm/) when they are stressed and with schwa /ə/ (i.e., /wəz/, /əv/, /frəm/) when they are unstressed, these words can also be considered to have weak forms. For learners, however, it is simpler to use the more common forms with schwa /ə/ when both stressed and unstressed, in which case, *was, of,* and *from* are not weak form words.

8.4 The use of strong forms

As stated earlier, weak forms are the norm, but note that strong forms are used in the following contexts:

1   When a word is stressed for emphasis or contrast:

- *I didn't tell **him**; I told **her**.*   /aɪ ˈdɪdn̩ ˈtɛl ˈhɪm | aɪ ˈtoʊld ˈhər/
- *He really **had** seen her.*   /hi ˈriəli ˈhæd ˈsin ər/
- *I'm looking **at** John, not **for** John.*   /aɪm ˈlʊkɪŋ ˈæt ˈdʒɑn | ˈnɑt ˈfor ˈdʒɑn/

2   When prepositions are separated from the noun phrases they relate to:

- *What are you looking at?* /ˈwɒt̬ ər ju ˈlʊkɪŋ ˈæt/
- *He was sent for at once.* /hi wəz ˈsɛnt ˈfor ət ˈwəns/
- *The one that I spoke to* /ðə ˈwən ðət̬ aɪ ˈspoʊk ˈtu/

3   When auxiliary verbs are used without their main verb:

- *You can swim, and I can too.* /ˈju kən ˈswɪm | ən ˈaɪ ˈkæn ˈtu/
- *I've seen it; you know I have.* /aɪv ˈsin ɪt | ju ˈnoʊ aɪ ˈhæv/
- *Are you here? Yes, I am.* /ər ju ˈhir | ˈjɛs aɪ ˈæm/

But *have* is weak when preceded by a modal auxiliary:

- *I didn't do it, but I should have.* /aɪ ˈdɪdn̩ ˈdu ɪt | bət̬ aɪ ˈʃʊd əv/
- *He did it? He couldn't have.* /hi ˈdɪd ɪt | hi ˈkʊdn̩ əv/

4   At the ends of sentences, preposition + pronoun sequences tend to have a weak preposition if a stressed syllable precedes and a strong preposition if one or more unstressed syllables precede:

- *Look at him!* /ˈlʊk ət̬ ɪm/
- *I took all of them.* /aɪ ˈtʊk ˈɑl ə ðəm/
- *He repeated it for me.* /hi rəˈpit̬əd ɪt ˈfor mi/
- *They pointed it at him.* /ðeɪ ˈpɔɪntəd ɪt̬ ˈæt̬ ɪm/

5   In yes/no questions, auxiliary verbs tend to be stressed in slower, more deliberate speech and unstressed in freer, more conversational speech. Another influencing factor is the location of following stresses. If the next syllable is stressed, the auxiliary verb tends to be unstressed, but if two or more unstressed syllables follow, the auxiliary verb tends to be stressed:

- *Am I the only one?* /əm ˈaɪ ði ˈoʊnli ˈwən/
- *Am I amusing you?* /ˈæm aɪ əˈmjuzɪŋ ju/
- *Can someone ask?* /kən ˈsəmwən ˈæsk/
- *Can you repeat that?* /ˈkæn ju rəˈpit ˈðæt/

8.5 Weak form contractions

The weak forms of some auxiliary verbs (and *am/are/is* as main verbs) consist of a single consonant in certain contexts. Since a consonant can't usually form a syllable on its own, the weak form combines with a preceding word, forming a **contraction**. In informal writing, such contractions are usually indicated with an apostrophe. The present tense forms of the verb *be* (*am*, *are*, and *is*), auxiliary *have* (*have*, *has*, and *had*), and the modal verbs *will* and *would* readily form contractions with personal pronouns:

am: *I'm* /aɪm/
are: *you're* /jor/ or /jər/, *we're* /wir/ or /wər/, *they're* /ðer/
is: *he's* /hiz/ or /iz/, *she's* /ʃiz/, *it's* /ɪts/
have: *I've* /aɪv/, *you've* /juv/, *we've* /wiv/, *they've* /ðeɪv/
has: *he's* /hiz/ or /iz/, *she's* /ʃiz/, *it's* /ɪts/
had: *I'd* /aɪd/, *you'd* /jud/, *he'd* /hid/ or /id/, *she'd* /ʃid/, *we'd* /wid/, *they'd* /ðeɪd/

will: *I'll* /aɪl/, *you'll* /jul/, *he'll* /hil/ or /il/, *she'll* /ʃil/, *we'll* /wil/ or /wəl/, *they'll* /ðeɪl/
would: *I'd* /aɪd/, *you'd* /jud/, *he'd* /hid/ or /id/, *she'd* /ʃid/, *we'd* /wid/, *they'd* /ðeɪd/

Note that:

1   The contracted forms of *is* and *has*, and *had* and *would*, are identical. The forms *he's*, *she's*, and *it's* can represent *he/she/it* + *is* or *he/she/it* + auxiliary *has*, while *I'd, you'd, he'd, she'd, we'd*, and *they'd* can represent these personal pronouns combined with either *would* or auxiliary *had*. The grammatical context usually makes it clear which word is intended.

2   Contractions with *is* and auxiliary *has* are not limited to personal pronouns but can occur with a wide range of words:

   - *Here's John.*   /ˈhirz ˈdʒɑn/
   - *What's happened?*   /ˈwɑts ˈhæpənd/
   - *That's right.*   /ˈðæts ˈraɪt/
   - *The guy I lent it to's left.*   /ðə ˈgaɪ aɪ ˈlɛnt ɪt ˈtuz ˈlɛft/
   - *The one I bought's great.*   /ðə ˈwən aɪ ˈbɑts ˈgreɪt/

3   The forms of the contractions of *is* and auxiliary *has* follow the same pattern as those for plural, possessive, and third person singular <s> (see Section 2.30). When the preceding word ends with a voiced sound (i.e., a vowel or a voiced consonant), the pronunciation is /z/:

   - *Mine's broken.*   /ˈmaɪnz ˈbroʊkən/
   - *The glue's run out.*   /ðə ˈgluz ˈrən ˈaʊt/

When the preceding word ends with a voiceless consonant, the pronunciation is /s/:

   - *This rock's heavy.*   /ˈðɪs ˈrɑks ˈhɛvi/
   - *Jack's gone home.*   /ˈdʒæks ˈgɑn ˈhoʊm/

When the preceding word ends with one of the consonants /s z ʃ ʒ ʧ ʤ/, *is* and *has* can't form contractions (see next paragraph):

   - *My wish has come true.*   /maɪ ˈwɪʃ əz ˈkəm ˈtru/
   - *The bridge is closed.*   /ðə ˈbrɪʤ əz ˈkloʊzd/

4   Contraction formation is restricted by the syllable-final clusters that are possible in English (see Section 10.3). Thus the /d/ of *would* and *had* can't form a phonetic contraction with *it* because /td/ is not a possible English cluster, while the /l/ of *will* can't contract with *it* because a /tl/ cluster is also not a possibility in English. Likewise, *is* and *has* don't form contractions with words ending with /s z ʃ ʒ ʧ ʤ/ because the alveolar fricatives /s/ and /z/ can't follow these consonants in a word-final cluster.

5   As the previous point demonstrates, a phonetic contraction is not the same thing as an orthographic contraction. Although *it would* /ɪt̮ əd/, *it had* /ɪt̮ əd/, and *it will* /ɪt̮ əl/ are not phonetic contractions (because the weak form is a syllable, not a lone consonant), they are often written *it'd* and *it'll*. Other non-phonetic orthographic contractions are common in informal writing (e.g., *should've* /ʃʊd əv/, *what'll* /wɑt̮ əl/, *might've* /maɪt̮ əv/). Such "double contractions" as *I'll've* /aɪl əv/ or *we'd've* /wid əv/ are a mix of phonetic contractions with orthographic contractions.

6   The second element of a contraction is an unstressed function word that has been reduced to a single consonant that attaches to the preceding word to form a single unit. As we have seen, the first element is often a personal pronoun, but it doesn't have to be in the case of *is* and *has*. Consequently, the first element may or may not be an unstressed function word. When the first element is a personal pronoun, the contraction isn't usually stressed, but like personal pronouns that aren't part of a contraction, it can be stressed for emphasis or contrast:

- *I said **I'll** do it.*   /aɪ ˈsɛd ˈaɪl ˈdu ɪt/
- *Now **I've** had enough.*   /ˈnaʊ ˈaɪv ˈhæd əˈnəf/
- ***He's** the one!*   /ˈhiz ðə ˈwən/

In such cases, it is the personal pronoun that is emphasized or contrasted, not the auxiliary verb that has contracted with it. Thus ***He's** the one!* /ˈhiz ðə ˈwən/ is equivalent to *He **is** the one!* /ˈhi ɪz ðə ˈwən/, not *He **is** the one!* /hi ˈɪz ðə ˈwən/ or *He **is** the one!* /ˈhi ˈɪz ðə ˈwən/.

When the second element is *is* or *has*, the contraction is often stressed, not for emphasis or contrast, but because the first element is the kind of word, a lexical word, that is usually stressed:

- *The **dog's** hiding.*   /ðə ˈdɑgz ˈhaɪdɪŋ/
- *The **cat's** died.*   /ðə ˈkæts ˈdaɪd/
- *My **teacher's** amazing.*   /maɪ ˈtiʃɚz əˈmeɪzɪŋ/
- *My **uncle's** eaten it.*   /maɪ ˈəŋkl̩z ˈitn̩ ɪt/

7   Since contractions formed with personal pronouns are so often unstressed, some of them have developed weak forms of their own, notably *you're*, *we're*, and *we'll*. When stressed, they have the strong forms /jor/, /wir/, and /wil/, and when unstressed, they have the weak forms /jər/, /wər/, and /wəl/:

- *You're silly.*   /jər ˈsɪli/
- *No, **you're** silly.*   /ˈnoʊ ˈjor ˈsɪli/
- *We're sorry, but we'll be late.*   /wər ˈsɑri bət wəl bi ˈleɪt/
- ***We're** sorry too.*   /ˈwir ˈsɑri ˈtu/
- ***We'll** be late too.*   /ˈwil bi ˈleɪt ˈtu/

8   When *are* contracts with *you* and *they*, there is a change of vowel. *You* /ju/ plus *are* /r/ becomes /jor/, while *they* /ðeɪ/ plus *are* /r/ becomes /ðɛr/.

8.6 Weak forms of BE (main verb and auxiliary)

8.6.1 Am

When *am* is preceded by the pronoun *I*, it is reduced to /m/, which contracts with *I*, resulting in the contraction *I'm* /aɪm/.

- *I'm fine.*   /aɪm ˈfaɪn/
- *I'm waiting.*   /aɪm ˈweɪṭɪŋ/

In other positions, unstressed *am* has the weak form /əm/.

• *Am I right?*	/əm aɪ ˈraɪt/
• *So am I.*	/ˈsoʊ əm ˈaɪ/
• *Why am I here?*	/ˈwaɪ əm aɪ ˈhir/

8.6.2 Are

When unstressed *are* is preceded by the pronouns *you*, *we*, or *they*, it is reduced to /r/, which contracts with the pronouns, resulting in the contractions *you're*, *we're*, and *they're*. In the case of *you're* and *they're*, the formation of the contraction is accompanied by a change of vowel, /u/ to [o] for *you're* and /eɪ/ to /ɛ/ for *they're*. When unstressed, as they usually are, the contractions *you're* and *we're* are further reduced to /jər/ and /wər/.

• **You're** *wrong, and* **we're** *right.*	/ˈjor ˈraŋ | ən ˈwir ˈraɪt/
• *You're late.*	/jər ˈleɪt/
• *We're lost.*	/wər ˈlɑst/
• *They're safe.*	/ðɛr ˈseɪf/

In other positions, *are* has the weak form /ər/.

• *When are you coming?*	/ˈwen ər ju ˈkəmɪŋ/
• *Are they mine?*	/ər ðeɪ ˈmaɪn/
• *The doors are locked.*	/ðə ˈdorz ər ˈlɑkt/

8.6.3 Is

Unlike *am* and *are*, *is* isn't limited to forming contractions with personal pronouns but can contract with a greater variety of words. The "rules" for the pronunciation of the contracted form of *is* are the same as those for plural, third person singular, and possessive <s> (see Section 2.30). *Is* is pronounced /z/ when it contracts with a word ending in a voiced sound (i.e., a vowel or one of the voiced consonants /b d g v ð m n ŋ l r/) or is pronounced /s/ when it contracts with a word ending in a voiceless sound (i.e., one of the voiceless consonants /p t k f θ/).

• *He's sad.*	/hiz ˈsæd/
• *She's dull.*	/ʃiz ˈdəl/
• *His dog's brown.*	/hɪz ˈdɑgz ˈbraʊn/
• *My car's new.*	/maɪ ˈkɑrz ˈnu/
• *It's good.*	/ɪts ˈgʊd/
• *This knife's blunt.*	/ðɪs ˈnaɪfs ˈblənt/
• *The cap's off.*	/ðə ˈkæps ˈɑf/

In other positions and when the preceding word ends in a sibilant, i.e., /s z ʃ ʒ ʧ ʤ/, unstressed *is* is pronounced /ɪz/ or /əz/.

- *Is it right?*
- *This is it.*
- *Hers is best.*
- *The dish is hot.*
- *My watch is slow.*
- *The bridge is closed.*

/ɪz ɪt ˈraɪt/ or /əz ɪt ˈraɪt/
/ˈðɪs ɪz ˈɪt/ or /ˈðɪs əz ˈɪt/
/ˈhɜrz ɪz ˈbɛst/ or /ˈhɜrz əz ˈbɛst/
/ðə ˈdɪʃ ɪz ˈhɑt/ or /ðə ˈdɪʃ əz ˈhɑt/
/maɪ ˈwɑʧ ɪz ˈsloʊ/ or /maɪ ˈwɑʧ əz ˈsloʊ/
/ðə ˈbrɪʤ ɪz ˈkloʊzd/ or /ðə ˈbrɪʤ əz ˈkloʊzd/

8.7 Weak forms of auxiliary HAVE and DO

8.7.1 Have

As an auxiliary verb, *have* forms contractions with the personal pronouns *I*, *you*, *we*, and *they*. *Have* loses its initial /h/ and its vowel, leaving only /v/, which combines with the personal pronouns.

- *I've won.*
- *You've done it.*
- *We've left.*
- *They've gone.*

/aɪv ˈwən/
/juv ˈdən ɪt/
/wiv ˈlɛft/
/ðeɪv ˈgɑn/

In other contexts, auxiliary *have* has a weak form with schwa /ə/, either /həv/ or /əv/. The initial /h/ is retained when auxiliary *have* occurs after a pause but dropped in all other unstressed contexts.

- *My friends have gone.*
- *The rest have left.*
- *What have you done?*
- *Have I passed?*
- *Have you seen it?*
- *Have we won?*

/maɪ ˈfrɛndz əv ˈgɑn/
/ðə ˈrɛst əv ˈlɛft/
/ˈwɑt̬ əv ju ˈdən/
/həv aɪ ˈpæst/
/həv ju ˈsin ɪt/
/həv wi ˈwən/

8.7.2 Has

The contracted forms of the auxiliary verb *has* are identical to those of *is*. As for *is*, the pronunciation of auxiliary *has* follows the "rules" for the pronunciation of plural, third person singular and possessive <s> (see Section 2.30). *Has* is pronounced /z/ when it contracts with a word ending in a voiced sound (i.e., a vowel or one of the voiced consonants /b d g v ð m n ŋ l r/) or is pronounced /s/ when it contracts with a word ending in a voiceless sound (i.e., one of the voiceless consonants /p t k f θ/).

- *He's gone away.*
- *She's broken it.*
- *My arm's gone numb.*
- *The car's been stolen.*
- *It's been found.*
- *My wife's left me.*
- *The cat's made a mess.*

/hiz ˈgɑn əˈweɪ/
/ʃiz ˈbroʊkən ɪt/
/maɪ ˈɑrmz gɑn ˈnəm/
/ðə ˈkɑrz bɪn ˈstoʊlən/
/ɪts bɪn ˈfaʊnd/
/maɪ ˈwaɪfs ˈlɛft mi/
/ðə ˈkæts ˈmeɪd ə ˈmɛs/

Unstressed auxiliary *has* doesn't form contractions when preceded by sibilants (i.e., /s z ʃ ʒ ʧ ʤ/) or when preceded by a pause. After sibilants, the weak form of *has* is /əz/, while after a pause, the /h/ is retained and the weak form is /həz/.

• *My boss has been fired.*	/maɪ ˈbɑs əz bɪn ˈfaɪərd/
• *The rose has wilted.*	/ðə ˈroʊz əz ˈwɪltəd/
• *My wish has come true.*	/maɪ ˈwɪʃ əz ˈkəm ˈtru/
• *The branch has snapped.*	/ðə ˈbrænʧ əz ˈsnæpt/
• *The badge has fallen off.*	/ðə ˈbæʤ əz ˈfɑlən ˈɑf/
• *Has he read it?*	/həz i ˈrɛd ɪt/
• *Has it happened?*	/həz ɪt ˈhæpənd/
• *Has the film started?*	/həz ðə ˈfɪlm ˈstɑrt̬əd/

8.7.3 Had

The auxiliary verb *had* forms contractions with the personal pronouns *I*, *you*, *he*, *she*, *we*, and *they*. When *had* contracts, it loses its initial /h/ and its vowel, leaving only /d/, which combines with the personal pronouns.

• *I'd finished.*	/aɪd ˈfɪnɪʃt/
• *You'd left.*	/jud ˈlɛft/
• *He'd gone.*	/hid ˈgɑn/
• *She'd arrived.*	/ʃid əˈraɪvd/
• *We'd eaten.*	/wid ˈitn̩/
• *They'd spent it.*	/ðeɪd ˈspɛnt ɪt/

In other contexts, auxiliary *had* has a weak form with schwa /ə/, either /həd/ or /əd/. The initial /h/ is retained when auxiliary *had* occurs after a pause but is dropped in all other unstressed contexts.

• *The doors had been closed.*	/ðə ˈdorz əd bɪn ˈkloʊzd/
• *I wish my team had won.*	/aɪ ˈwɪʃ maɪ ˈtim əd ˈwən/
• *What had happened?*	/ˈwɑt̬ əd ˈhæpənd/
• *Had he gone?*	/həd i ˈgɑn/
• *Had she left?*	/həd ʃi ˈlɛft/
• *Had they promised?*	/həd ðeɪ ˈprɑməst/

8.7.4 Do

The auxiliary verb *do* has the weak form /də/ when the following word begins with a consonant. Before vowels, unstressed auxiliary *do* is pronounced /du/, and therefore, we can consider it not to have a weak form in this context.

• *Where do we wait?*	/ˈwɛr də wi ˈweɪt/
• *Do they know?*	/də ðeɪ ˈnoʊ/
• *Where do I go?*	/ˈwɛr du aɪ ˈgoʊ/
• *Do animals dream?*	/du ˈænəml̩z ˈdrim/

8.8 Weak forms of modal verbs

8.8.1 Would

The modal verb *would* forms contractions with the personal pronouns *I, you, he, she, we,* and *they*. When *would* contracts, it loses its initial /w/ and its vowel, leaving only /d/, which attaches to the personal pronouns. The contracted forms of *would* (*he'd* /hid/, *you'd* /jud/, and so on) are written and pronounced in the same way as the contracted forms of *had*.

• *I'd buy one.*	/aɪd ˈbaɪ ˈwən/
• *You'd like it.*	/jud ˈlaɪk ɪt/
• *He'd do it.*	/hid ˈdu ɪt/
• *She'd see it.*	/ʃid ˈsi ɪt/
• *We'd get better.*	/wid ˈgɛt ˈbɛt̬ər/
• *They'd help.*	/ðeɪd ˈhɛlp/

In other contexts, *would* has a weak form with schwa /ə/, either /wəd/ or /əd/. The initial /w/ is retained when *would* occurs after a pause but dropped in other unstressed contexts.

• *It'd work.*	/ɪt̬ əd ˈwərk/
• *The boss would hate it.*	/ðə ˈbɑs əd ˈheɪt̬ ɪt/
• *The top would fall off.*	/ðə ˈtɑp əd ˈfɑl ˈɑf/
• *Would he try?*	/wəd i ˈtraɪ/
• *Would it matter?*	/wəd ɪt ˈmætər/
• *Would they come?*	/wəd ðeɪ ˈkəm/

8.8.2 Will

The modal verb *will* forms contractions with the personal pronouns *I, you, he, she, we,* and *they*. When *will* contracts, it loses its initial /w/ and its vowel, leaving only /l/, which attaches to the personal pronouns. When unstressed, as it usually is, *we'll* has the weak form /wəl/, which is distinct from the form it has when stressed, i.e., /wil/. Unstressed *he'll* usually has the weak form /il/, except after a pause, when it's pronounced /hil/.

• *He'll wait. I'm sure he'll wait.*	/hil ˈweɪt | aɪm ˈʃər il ˈweɪt/
• *You'll see. I'll show you.*	/jul ˈsi | aɪl ˈʃoʊ ju/
• *She'll do her best.*	/ʃil ˈdu ər ˈbɛst/
• *We'll leave early.*	/wəl ˈliv ˈərli/
• *We'll leave, and then they'll leave.*	/ˈwil ˈliv | ən ˈðɛn ˈðeɪl ˈliv/
• *They'll finish soon.*	/ðeɪl ˈfɪnɪʃ ˈsun/

In other contexts, *will* has a weak form with schwa /ə/, either /wəl/ or /əl/. The initial /w/ is retained when *will* occurs after a pause but is dropped in other unstressed contexts. This /əl/ form is often realized as syllabic /l̩/ when the preceding word ends with a consonant; see Section 8.2.1.

• *It'll work.*	/ɪt̬ əl ˈwərk/
• *That will do.*	/ˈðæt̬ əl ˈdu/

- *Mike will go.*   /'maɪk əl 'goʊ/
- *Will you help?*   /wɪl ju 'hɛlp/
- *Will he say?*   /wɪl i 'seɪ/

8.8.3 Can

The weak form of the modal verb *can* is /kən/.

- *Tom can drive.*   /'tɑm kən 'draɪv/
- *You can try.*   /ju kən 'traɪ/
- *Can you come?*   /kən ju 'kəm/

8.9 Weak forms of prepositions

8.9.1 At

The weak form of *at* is /ət/.

- *Look at that.*   /'lʊk ət 'ðæt/
- *At long last.*   /ət 'lɑŋ 'læst/

8.9.2 For

The weak form of *for* is /fər/.

- *He took it for granted.*   /hi 'tʊk ɪt fər 'græntəd/
- *For hire.*   /fər 'haɪər/

8.9.3 To

Both as a preposition and as the to-infinitive, *to* has the weak form /tə/ before a word beginning with a consonant. Before vowels, the weak form of *to* is /tu/, and therefore, we can consider it not to have a weak form in this context.

- *I go to work to make money.*   /aɪ 'goʊ tə 'wɔrk tə 'meɪk 'məni/
- *I told him to go to hell.*   /aɪ 'toʊld ɪm tə 'goʊ tə 'hɛl/
- *I go to a gym to exercise.*   /aɪ 'goʊ tu ə 'dʒɪm tu 'ɛksərsaɪz/
- *I went to a diner to eat.*   /aɪ 'wɛnt tu ə 'daɪnər tu 'it/

8.10 Weak forms of personal pronouns and possessive determiners

8.10.1 He

The weak form of *he* is /i/. The initial /h/ of unstressed *he* is retained, however, when it is preceded by a pause, and therefore we can consider *he* not to have a weak form in this context.

- *I know he thinks so.*   /aɪ 'noʊ i 'θɪŋks 'soʊ/
- *He thinks so.*   /hi 'θɪŋks 'soʊ/
- *They said he left.*   /ðeɪ 'sɛd i 'lɛft/
- *He left.*   /hi 'lɛft/

8.10.2 Him

The weak form of *him* is /ɪm/.

- *Tell him.*   /'tɛl ɪm/
- *They made him leave.*   /ðeɪ 'meɪd ɪm 'liv/

8.10.3 His

The weak form of *his* is /ɪz/. The initial /h/ of unstressed *his* is retained, however, when it is preceded by a pause, and therefore, we can consider *his* not to have a weak form in this context. *His* only has a weak form as a possessive determiner (e.g., *I've read his book*) but not as a possessive pronoun (e.g., *I've read his*).

- *I took his watch.*   /aɪ 'tʊk ɪz 'wɑʧ/
- *His watch was stolen.*   /hɪz 'wɑʧ wəz 'stoʊlən/
- *They know his name.*   /ðeɪ 'noʊ ɪz 'neɪm/
- *His name was known.*   /hɪz 'neɪm wəz 'noʊn/

8.10.4 Her

Both as a personal pronoun (e.g., *I found her*) and as a possessive determiner (e.g., *I found her bag*), *her* has the weak form /ər/. The initial /h/ of unstressed *her* is retained, however, when it is preceded by a pause, and therefore, we can consider *her* not to have a weak form in this context.

- *I've never met her.*   /aɪv 'nɛvər 'mɛt̬ ər/
- *I've met her mother.*   /aɪv 'mɛt̬ ər 'məðər/
- *I've read her book.*   /aɪv 'rɛd ər 'bʊk/
- *Her book's good.*   /hər 'bʊks 'gʊd/
- *Her dog died.*   /hər 'dɑg 'daɪd/

8.10.5 Them

The weak form of *them* is /ðəm/. When unstressed *them* is preceded by a word ending in a consonant, the initial /ð/ is often dropped in more casual speech styles, leaving /əm/.

- *I saw them.*   /aɪ 'sɑ ðəm/
- *He bought them.*   /hi 'bɑt ðəm/
- *Go get 'em!*   /'goʊ 'gɛt̬ əm/

8.11 Weak forms of articles

8.11.1 A and An

The weak forms of *a* and *an* are /ə/ and /ən/. *A*, of course, is used before consonants and *an* before vowels.

* *A banana.*   /ə bəˈnænə/
* *An apple.*   /ən ˈæpl̩/
* *A unit.*   /ə ˈjunət/
* *An hour.*   /ən ˈaʊər/

8.11.2 The

Before a consonant, *the* has the weak form /ðə/, but before a vowel, it's /ði/, and therefore, we can consider *the* not to have a weak form in this context.

* *The police.*   /ðə pəˈlis/
* *The moon.*   /ðə ˈmun/
* *The answer to the question.*   /ði ˈænsər tə ðə ˈkwɛstʃən/

8.12 Weak forms of conjunctions

8.12.1 And

The most common weak form of *and* is /ən/, while /ənd/ is also a possibility but much less usual. It's sometimes said that /ən/ occurs before consonants and /ənd/ before vowels, but this isn't true – the form without /d/ is much more common no matter what follows.

* *A burger and fries.*   /ə ˈbərgər ən ˈfraɪz/
* *Stop and wait.*   /ˈstɑp ən ˈweɪt/
* *In and out.*   /ˈɪn ən ˈaʊt/

8.12.2 As

The weak form of *as* is /əz/.

* *As old as the hills.*   /əz ˈoʊld əz ðə ˈhɪlz/
* *As far as I can see.*   /əz ˈfɑr əz ˈaɪ kən ˈsi/

8.12.3 Than

The weak form of *than* is /ðən/.

* *He left earlier than I did.*   /hi ˈlɛft ˈərliər ðən ˈaɪ ˈdɪd/
* *More than enough.*   /ˈmor ðən əˈnəf/

8.12.4 That

That has the weak form /ðət/ when it's a conjunction (e.g., *I know that it's true*) or relative pronoun (e.g., *the man that I saw*) but has no weak form when it's a demonstrative determiner (e.g., *I know that* /ðæt/ *man*) or a demonstrative pronoun (e.g., *I know that* /ðæt/).

- *They said that it's good.*   /ðeɪ ˈsɛd ðət̪ ɪts ˈɡʊd/
- *I've heard that he's back.*   /aɪv ˈhɜrd ðət̪ iz ˈbæk/
- *The dog that bit me*   /ðə ˈdɑɡ ðət ˈbɪt mi/
- *The man that I saw*   /ðə ˈmæn ðət̪ aɪ ˈsɑ/

8.13 Variable weak forms

In the preceding section, we have included only those words that reliably alternate between strong and weak forms in stressed and unstressed syllables. A number of other words are more variable. Some have weak forms that occur relatively rarely, such as when *I*, *my*, and *so* are weakened to /ə/, /mə/, and /sə/. Others have weak forms that are quite common, such as /jə/ and /jər/ for *you* and *your* but not so common that they are the norm in unstressed contexts. Words with variable weak forms include:

I	/ə/	**their**	/ðər/	**she'll**	/ʃəl/
you	/jə/	**I'm**	/əm/	**they'll**	/ðəl/
my	/mə/	**you're**	/jər/	**or**	/ər/
your	/jər/	**they're**	/ðər/	**so**	/sə/

8.14 Non-phonemic weakening

Some writers on English phonetics use strong/weak systems of transcription (see Section 5.3) that assign different symbols to strong (i.e., stressed) and weak (i.e., unstressed) variants of the same phoneme. In stressed syllables, they transcribe schwa /ə/, schwar /ər/, FLEECE /i/, and GOOSE /u/ with [ʌ], [ɚ], [iː], and [uː], while in unstressed syllables, they transcribe them [ə], [ɚ], [i] and [u]. Consequently, they are obliged to transcribe certain grammatical words in two different ways depending on whether they are stressed or not, even though there is no phonemic difference between the pronunciations. This is misleading because it confuses true phonemic weak forms, which are important for learners, with the slight non-phonemic changes that occur when vowels are unstressed, which is of relatively minor importance.

Words whose transcription would vary if different symbols were used for stressed and unstressed schwa include *was*, *does*, *must*, *from*, *of*, *us*, *some*, and *but*, for example:

was:	*I was right.* /aɪ wəz ˈraɪt/	*I was.* /aɪ ˈwʌz/
does:	*Does it work?* /dəz ɪt ˈwɜrk/	*It does.* /ɪt ˈdʌz/
must:	*I must ask.* /aɪ məst ˈæsk/	*I must.* /aɪ ˈmʌst/
from:	*It's from Bob.* /ɪts frəm ˈbɑb/	*Where from?* /ˈwɛr ˈfrʌm/
of:	*One of each.* /ˈwʌn əv ˈiʧ/	*The one I thought of.* /ðə ˈwʌn aɪ ˈθɑt̪ ʌv/
us:	*Tell us.* /ˈtɛl əs/	*It's us.* /ɪts ˈʌs/
some:	*Buy some milk.* /ˈbaɪ səm ˈmɪlk/	*Buy me some.* /ˈbaɪ mi ˈsʌm/
but:	*Slow but steady.* /ˈsloʊ bət ˈstɛdi/	*No buts.* /ˈnoʊ ˈbʌts/

Words whose transcription would vary if different symbols were used for stressed and unstressed schwar /ɚ/ include *were* and *her*, for example:

were: *You were late.* /ju wɚ ˈleɪt/   *We were.* /wi ˈwɝ/
her: *Her name's Kim.* /hɚ ˈneɪmz ˈkɪm/   ***Her** name's Kim (not his).* /ˈhɝ ˈneɪmz ˈkɪm/

Words whose transcription would vary if different symbols were used for stressed and unstressed FLEECE include *me*, *we*, *she*, and *the*, for example:

me: *Tell me.* /ˈtɛl mi/   *It's me.* /ɪts ˈmiː/
we: *We left.* /wi ˈlɛft/   *And **we** left.* /ən ˈwiː ˈlɛft/
she: *She tried.* /ʃi ˈtraɪd/   *So did she.* /ˈsoʊ dɪd ˈʃiː/
he: *He knows.* /hi ˈnoʊz/   *Nor does he.* /ˈnor dəz ˈhiː/
the: *The end.* /ði ˈɛnd/   *I said "the" end.* /aɪ ˈsɛd ˈðiː ˈɛnd/

Words whose transcription would vary if different symbols were used for stressed and unstressed GOOSE include *you*, *do*, and *to*, for example:

you: *You can't.* /ju ˈkænt/   *It's you.* /ɪts ˈjuː/
do: *Why do I try?* /ˈwaɪ du aɪ ˈtraɪ/   *I do.* /aɪ ˈduː/
to: *Go to England.* /ˈgoʊ tu ˈɪŋglənd/   *Where to?* /ˈwɛr ˈtuː/

8.15 Weak forms and connected speech

The preceding weak forms have been given in their most neutral forms, but it's common for such high-frequency words to appear in phonetic contexts that alter their phonetic structure.

Since *and*, *an*, and *will* have the weak forms /ən/ and /əl/, these can form syllabic consonants more or less readily depending on the final consonant of the preceding word (see Section 8.2).

- *bread and butter*   /ˈbrɛd n̩ ˈbətər/
- *knife and fork*   /ˈnaɪf n̩ ˈfork/
- *bought and sold*   /ˈbɑt n̩ ˈsoʊld/
- *I had an answer.*   /aɪ ˈhæd n̩ ˈænsər/
- *cause an accident*   /ˈkɑz n̩ ˈæksədənt/
- *eat an orange*   /ˈit n̩ ˈorɪndʒ/
- *That'll do.*   /ˈðæt l̩ ˈdu/
- *Help'll come.*   /ˈhɛlp l̩ ˈkəm/
- *Time'll tell*   /ˈtaɪm l̩ ˈtɛl/

8.16 Contractions with NOT

A second class of contractions is quite different from those we have discussed so far. The negative contractions are a combination of *not* and an auxiliary verb, which result in the following forms:

isn't	/ˈɪzn̩t/	**didn't**	/ˈdɪdn̩t/	**mustn't**	/ˈməsn̩t/
aren't	/ɑrnt/	**haven't**	/ˈhævn̩t/	**shouldn't**	/ˈʃʊdn̩t/
wasn't	/ˈwɔzn̩t/	**hasn't**	/ˈhæzn̩t/	**couldn't**	/ˈkʊdn̩t/

weren't	/wərnt/	**hadn't**	/ˈhædn̩t/	**wouldn't**	/ˈwʊdn̩t/
don't	/doʊnt/	**won't**	/woʊnt/		
doesn't	/ˈdəzn̩t/	**can't**	/kænt/		

These contractions are best considered as individual words in their own right that have developed through historical processes of word formation and grammaticalization and not as present-day weak forms of *not* that occur through processes of weakening during connected speech. They differ from the first group of contractions in a number of ways:

1   In terms of stress, *not* does not behave like a weak form word. As we have seen, such words are unstressed in all but exceptional circumstances. Consequently, they have pronunciations typical of unstressed syllables (i.e., with centralized vowels and dropped consonants). Their reduction in certain contexts to a single consonant that contracts with a preceding word is an extension of the same process. *Not*, in contrast, is a grammatical word that is usually stressed, like for example the demonstratives (*this, that, these, those*) and possessive pronouns (*mine, yours,* and so on):

- I'm not ready.   /aɪm ˈnɑt ˈrɛdi/
- He's big but not strong.   /hiz ˈbɪg bət ˈnɑt ˈstrɑŋ/
- Try not to forget.   /ˈtraɪ ˈnɑt tə fərˈgɛt/
- It's not knowing that's worst.   /ɪts ˈnɑt ˈnoʊɪŋ ðəts ˈwərst/

When an unstressed auxiliary verb contracts with a preceding word, the resulting contraction has the stressing that word would have had if the auxiliary had not contracted. If the word is a personal pronoun, then the contraction, like the pronoun, is usually unstressed. If the word is a lexical word, as it could be in cases of contraction with *is* or *has*, then the contraction, like the lexical word, is usually stressed. In the case of contractions with *not*, however, the situation is reversed. The contraction takes the stressing of the contracting word *not* and is stressed even though the preceding word is of a type that is usually unstressed:

- Don't go.   /ˈdoʊnt ˈgoʊ/
- He can't stay.   /hi ˈkænt ˈsteɪ/
- It doesn't work.   /ɪt ˈdəzn̩t ˈwərk/
- I won't ask.   /aɪ ˈwoʊnt ˈæsk/

2   Most of the negative contractions do not conform to our definition of a phonetic contraction. In *isn't, didn't, haven't,* and others, the *not* element isn't reduced to a single consonant but has the form of a syllable, /ənt/, which is usually realized with a syllabic consonant, /n̩t/. Only *aren't, weren't,* and *can't* can be analyzed as consisting of a word reduced to a consonantal element and attached to a preceding word, /nt/ in the case of *aren't* and *weren't,* and /t/ in the case of *can't.*

3   Two of the negative contractions, *don't* and *won't,* have completely unpredictable forms. The /u/ and /ɪl/ of *do* and *will* become /oʊ/ in *don't* and *won't.*

4   The final /t/ of negative contractions only regularly occurs before a pause. In other contexts (i.e., before a word beginning with a vowel or a consonant), /t/ is frequently dropped. This is particularly common in the case of disyllabic contractions, *isn't, haven't, couldn't,* and so on, though it is less usual in the case of the five monosyllabic contractions, *aren't, weren't, don't, won't,* and *can't.*

Chapter 9

Practice
Weak vowels and weak forms

9.1 Syllabic consonants: practice

This section provides practice in pronouncing syllabic consonants in the phonetic contexts that favor their use. The exercise material includes the target sounds in words, phrases, and sentences.

9.2 Syllabic /l̩/

9.2.1 Words

a) /pl̩/, /bl̩/

apple, chapel, couple, example, nipple, opal, people, pupil, purple, ripple, sample, simple, scalpel, staple, triple, cripple; bubble, cable, crumble, double, gamble, global, herbal, humble, marble, mumble, noble, pebble, ramble, rubble, stable, stumble, table, tremble, trouble, label, rumble, cannibal, horrible

b) /tl̩/, /dl̩/

battle, beetle, bottle, brutal, cattle, crystal, fatal, hostel, little, metal, nettle, petal, pistol, postal, rattle, settle, shuttle, startle, subtle, title, total, turtle, vital; bridal, candle, cradle, cuddle, doodle, fiddle, huddle, ladle, medal, middle, model, muddle, needle, paddle, pedal, puddle, riddle, saddle, scandal

c) /kl̩/, /gl̩/, /tʃl̩/, /dʒl̩/

ankle, buckle, circle, crackle, cycle, knuckle, snorkel, sparkle, sprinkle, tickle, trickle, twinkle, wrinkle, local, uncle, vocal, article, chemical, medical, miracle; angle, bangle, burgle, eagle, gargle, giggle, haggle, jingle, juggle, jungle, legal, single, smuggle, squiggle, strangle, struggle, tangle, wriggle; satchel, Rachel; angel, cudgel

d) /ml̩/, /nl̩/

camel, dismal, formal, mammal, normal, thermal, animal; channel, colonel, final, funnel, journal, kennel, panel, signal, tunnel, criminal, eternal

e) /fḷ/, /vḷ/, /θḷ/, /ðḷ/

baffle, muffle, stifle, trifle, waffle, raffle, rifle, shuffle, awful; civil, devil, drivel, evil, gravel, grovel, hovel, level, naval, novel, oval, rival, shovel, travel, approval, arrival, festival, interval, removal; lethal, brothel; betrothal

f) /sḷ/, /zḷ/, /ʃḷ/

axle, bristle, cancel, castle, fossil, gristle, hassle, muscle, parcel, pencil, rustle, stencil, thistle, whistle, wrestle, universal; chisel, dazzle, drizzle, diesel, easel, fizzle, nasal, nozzle, puzzle, weasel, proposal, refusal; crucial, partial, social, special, commercial, essential, initial, official, potential

9.2.2 Phrases

a social animal, universal approval, a controversial article, a provincial capital, harmful chemicals, a professional criminal, social disapproval, the local hospital, an impossible obstacle, a controversial proposal, a little puzzled, facial muscles, normal levels, a historical novel, a political rival, international travel, a journal article, verbal signals, a nocturnal mammal, a little angel, a tropical jungle, a political struggle, social circles, a skillful tackle, a statistical model, a financial muddle, a bicycle pedal, a political scandal, a legal battle, the final total, a political gamble, a beautiful couple, a typical example, local people, an able pupil, a classical temple, official approval

9.2.3 Sentences

(1) I was a trifle puzzled by his refusal. (2) Rachel was unable to stifle a giggle. (3) She made a simple but special apple crumble. (4) He feels comfortable in multiple social circles. (5) It's an unmistakable signal of financial trouble. (6) My uncle wobbled home on his unstable bicycle. (7) The title of his article was "The Maximal Syllable." (8) It was crucial to get approval from the local council. (9) Our principal is responsible, respectable, and reliable. (10) The pupils found it difficult to give examples of ethical principles.

9.3 Syllabic /n/

9.3.1 Words

a) /tn̩/, /dn̩/

bitten, brighten, button, carton, certain, cotton, curtain, fatten, flatten, frighten, glutton, kitten, lighten, mitten, mutton, rotten, shorten, straighten, tartan, threaten, tighten; burden, garden, harden, pardon, sudden, warden, wooden, rodent, student, couldn't, shouldn't, didn't, wouldn't, hadn't, guidance

b) /fn̩/, /vn̩/, /ðn̩/, /θn̩/

deafen, hyphen, often, orphan, soften, stiffen, toughen, infant; driven, even, given, heaven, oven, proven, raven, seven, servant, eleven, relevant, convent; heathen; strengthen, lengthen

c) /sn̩/, /zn̩/

arson, basin, fasten, glisten, listen, loosen, person, vixen, recent, comparison, absent, innocent, magnificent; chosen, cousin, crimson, dozen, frozen, poison, prison, raisin, reason, risen, season, treason, doesn't, isn't, peasant, present, horizon, citizen

d) /ʃn̩/, /ʒn̩/

caution, cushion, fashion, lotion, mission, motion, nation, ocean, passion, portion, session, station, action, fiction, option, section, patient, pension, mention, mansion, function, profession, operation, information, foundation, education, creation, accommodation, tradition, position, ambition, condition, revolution, politician, magician, musician, technician, attention, attraction, collection, description, election, instruction, introduction, protection, reception, ancient, sufficient, efficient, emotion, solution, suspicion; vision, provision, division, collision, decision, conclusion, confusion, illusion, conversion, diversion, excursion, occasion, invasion, persuasion, explosion

9.3.2 Phrases

fasten a button, a prison warden, an ancient nation, a session musician, heightened tension, pension contributions, an important function, my chosen profession, a sudden resignation, tighten regulations, a pleasant sensation, an unpleasant situation, sudden inspiration, a written examination, a student demonstration, an ancient civilization, pleasant associations, an important collection, a wooden construction, written instructions, a television production, a sudden vision, pension provision, an important decision, a sudden conversion, a population explosion, an important lesson, listen patiently, a decent person

9.3.3 Sentences

(1) Jason met his relations at the station. (2) Read this important information about depression medication. (3) He studied the representation of adolescence in Asian fiction. (4) Gordon listened in growing confusion to his cousin's objections. (5) Seven patients developed infections and required hospitalization. (6) There was a population explosion due to immigration and urbanization. (7) His frightened expression strengthened my impression of his innocence. (8) Nathan's dedication to his chosen profession is an inspiration to all of us. (9) Information about my former positions is given in the written application. (10) What expectations does the present generation of students have from education?

9.4 Weak forms and contractions: practice

The following sections provide practice in using English weak forms and contractions in short phrases and sentences.

9.5 Forms of BE (main verb and auxiliary)

9.5.1 Am and Are

a) /aɪm/

I'm fine. I'm here. I'm tired. I'm leaving. I'm busy. I'm having dinner. I'm waiting. I'm taking my time. I'm seeing John later. I'm doing my best. I think I'm lost. I'm trying. I'm worn out. You know I'm right.

b) /əm/

Am I late? Am I right? Am I wrong? Am I winning? Am I under arrest? Am I boring you? Am I making myself clear? What am I waiting for? Where am I going? Who am I talking to? How am I doing? When am I expected?

c) /jər/

You're wonderful. You're learning. You're a real friend. You're almost there. You're doing well. You're close. You're getting better. You're being silly. You're seeing things. You're annoying me. You're making a mistake. You're late. You're very brave. Now you're talking. I think you're great. I know you're busy. He said you're trying hard. She knows you're interested.

d) /wər/

We're coming. We're running late. We're getting along well. We're making good progress. We're finding it difficult. We're having problems. We're leaving soon. We're thinking about it. We're doing it again. We're meeting later. We're happy together. He knows we're here. She thinks we're a couple. They said we're allowed.

e) /ðɛr/

They're awful. They're here. They're on their way. They're taking it easy. They're nearly there. They're plotting. They're out. They're starting. They're both teachers. They're difficult. They're gone. She said they're coming. He knows they're cheating. They think they're special. It sounds like they're serious.

f) /ər/

Are you ready? Are you there? Are you sure? Are you all right? Are you comfortable? Are you joking? Are they lost? What are you waiting for? What are you doing? What are you looking at? What are you talking about? Where are you going? Where are you from? Where are they made? Where are we staying? When are we going? When are you leaving? When are we meeting? When are you getting up? Why are you angry? Why are they broken? Why are we waiting? Why are they laughing? Why are you smiling? What are they eating? What are you carrying? What are they hiding? What are we doing?

9.5.2 Is

a) /z/

The job's easy. His dad's rich. This bag's heavy. The cave's very dark. The game's over. The gun's loaded. This ring's very expensive. The bill's wrong. The door's locked. My knee's aching. The glue's drying. Who's there? My pay's too low. Why's that? That boy's lazy. My toe's hurting. Now's the time.

b) /s/

The tap's leaking. The shop's closed. The ship's sinking. The cat's sleeping. That's incredible. His boat's very big. What's the problem? My back's itching. This cake's too sweet. This lock's useless. This fork's bent. My life's amazing. My cough's getting worse. This knife's very sharp. That tooth's rotten.

c) /ɪz/ *or* /əz/

This is it. The case is closed. The choice is yours. This place is awful. His voice is breaking. Hers is better. His is worse. The news is exciting. The cause is unknown. The hose is leaking. My nose is bleeding. The quiz is too difficult. The brush is dirty. English is fun! This fish is rotten. The varnish is still wet. Beige is my favorite color. The beach is empty. Bleach is dangerous. The branch is breaking. Your brooch is lovely. My watch is very old. The bridge is collapsing. The cage is open. The damage is done. This language is easy. The last page is missing.

9.6 Forms of HAVE (auxiliary)

9.6.1 Have

a) /aɪv/

I've seen it. I've finished. I've done it. I've been waiting all day. I've been robbed. I've made dinner. I've been there. I've found it. I've had enough. I've done my best. I've had a shower. You know I've tried.

b) /juv/

You've broken it. You've made a mess. You've succeeded. You've made it. You've taken too long. You've missed one. You've spilled some. You've dropped something. You've said that before. You've lost. I think you've had enough.

c) /wiv/

We've never met. We've arrived. We've changed. We've prepared everything. We've done our best. We've had it fixed. We've worn it out. We've turned it off. We've given up. We've bought a new one. You think we've cheated?

d) /ðeɪv/

They've seen it. They've left. They've done it before. They've made a mistake. They've already eaten. They've gotten lost. They've been stolen. They've been welcomed. They've split up. I bet they've gone.

e) /əv/

People have complained. The sheep have wandered off. The children have gone to bed. The men have been arrested. The women have vanished. My feet have gone numb. His teeth have fallen out. The geese have flown away. The mice have eaten all the cheese. The police have been asking about you. My parents have gone on holiday. Ten cars have been stolen. Where have you been? It might have happened. What have you done? You shouldn't have left.

f) /həv/

Have I missed something? Have you noticed anything? Have we won? Have they replied? Have the kids come home? Have you finished? Have the police been called? Have we passed the exam? Have you seen it?

9.6.2 Has

a) /z/

The job's been done. The bread's gone moldy. The dog's died. My glove's disappeared. A crime's been committed. The machine's stopped working. The building's fallen down. The well's run dry. His knee's gotten worse. My coffee's gone cold. Who's bought one? The car's broken down again. My pay's disappeared. The sky's gotten darker. The joy's gone out of it. The snow's all melted. The cow's been milked.

b) /s/

My cap's blown away. The group's fallen apart. The cat's been run over. A jet's just crashed. My snake's shed its skin. The clock's stopped. My wife's left me. The roof's collapsed. The moth's flown away. My rotten tooth's been pulled out. Ruth's left.

c) /əz/

The address has changed. The bus has broken down. His has been replaced. My nose has been itching all day. My wish has come true. The bush has grown too big. The camouflage has fooled them. The barrage has started. My watch has stopped. Your brooch has fallen off. The cottage has burnt down. The urge has passed.

d) /həz/

Has it worked? Has she left? Has he done it? Has the train arrived yet? Has your headache gone? Has my mother called? Has the baby gone to sleep? Has the rain stopped? Has it helped?

9.6.3 *Had*

a) /aɪd/

I'd already finished. I'd done all I could. I wish I'd told him. I'd already left. I'd seen it before. I'd better go. If only I'd known. He said I'd spoiled it. She thought I'd taken it. I knew I'd made a mistake. I'd wrecked it.

b) /jud/

You'd been before. You'd never seen it. I wish you'd come earlier. If only you'd said. You'd made a mess. She said you'd left. I thought you'd finished. I knew you'd been tricked. You'd already eaten it.

c) /hid/

He'd already gone. He'd left. He'd seen it. He'd been there before. He'd hardly started. He'd done it again. He'd spoiled it. He'd already bought it. He'd crashed the car. He'd lost it. He'd fallen over.

d) /ʃid/

She'd said everything. She'd been there all day. She'd already finished. I wish she'd done better. If only she'd listened. She'd given up. She'd arrived early. I knew she'd failed. I thought she'd done better.

e) /wid/

We'd better leave. We'd finished early. We'd taken a long time. We'd already opened it. I wish we'd tried that first. If only we'd met ten years ago. I thought we'd passed. I knew we'd gone too far. We'd missed it.

f) /ðeɪd/

They'd broken it. They'd done it before. They'd tried their best. They'd broken new ground. They'd set a new record. If only they'd said so. I wish they'd left earlier. They said they'd been invited. I thought they'd gone.

g) /əd/

The gap had widened. The job had gotten worse. It had broken down. The fad had passed. My back had gone. The dog had run off. The coach had gone home. The bridge had been repaired. His cough had cleared up. The love had gone. The myth had grown. The boss had left. The prize had been won. My wish had been granted. Its prestige had lessened. The dam had been built. The phone had been ringing. The song had finished. Bill had arrived. The bar had closed. The sea had been polluted. My money had run out. The zoo had closed down. The day had gone well. The lie had been discovered. The toy had broken. The plough had rusted. The show had finished.

h) /həd/

Had she already left? Had it been going on long? Had it been a success? Had they tidied up? Had they done it before? Had it been prepared? Had you been there before? Had it worked? Had it been stolen?

9.7 Forms of DO (auxiliary)

a) /də/

Do they know? Do we park here? Do people like that? Do pandas eat meat? Do rabbits hibernate? Where do penguins live? How do birds fly? When do babies start talking? Which do they like? What do the police want?

b) /du/

Do apples grow on trees? Do elephants really never forget? Do onions make you cry? Do old people sleep more? Where do Ann's parents live? When do I start? What do owls eat?

9.8 Modal verbs

9.8.1 *Would*

a) /aɪd/

I'd like to go. I'd enjoy it. I'd do it. I'd have a go. I'd open it. I'd take one. I'd like one. I'd win easily. I'd eat it all. I'd laugh my head off. I'd leave it alone. I'd love to come. I'd make a difference. You know I'd love it.

b) /jud/

You'd find it difficult. You'd notice the difference. You'd get it wrong. You'd eat it all. You'd spoil it. You'd easily win. You'd never finish in time. You'd never understand. You'd love it. I think you'd like it.

c) /(h)id/

He'd steal it. He'd never do it. He'd waste our time. He'd make a mess. He'd work it out. He'd take a long time. He'd help. He'd try. He'd make you proud. He'd drive you crazy. He'd buy it all. I think he'd get lost. She said he'd wait.

d) /ʃid/

She'd get angry. She'd see the funny side. She'd throw it away. She'd lose it. She'd take it all. She'd take it home. She'd make a fortune. She'd say what she thinks. She'd like to keep it. She'd like one. I think she'd hate it.

e) /wid/

We'd break the record. We'd have a great time. We'd like to join you. We'd get lost. We'd be wasting our money. We'd win. We'd get away with it. We'd be rich. We'd be able to do it. We'd enjoy it. I know we'd do well.

f) /əd/

The top would fall off. The lab would close down. The debt would increase. The bed would be too big. The itch would get worse. The cage would rust. The knife would be found. The drive would be tiring. The myth would grow. A kiss would be nice. A snooze would be good. I wish this rash would go away. Beige would look nice. I said Pam would do it. The bone would break. The ring would get lost. The coal would run out. A year would be enough. The tea would get cold. A party would be great. A few would be enough. That way would be quicker. A pie would be too much. That boy would be suitable. If only the snow would melt. I wish that cow would move.

9.8.2 Will

a) /aɪl/, /jul/, /(h)il/, /ʃil/, /wəl/, /ðeɪl/

I'll let you know. I think I'll leave. You'll understand. I know you'll do well. He'll never admit it. I think he'll leave early. She'll never know. Now she'll feel better. We'll work it out. I know we'll manage. They'll never find it. I think they'll stop looking.

b) /l̩/ *(after consonants)*

The top'll break. A cab'll stop. That'll do. It'll never work. The mood'll change. The park'll close. The egg'll break. Which'll fit? The bridge'll collapse. Crime'll increase. When'll that happen? Half'll be enough. The cave'll be dark. Your teeth'll rot. The bus'll be late. The surprise'll kill him. My cash'll run out. Sabotage'll work. This one'll do. My room'll be big enough. The string'll snap.

c) /əl/ *(after /l/ or /r/)*

The bill will be high. The bell will ring soon. The fool will get hurt. The smell will get worse. The wall will be demolished. The wheel will fall off. The car will break down. The floor will collapse. The chair will break. The fear will go away. His brother will help. Four will be enough.

d) /əl/ *(after vowels)*

The sea will be cold. Three will be enough. The fee will be high. The zoo will be closed. The tray will be too heavy. The day will fly by. The sky will clear up. That boy will do well. The snow will soon melt. I'm sure the show will be great. Now will be fine.

e) /wɪl/

Will you give it a try? Will it work? Will she make it? Will they do it? Will it be enough? Will that do?

9.8.3 Can

a) /kən/

I can swim. You can try. It can wait. I can tell. Dave can do it. Can we go? Jack can take the train. The neighbors can hear you. Can you say that again? Where can I park? What can I say? Who can it be? Which can I take? You can say that again! As far as I can see. I can barely hear myself think. I can live with it. I can take it or leave it. You've bitten off more than you can chew.

9.9 Prepositions

9.9.1 At and For

a) /ət/

clutch at straws, asleep at the wheel, young at heart, choose at random, talk at length, take something at face value, burn the candle at both ends, fall at the first hurdle, howl at the moon, ill at ease, at a moment's notice, weak at the knees, at the drop of a hat, in the right place at the right time

b) /fər/

one for luck, for the sake of argument, a recipe for disaster, word for word, for better or for worse, good for nothing, lost for words, spoiled for choice, food for thought, a cry for help, take for granted, a sight for sore eyes, an A for effort, a man for all seasons, tit for tat, a free for all, once and for all

9.9.2 To

a) /tə/

a hard nut to crack, a tough act to follow, back to square one, up to date, a score to settle, agree to disagree, back to basics, close to home, a bitter pill to swallow, bored to tears, a shoulder to cry on, raring to go, too hot to handle, A to Z, day to day, man to man, well to do, a bride to be, face to face, head to head, a mother to be, wall to wall, door to door, ready to wear, heart to heart

b) /tu/

a bite to eat, a means to an end, afraid to ask, end to end, down to earth, made to order, a call to action

9.10 Personal pronouns and possessive determiners

9.10.1 He, Him, His, Her, Them

a) /i/

So he knows, does he? Has he seen it? Will he know? Can he help? Where did he go? What does he want? Should he try? Could he answer? I know he does. She said he did. I thought he knew.

b) /hi/

He told us everything. He knows a lot. He ran off. He did it well. He told me so. He thought about it.

c) /ɪm/

Help him. Don't rob him. We've got him. They hated him. I woke him up. They had to drag him. I can't reach him. They didn't charge him anything. It drove him mad. He said it was beneath him. She tried to soothe him. I don't miss him. It didn't faze him. Please don't push him. I can't name him. I'll phone him later. Sing him a song. Let's call him. I can see him. They adore him.

d) /ɪz/

I know his mother. I caught his cold. She took his details. I believed his story. It's near his house. Can you see his car? Has he learned his lesson? Does his brother live there? They took his keys. Give me his stuff.

e) /hɪz/

His coat's wet. His car's gone. His mother called. His house is on fire. His brother took it. His wife left.

f) /ər/

I can't find her. Just ask her. They gave her a prize. I'll phone her later. He met her. Tell her again. She said she'll miss her. I hardly know her. I bought her one. I can see her. What's her name? Take her bag. I found her number. Will her brother come? Is her mother okay? I know her aunt. I've read her book. She took her time. Someone took her coat.

g) /hər/

Her mother left. Her bag's over there. Her brother said so. Her finger's swollen. Her car's been stolen.

h) /ðəm/

Help them. Nobody mentioned them. I know them. Jack found them. Show them again. I took them home. He broke them. Put them over there. Can I borrow them? Will you look after them? He stood behind them.

9.11 Articles

9.11.1 A, An, The

a) /ə/

a pocket, a bat, a table, a dog, a coat, a guess, a cheat, a joke, a farm, a vote, a thing, a sock, a zoo, a shop, a hobby, a minute, a note, a letter, a robot, a university, a unit, a uniform, a yacht, a window; a proud father, a big decision, a tricky question, a dirty mind, a close shave, a good time, a cheap ticket, a gentle breeze, a frank answer, a vulgar attitude, a thin line, a soft landing, a short walk, a hot drink, a misty morning, a naughty child, a loud bang, a rough plan, a useful tip, a united country, a unique situation, a universal truth, a young man, a one-eyed dog, a wonderful achievement

b) /ən/

an idiot, an elephant, an animal, an uncle, an offer, an eagle, an alien, an item, an oyster, an ocean, an hour; an interesting story, an envious friend, an angry stranger, an odd couple, an easy task, an ordinary day, an aching back, an idle moment, an oily rag, an open door, an outdoor swimming pool

c) /ðə/

the police, the beach, the time, the kitchen, the ground, the champion, the gym, the French, the Vatican, the thirties, the sky, the zoo, the shower, the heart, the moon, the knowledge, the last, the radio, the United States, the world

d) /ði/

the Internet, the entrance, the attic, the others, the office, the East, the eighties, the ice caps, the oil crisis, the owner, the outback

9.12 Conjunctions

9.12.1 And, As, Than, That

a) /ən/

up and down, ebb and flow, cat and dog, food and drink, through thick and thin, big and bold, knife and fork, alive and well, north and south, smooth and silky, this and that, his and hers, flesh and blood, an arm and a leg, again and again, willing and able, all and sundry, wear and tear, free and easy, few and far between, day and night, high and dry, slow and steady, now and again

b) /əz/

as far as the eye can see, as old as the hills, as soon as possible, as clean as a whistle, as good as new, as smooth as silk, as cold as ice, as fit as a fiddle, as light as a feather, as gentle as a lamb, as busy as a bee, as dry as a bone, as flat as a pancake, as quiet as a mouse, as strong as an ox, as white as snow

c) /ðən/

larger than life, more trouble than it's worth, better than nothing, a fate worse than death, better safe than sorry, larger than life, rather you than me, easier said than done, more often than not, better late than never

d) /ðət/

I know that he did it. He said that she knew. They agreed that it was wrong. She claimed that she understood. They pretended that they were working. They hoped that it was true. the man that they saw, the meal that they had, a question that they answered, the man that lives next door, the woman that found it, the boy that left early, the girl that works there, the people that made it

Chapter 10

Consonant clusters

10.1 Consonant clusters vs. consonant sequences

English consonants can occur in groups, known as **consonant clusters**. For example, there are consonant clusters at the beginning of the words *float*, *cream*, *sprout*, *stream*, and at the end of the words *bank*, *past*, *wasps*, *instincts*. Words such as *sing*, *knife*, *gnome*, and *receipt*, of course, don't contain consonant clusters because clusters are a matter of pronunciation, not spelling. Groups of consonants occurring between words also don't count as consonant clusters. For example, the /st/ of *past* is a cluster, while the /st/ of *this time* isn't, because the /s/ and the /t/ belong to different words and therefore to different syllables. The consonants of a true cluster must belong to the same syllable. Consonants that are merely adjacent to each other with a syllable boundary between them are known as consonant **sequences**. This is why /st/ in *disturb*, where the syllable boundary is before /st/, is a cluster, while /st/ in *mistime*, where the syllable boundary is between /s/ and /t/, is a sequence.

The clusters permissible in English differ according to whether they are at the beginning of a syllable or the end of a syllable. What follows is a summary of the clusters commonly found in the core vocabulary of English. Further clusters would be possible if we included foreign borrowings (/ʃm/ in *schmuck*), rare words (word-initial /smj/ in *smew*), technical words (/skl/ in *sclerosis*), onomatopoeic words (/vr/ in *vroom*), or proper nouns (word-initial /gw/ in *Gweek*, /ʃl/ in *Shlaen*), but for practical purposes, we exclude these.

10.2 Initial clusters

Two-consonant clusters are of three main types:

1   A plosive followed by an approximant:

	/p/	**/b/**	**/t/**	**/d/**	**/k/**	**/g/**
/j/	/pj/ *pure*	/bj/ *beauty*			/kj/ *cute*	
/w/			/tw/ *twice*	/dw/ *dwell*	/kw/ *quick*	
/r/	/pr/ *price*	/br/ *bright*	/tr/ *try*	/dr/ *drive*	/kr/ *cry*	/gr/ *grow*
/l/	/pl/ *play*	/bl/ *blue*			/kl/ *clock*	/gl/ *glad*

Note that /gj/ occurs word-internally (*singular* /ˈsɪŋgjələ/), and /gw/ occurs initially in Welsh (*Gwen* /gwen/) and foreign borrowings (*guava* /ˈgwɑvə/), as well as word-internally (*anguish* /ˈæŋgwɪʃ/).

2   A voiceless fricative (and /v/) or a nasal followed by an approximant:

	/f/	/v/	/θ/	/s/	/ʃ/	/h/	/m/
/j/	/fj/ few	/vj/ view				/hj/ hue	/mj/ mute
/w/				/sw/ swim			
/r/	/fr/ fry		/θr/ throw		/ʃr/ shred		
/l/	/fl/ fly			/sl/ slip			

Note that /θw/ occurs initially in *thwart*.

3   /s/ followed by a plosive or a nasal:

	/p/	/t/	/k/	/m/	/n/
/s/	/sp/ spot	/st/ stop	/sk/ skip	/sm/ small	/sn/ snow

Initial three-consonant clusters are a combination of the first and third types of two-consonant clusters: a plosive preceded by /s/ and followed by an approximant.

		/p/	/t/	/k/
/s/	/j/	/spj/ spew		/skj/ skew
	/w/			/skw/ square
	/r/	/spr/ spring	/str/ street	/skr/ scratch
	/l/	/spl/ splash		

10.3 Final clusters

Two-consonant clusters are of three types: (1) obstruent + obstruent, (2) sonorant + obstruent, (3) sonorant + sonorant.

Obstruent	**Obstruent**	
plosive	plosive	/kt/ *act*, /pt/ *accept*
plosive	fricative	/ps/ *collapse*, /ts/ *blitz*, /dθ/ *width*, /ks/ *axe*
fricative	plosive	/sp/ *wasp*, /sk/ *mask*, /st/ *list*, /ft/ *left*
Sonorant	**Obstruent**	
nasal	stop	/mp/ *dump*, /nt/ *hint*, /nd/ *hand*, /ŋk/ *thank*, /ntʃ/ *lunch*, /ndʒ/ *sponge*
nasal	fricative	/mf/ *lymph*, /nθ/ *month*, /ns/ *once*, /nz/ *lens*
approximant	stop	/lp/ *help*, /lb/ *bulb*, /lt/ *tilt*, /ld/ *cold*, /lk/ *milk*, /ltʃ/ *belch*, /ldʒ/ *bulge*, /rp/ *harp*, /rb/ *blurb*, /rt/ *heart*, /rd/ *hard*, /rtʃ/ *march*, /rdʒ/ *large*, /rk/ *cork*
approximant	fricative	/lf/ *golf*, /lv/ *solve*, /lθ/ *health*, /ls/ *false*, /rf/ *scarf*, /rv/ *starve*, /rθ/ *earth*, /rs/ *horse*, /rʃ/ *harsh*

Sonorant	Sonorant	
approximant	nasal	/lm/ *film*, /rm/ *arm*, /rn/ *barn*
approximant	approximant	/rl/ *girl*

Note that /pθ/ occurs in *depth*, /mθ/ in *warmth*, /ŋθ/ in *strength* and *length*, /rg/ in *morgue*, /lʃ/ in *Welsh*, /ln/ in *kiln*, and /rz/ in *Mars*.

Three-consonant clusters are of two types: (1) obstruent + obstruent + obstruent, (2) sonorant + obstruent + obstruent.

Obstruent	Obstruent	Obstruent	
plosive	fricative	plosive	/kst/ *text*

Sonorant	Obstruent	Obstruent	
nasal	plosive	plosive	/mpt/ *prompt*, /ŋkt/ *instinct*
nasal	plosive	fricative	/mps/ *glimpse*, /ŋks/ *lynx*

The medial plosives of /mpt/, /mps/, /ŋkt/, and /ŋks/ are often not pronounced. A number of clusters only occur in one word or a very small group of words: /lpt/ *sculpt*, /lts/ in *waltz* (which has an alternative pronunciation with /ls/), /dst/ in *amidst*, /nz/ in *cleanse*, /nst/ in *against*, /ŋst/ in *amongst*, /rst/ in *first*, *thirst*, *burst*, *worst*, /rld/ in *world*, /rps/ in *corpse*, and /rts/ in *quartz*.

The addition of the <-s>, <-ed>, and <-th> suffixes to words increases the number of cluster possibilities. The following two-consonant clusters occur only when one of these suffixes is added:

Obstruent	Obstruent	
stop	plosive	/gd/ *jogged*, /bd/ *robbed*, /tʃt/ *watched*, /dʒd/ *caged*
stop	fricative	/bz/ *robs*, /gz/ *bags*
fricative	plosive	/θt/ *frothed*, /ðd/ *bathed*, /vd/ *lived*, /zd/ *gazed*, /ʃt/ *wished*
fricative	fricative	/fs/ *cliffs*, /vz/ *gives*, /θs/ *myths*, /ðz/ *breathes*

Sonorant	Obstruent	
nasal	plosive	/md/ *blamed*, /ŋd/ *pinged*
nasal	fricative	/mz/ *times*, /nθ/ *ninth*
approximant	fricative	/lz/ *falls*, /rz/ *cars*

Note that /tθ/ appears in *eighth* and /fθ/ in *fifth*.

The following three-consonant clusters occur only when an inflectional ending is added to a two-consonant cluster:

Obstruent	Obstruent	Obstruent	
plosive	fricative	plosive	/pst/ *lapsed*

Sonorant	Obstruent	Obstruent	
nasal	stop	plosive	/nʧt/ *wrenched*, /ndʒd/ *lunged*
nasal	stop	fricative	/nts/ *hunts*, /ndz/ *hands*
approximant	stop	plosive	/lʧt/ *squelched*, /ldʒd/ *indulged*, /rʧt/ *searched*, /rdʒd/ *merged*
approximant	plosive	fricative	/lps/ *helps*, /ldz/ *fields*, /lks/ *milks*, /rdz/ *birds*, /rks/ *marks*
approximant	fricative	plosive	/lvd/ *revolved*, /rvd/ *reserved*, /rst/ *first*

Note that /nzd/ occurs in *cleansed*, /ndθ/ in *thousandth*, and /lbz/ in *bulbs*.

The following three-consonant cluster *types* (e.g., plosive + plosive + fricative, nasal + fricative + fricative) occur only when a suffix is added to a two-consonant cluster:

Obstruent	Obstruent	Obstruent	
plosive	plosive	fricative	/pts/ *accepts*, /kts/ *rejects*
fricative	plosive	fricative	/sps/ *gasps*, /sts/ *fists*, /sks/ *risks*, /fts/ *lifts*
fricative	plosive	plosive	/spt/ *grasped*, /skt/ *tasked*
Sonorant	**Obstruent**	**Obstruent**	
nasal	fricative	fricative	/mfs/ *triumphs*, /nθs/ *tenths*
approximant	fricative	fricative	/lvz/ *involves*
approximant	nasal	fricative	/lmz/ *films*, /rmz/ *harms*

Note that /lmd/ occurs in *filmed* and *overwhelmed*, /lnz/ in *kilns*, /lfθ/ in *twelfth*, /lfs/ in *gulfs*, /ŋθs/ in *lengths* and *strengths*, /fθs/ in *fifths*, /ksθ/ in *sixth*, /dθs/ in *widths* and *breadths*, /tθs/ in *eighths*, /pθs/ in *depths*.

All four-consonant final clusters require one or more inflectional endings and only /ŋkts/ occurs in more than a single word (*instincts, precincts, adjuncts*). /ksts/ is found in *texts*, /ksθs/ in *sixths*, /ŋkst/ in *jinxed*, /ndθs/ in *thousandths*, /lpts/ in *sculpts*, and /lfθs/ in *twelfths*.

10.4 Elision

A number of syllable-final clusters can be simplified through the process of **elision** described in Section 12.2. The /t/ can be elided from /pts/, /kts/, /sts/, /fts/, /ksts/, /ŋkts/, /ŋsts/, and /lpts/; the /d/ elided from /ndz/, /ndθ/, /ldz/, and /ndθs/; and the /k/ elided from /skt/. When immediately followed by a word beginning with a consonant, /t d/ can be elided from all clusters in which they appear in final position (except for /lt/ and /nt/), and /k/ elided when it's preceded by /s/.

10.5 Epenthesis

Sounds can also be inserted into clusters, a phenomenon known as **epenthesis**. This usually involves the insertion of a voiceless plosive (/p/, /t/, or /k/) between a nasal and a following voiceless fricative. It happens for straightforward articulatory reasons. Figure 10.1 shows

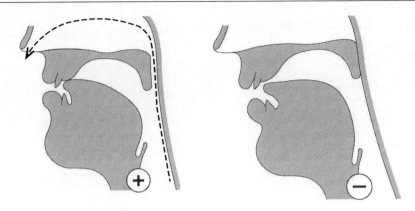

Figure 10.1 Transition from English /n/ (left) to /s/ (right); the arrow indicates escape of airstream through nose

that three changes have to be made simultaneously when moving from the position for /n/ to that for /s/: (1) vocal fold vibration stops; (2) the soft palate rises, closing off the nasal cavity; and (3) the closure between the tip of the tongue and the alveolar ridge opens into a narrow gap. If steps 2 and 3 aren't carried out at precisely the same moment, and step 3 lags behind, then pressure builds up in the oral cavity. When the alveolar closure is released, a plosive /t/ occurs. Note that the epenthetic voiceless plosive occurs at the same place of articulation as the nasal and so when the nasal is bilabial /m/, the plosive is bilabial /p/, and when the nasal is velar /ŋ/, the plosive is velar /k/.

- **Epenthetic /p/:** /mf/ becomes /mpf/ in *lymph*; /mfs/ becomes /mpfs/ in *triumphs*; /mθ/ becomes /mpθ/ in *warmth.*
- **Epenthetic /t/:** /ns/ becomes /nts/ in *once*; /nst/ becomes /ntst/ *against*; /nθ/ becomes /ntθ/ *month*; /nθs/ becomes /ntθs/ *tenths.*
- **Epenthetic /k/:** /ŋθ/ becomes /ŋkθ/ in *length*; /ŋθs/ becomes /ŋkθs/ in *strengths*; /ŋsts/ becomes /ŋksts/ in *angsts.*

Epenthesis with /t/ is more common than with /p/ or /k/ because there are more words with the /ns/ cluster, and these words also tend to be in more frequent use. This leads to *prince* being pronounced like *prints*, *sense* like *scents*, *chance* like *chants*, and *dense* like *dents*.

Chapter 11

Practice

Consonant clusters

11.1 Initial clusters ending in /j/ or /w/

11.1.1 /pj spj bj kj skj fj vj mj hj/ and /tw dw kw skw sw/

a) Words

puny, pupil, pure; spew; beautiful; cube, cucumber, cure, curious, cute; skewer; few, fuel, fume, funeral, furious, future; view; muesli, museum, music; huge, human, humid, humor; twelve, twice, twig, twin, twist; dwindle; quack, qualify, quality, quantity, queen, question, quick, quiet, quit, quite, quiz, choir, cuisine; square, squash, squeak, squeeze, squid, squirrel, squirt; swallow, swan, swap, swear, sweat, sweet, swim, swing, switch

b) Phrases

beauty treatments, a miraculous cure, genuinely curious, skewed results, breathtaking beauty, a long-standing feud, the distant future, a breathtaking view, as stubborn as a mule, a museum curator, a music stand, slapstick humor, classical music, a dry twig, twin brothers, a strange twist, a slum dweller, a school choir, French cuisine, quality control, a long-standing quarrel, a probing question, freshly squeezed orange juice, a grey squirrel, a black swan, stale sweat, a quick swig, the flick of a switch, an unexpected twist, a private dwelling, an awkward question, threaten to quit, switch places

c) Sentences 1

(1) They swore to contribute equally. (2) Switzerland's a beautiful country. (3) Hugh was miraculously cured. (4) He acquired a large Swedish vocabulary. (5) The twelve curious documents were quickly distributed. (6) It's purely a humanitarian question. (7) I'm furious that he refused twice.

Sentences 2

(1) Samuel questioned my future in the choir. (2) The review gave an overview of the dwindling figures. (3) Muriel quit after a quarrel. (4) The human population continued to dwindle. (5) We switched to Swahili quite quickly. (6) We watched the beautiful swans quietly swimming. (7) Dwayne spoke with an Oklahoma twang.

11.2 Initial clusters ending in /l/ or /r/

11.2.1 /pl spl bl kl gl fl sl/ and /pr spr br tr str dr kr skr gr fr θr/

a) Words

place, plan, plate, play, please, plus; splash, split; black, blame, block, blow; clap, clean, clock, cloud; glad, glass, globe, glue; flag, flat, flight, floor, fly; slap, sleep, sleeve, slice, slide, slim, slip, slow; press, price, print, prize; spray, spread, spring; brain, bread, break, bridge, bring; train, trap, tree, trip; straight, strange, street, stress; dream, dress, drink, drop, dry; cross, crowd, cry; scratch, screen, screw; grape, great, green, group, grow; frame, free, fresh, friend, front, fruit; threat, three, thrill, throat, through, throw

b) Phrases

clear plastic, swap places, a plane crash, tropical plants, a brilliant player, a school playground, a clever plot twist, blood pressure, a thriving black market, a huge blast, a drop of blood, broken glass, crystal clear, a tropical climate, a thrilling climax, a sports club, frosted glass, a brief glimpse, swollen glands, a slippery slope, flesh and blood, flash floods, squeaky floorboards, plain flour, fresh flowers, a flight of stairs, a snappy slogan, a steep slope, a strong flavor, bright flames, standard practice, gloomy predictions, blind prejudice, sliced bread, crime prevention, prim and proper, a gradual process, a quality product, steady progress, a Christmas present, spring cleaning, fly spray, a crime spree, a drunken brawl, fresh bread, a stone bridge, plum brandy, a beautiful bride, pronunciation drills, a brain scan, a fresh breeze, a breach of trust, a cruel trick, thriving trade, a crowded train, a grain of truth, a blocked drain, stomach cramps, a brutal crime, a blank screen, a splinter group, a mutual friend, fresh fruit, French fries

c) Sentences 1

(1) It improves students' employment prospects. (2) Please provide a credible explanation. (3) Fred grossly neglected his tasks. (4) The construction industry went through a dramatic decline. (5) A controversial new clause was included in the agreement. (6) He wiped the slate clean and started fresh. (7) The French flag was fluttering in the breeze. (8) Please drink plenty of fluids. (9) They criticized a crucial flaw in the project. (10) The flimsy plane flew through the gray clouds.

Sentences 2

(1) Fred brought Claire fresh spring flowers to celebrate. (2) The classes are spread over three weeks. (3) A lunch break improves productivity and creativity in the workplace. (4) I blame Craig for breaking his promise. (5) Greg was a complete stranger. (6) Drake slid the secret drawer closed. (7) The storm left a trail of destruction through Florida. (8) Trevor tried on a flowing black dress. (9) Three countries threatened to withdraw from the agreement. (10) Please stack the crates on the floor.

Sentences 3

(1) I regret drawing such trite conclusions. (2) It brought a slight increase in unemployment. (3) A comprehensive bibliography is included. (4) Graham applied for a grant. (5) The

player's hands were crippled with arthritis. (6) The slimy green frog croaked. (7) My gran is too frail to travel. (8) The tree trunks creaked and groaned strangely.

11.3 Initial two-consonant clusters beginning with /s/ or /ʃ/

11.3.1 /sp st sk sf sm sn ʃr/

a) Words

space, speak, special, spend, spin, spoon, sport, spot; stage, stand, star, start, still, stop, story; school, skill, skirt, sky; sphinx, sphere; small, smell, smile, smoke, smooth; snack, snake, sneeze, snore, snow; shrimp, shrink, shrug

b) Phrases

storage space, a broad spectrum, slurred speech, ground spices, a huge spider, a fluent speaker, steep stairs, a sweeping statement, grilled steak, a true story, stage fright, stale bread, stand up straight, stainless steel, stand still, a study group, a blind spot, a spectacular stunt, a flaky scalp, a crazy scheme, a human skeleton, clear skin, study skills, a cloud of smoke, a spiral staircase

c) Sentences

(1) Skiing equipment is extremely expensive. (2) He smiled from behind his spectacles. (3) She studies the speech of small children. (4) He stumbled over a stone in the snow. (5) The stage was shrouded in smoke. (6) He shrugged and started to stand. (7) They speculated without a shred of substantial evidence. (8) The snake's skin was smooth. (9) It stopped snowing before school started. (10) The smell of smoke makes me sneeze.

11.4 Final clusters

As in the case of the initial clusters, the final clusters have been combined into larger groups. The exercise material, which includes words, phrases, and sentences, has been presented in the following order: (1) clusters beginning with a stop; (2) clusters beginning with a fricative; (3) clusters beginning with a nasal; (4) clusters beginning with an approximant; and (5) clusters containing dental fricatives.

11.5 First consonant = stop

11.5.1 /pt pts kt kts bd bz gd gz tʃt dʒd ps pst ts dz ks kst ksts/

a) Words

accept, adapt, concept, except, interrupt; dropped, hoped, kept, slept, stopped; adopts, disrupts, scripts; act, collect, connect, correct, fact; checked, liked, looked, talked; acts, collects, expects, insects; described, rubbed; jobs, pubs, tubes, webs; begged, hugged; bags, dogs, eggs, legs; attached, reached, scratched, touched, watched; damaged, managed; collapse, perhaps;

chips, cups, gaps, groups, keeps, lips, sleeps, steps; collapsed, elapsed; blitz; bits, boats, cats, coats, eats, forgets, lights, pets, puts, seats; beds, clouds, feeds, heads, needs; box, fix, mix, six, tax; books, jokes, likes, makes, socks, weeks; next, text; fixed, mixed, taxed; texts

b) Phrases

adopt a child, a film script, a conflict of interests, change the subject, acts of violence, resolve a conflict, test tubes, a sports club, cats and dogs, soft-boiled eggs, soft drugs, caged birds, hopes and dreams, lapse into silence, armed troops, bend over backward, dense clouds, a draft text, mixed feelings, a range of topics

c) Sentences

(1) I slept wrapped in a soft blanket. (2) They joked and laughed as they looked at the screen. (3) I've booked six tickets for tonight's performance. (4) He stretched and crossed his legs. (5) I had cornflakes and boiled eggs for breakfast. (6) The traffic clogged the streets. (7) Alex grabbed the suspect's wrist, but he managed to escape. (8) She shrugged and lapsed into silence. (9) We changed the dates of our flights. (10) The roads were blocked by landslides. (11) He always takes my remarks out of context. (12) The players' contracts expire next spring. (13) Abstract words make texts difficult to follow.

11.6 First consonant = fricative

11.6.1 /sp sps spt sk sks skt st sts zd ʃt ft fts vd fs vz/

a) Words

crisp, gasp, lisp, wasp; gasps, grasps, lisps, wasps; gasped, lisped; ask, desk, disk, mask, risk, task; asks, desks, disks, masks, risks, tasks; asked, masked, risked; best, cost, fast, fist, last, lost, most, nest, rest, test; based, crossed, dressed, forced, kissed; boasts, costs, forests, ghosts, guests, rests; amazed, caused, paused, realized, refused, sneezed; crashed, finished, pushed, rushed, smashed, washed, wished; craft, gift, left, lift, soft; coughed, laughed; crafts, gifts, shifts, thefts; arrived, improved, loved, moved, received, saved, shaved, waved; cliffs, coughs, laughs; arrives, believes, caves, detectives, drives, gives, gloves, loves, moves, saves, waves, knives, wives

b) Phrases

clasp hands, speak with a lisp, gasp in astonishment, a desk lamp, a slipped disk, health risks, an arrest warrant, count the costs, a dense forest, a conflict of interests, built to last, an ant's nest, a speck of dust, a wasp's nest, arts and crafts, a draft agreement, a gift box, damaged nerves, a first draft, exchange gifts

c) Sentences

(1) I asked for breakfast. (2) Mix in the paste with a whisk. (3) He was teased because of his lisp. (4) I gasped when I realized the risk. (5) My cheeks flushed when I was embarrassed.

(6) He who laughs last laughs longest. (7) His enthusiasm lifts my spirits and takes my mind off life's problems.

11.7 First consonant = nasal

11.7.1 /md mz mp mpt mps mf mfs/, /nz nzd nd ndz nt nts ns nst ntʃ ntʃt ndʒ ndʒd/, and /ŋz ŋd ŋk ŋkt ŋkts ŋks/

a) Words

ashamed, climbed, formed, named, screamed, seemed, welcomed; crimes, crumbs, dreams, drums, exams, games, gums, names, problems, rooms, thumbs; bump, camp, jump, lamp, lump, stamp; attempt, prompt, tempt; bumped, dumped, jumped, limped; glimpse; bumps, camps, jumps, lamps, limps, lumps, stamps; triumph; triumphs; bronze, cleanse; beans, chains, cleans, fans, fines, guns, lines, opens, pens, towns, trains, wins; cleansed; band, end, find, friend, hand, kind, land, mind, stand; cleaned, opened, phoned; defends, depends, ends, finds, friends, hands, lands, minds, sends, stands; aunt, count, faint, hint, mint, paint, point, tent; amounts, counts, giants, paints, prints, wants; bounce, chance, dance, fence, once, since, tense; against; convinced, glanced, sensed; bench, bunch, inch, punch; clenched, crunched, launched, pinched; change, range, strange; arranged, exchanged; bangs, brings, gangs, gongs, hangs, kings, rings, songs, things; belonged; bank, think; distinct, instinct; blinked, linked, thanked; instincts; larynx, minx; drinks, shrinks, stinks, thanks

b) Phrases

violent crimes, solve problems, innocent victims, household items, a botched attempt, a moment of triumph, the merest glimpse, jump to conclusions, cramped quarters, a strange blend, distant lands, myths and legends, a round of golf, a gust of wind, husbands and wives, cleanse a wound, contact lenses, gold coins, pots and pans, twists and turns, a wrist band, find fault, a sound mind, second best, a round of drinks, a fox hunt, specks of paint, a prolonged absence, a guest appearance, a twinge of conscience, a grand entrance, a profound influence, blind obedience, a sequence of events, against all odds, a second chance, salient points, accept a challenge, orange zest, an act of revenge, a clenched fist, change your mind, exchange words, no strings attached, the kings and queens of England, a bank account, a direct link, sink fast

c) Sentences 1

(1) His parents were profoundly ashamed. (2) Since the accident, he walks with a limp. (3) It was a triumph of science. (4) They dumped the guns in the swamp. (5) Let's pretend it never happened. (6) I wasn't convinced by his arguments. (7) Different clients have different needs. (8) There was a distinct improvement.

Sentences 2

(1) She doesn't stand a chance against her opponents. (2) Her husband still clings to the past. (3) I longed for a moment of silence. (4) He flinched when the verdict was announced.

(5) My instincts told me to trust my friend. (6) His response was succinct and to the point. (7) When did the lynx become extinct in Scotland?

11.8 First consonant = approximant

11.8.1 /lp lps lpt lt lts ld ldz ltʃ ltʃt ldʒ ldʒd lk lks lkt lm lmz lf lv lvz lvd ls lst lz/

a) Words

help, pulp, scalp; helps, scalps; sculpt; helped, yelped; belt, fault, melt, salt; waltz; bolts, halts, results; child, hold, old, wild; called, fooled, pulled; fields, holds, shields; belch, squelch; belched, squelched; bulge, indulge; bulged, indulged; milk, silk; elks, sulks; milked, sulked; elm, film; elms, films; self, shelf, wolf; solve, twelve, valve; shelves, wolves; dissolved, solved; else, false, pulse; repulsed; bills, calls, dolls, pulls, rules, schools, smiles, tells, walls

b) Phrases

beyond help, nuts and bolts, a pinch of salt, a spoiled child, dance a waltz, find faults, a sense of guilt, adopt a child, a bold statement, cold hands, an old friend, wild animals, a twinge of guilt, a silent film, goat's milk, a film script, the Gulf states, a first impulse, the sound of bells, bend the rules, a faint pulse

c) Sentences

(1) Help me fold the sheets. (2) He gulped down the seltzer and belched. (3) Don't be lulled into a false sense of security. (4) He knelt and checked for a pulse. (5) The event was held in a field. (6) They protected themselves with shields. (7) The child drank the milk. (8) Carol's first impulse was to scream. (9) Paul's shelves were crammed with books.

11.8.2 /rp rps rpt rb rbz rbd rt rts rd rdz rtʃ rtʃt rdʒ rdʒd rk rks rkt rg rgz rm rmz rmd rn rnz rnd rl rlz rld rf rfs rv rvz rvd rθ rθs rs rst rz rʃ/

a) Words

carp, harp, sharp; corpse; harps, warps; warped; orb, rhubarb; absorbs; absorbed; chart, dart, fort, part, port, short, smart; carts, hearts, sorts, sports, starts; beard, card, guard, lord, weird, yard; boards, fords, rewards, swords; march, torch; marched, scorched; barge, charge, large; barged, charged; bark, dark, fork, mark, park; corks, sharks, sparks; barked, parked; morgue; morgues; arm, farm, storm, warm; forms, harms, norms, storms; armed, harmed, reformed; barn, born, horn, yarn; acorns, thorns; mourned, warned; snarl; snarls; snarled; dwarf, scarf; scarfs; carve, starve; carves, starves; carved, starved; fourth, hearth, north; fourths; course, divorce, horse, pierce, scarce; divorced, forced; cheers, yours; harsh, marsh

b) Phrases

airport lounge, a horse-drawn cart, a flow chart, a source of comfort, contempt of court, an armed escort, a change of heart, spare parts, a false passport, the world of sports, a means of support, beard growth, a greeting card, a cardboard box, cupboard space, closely guarded, a health hazard, a secret hoard, put the record straight, a drop in the standard, a double-edged sword, march in step, free of charge, a mark of respect, a park bench, an amusement park, flying sparks, a false alarm, my left arm, farm produce, storm clouds, a divorce court, pierced ears, tears of remorse, untapped resources, a marsh plant, at arm's length, a heart of gold

c) Sentences

(1) We had rhubarb tart for dessert. (2) He served on the Board of Education for six years. (3) My neighbors have a weird and warped sense of humor. (4) She held onto Robert's arm for support. (5) George was attacked by a shark. (6) She embarked on a research project as part of her master's thesis. (7) Their warm friendship was a source of comfort. (8) Mars is the planet most like earth. (9) He unearthed many ancient treasures. (10) They were warned to expect the worst. (11) The horse pricked up its ears.

11.9 Final clusters with dental fricatives

11.9.1 /θs ðd ðz dθ dθs ŋθ ŋθs lθ nθ nθs/

a) Words

deaths, moths, myths; breathed, bathed, clothed, loathed, mouthed, unscathed, soothed; bathes, breathes, loathes, soothes; breadth, hundredth, width; hundredths; length, strength; lengths, strengths; filth, health, stealth, wealth; hyacinth, labyrinth, month, plinth, millionth, ninth, tenth; hyacinths, months, plinths, ninths, tenths

b) Sentences

(1) She loathes stylish clothes. (2) My husband isn't in the best of health. (3) He emerged unscathed from the accident. (4) He summoned all the strength he had left. (5) The animals huddled together for warmth. (6) Tracy swims twelve lengths in six minutes. (7) The results have improved in recent months. (8) Find the length and the width of the rectangle. (9) The moths left holes in my clothes. (10) Add six-twelfths and three-sixths. (11) He amassed a vast amount of wealth.

Chapter 12

Connected speech

The following features are of a different type from those treated so far. Phonemes are realized in particular ways and are combined in particular orders to form words. This is relatively straightforward for learners. When it comes to features of connected speech, however, it cannot be said that these phenomena absolutely must occur in the contexts described but only that they very commonly do, which raises the question of whether the learner should attempt to imitate these patterns of native speech.

Firstly, it's certainly advisable to learn about connected speech because it will help with listening comprehension. It's easier to understand speakers if you know when to expect sounds to change, appear, or disappear. Secondly, connected speech phenomena are not unique to English, but at the same time, they are not universal. By this, we mean that learners have connected speech habits that are almost certainly different from English habits and that applying those patterns to English will result in mispronunciations. Thus, one reason to learn about English patterns of connected speech is to help avoid this. Finally, depending on the learner's background, certain connected speech processes can make English pronunciation easier: why make such an effort to pronounce /skt/ in *asked* when you don't have to?

12.1 Citation forms vs. connected speech forms

The pronunciation of a word can vary depending on its phonetic environment. We have seen an example of this in the case of words that have strong and weak forms (see Chapter 8), the strong form being used in stressed syllables and the weak form in unstressed syllables. The context of the surrounding sounds also has an important influence on a word's pronunciation. When we quote a word in isolation, we give what is known as the **citation form** of the word, and this is the pronunciation recorded in dictionaries. However, words are rarely uttered in isolation but are preceded and followed by other words. As a result, adjacent sounds influence each other across word boundaries, which often causes a change in the phonemic structure of a word. A pronunciation of a word influenced by the sounds in surrounding morphemes, syllables, or words is known as a **connected speech form**.

The two connected speech processes that occur in GA are:

Elision: A phoneme present in the citation form is lost in the connected speech form.
Assimilation: A phoneme in the citation form changes into another phoneme in the connected speech form.

12.2 Elision

12.2.1 Consonant elision

The most common kind of elision involves /t/ and /d/. The alveolar plosives can be elided when they stand between two consonants and belong to the same syllable as the preceding consonant. For example, /t/ can be elided in *last lesson* /ˈlæs ˈlɛsn̩/ and *facts* /fæks/ and /d/ in *brand new* /ˈbræn ˈnu/ and *hands* /hænz/ but not in *his twin* /hɪz ˈtwɪn/ or *this drink* /ˈðɪs ˈdrɪŋk/. The following consonant may be in a suffix, the second element of a compound or a following word:

/ft/ + C	*lifts* /lɪfs/	*software* /ˈsɑfwɛr/	*lift me* /ˈlɪf mi/
/st/ + C	*firstly* /ˈfɔrsli/	*coastguard* /ˈkoʊsgɑrd/	*best friend* /ˈbɛs ˈfrɛnd/
/kt/ + C	*collects* /kəˈlɛks/	*fact-finding* /ˈfækfaɪndɪŋ/	*react badly* /riˈæk ˈbædli/
/pt/ + C	*accepts* /əkˈsɛps/	*scriptwriter* /ˈskrɪpraɪt̬ər/	*kept quiet* /ˈkɛp ˈkwaɪət/
/nd/ + C	*hands* /hænz/	*grandfather* /ˈgrænfɑðər/	*stand still* /ˈstæn ˈstɪl/
/ld/ + C	*fields* /filz/	*childcare* /ˈtʃaɪlkɛr/	*hold tight* /ˈhoʊl ˈtaɪt/

Word-final alveolar plosives are often realizations of the <-ed> inflection, but this doesn't block elision:

/bd/ + C	They robbed the bank.	/ðeɪ ˈrɑb ðə ˈbæŋk/
/gd/ + C	I shrugged my shoulders.	/aɪ ˈʃrɑg maɪ ˈʃoʊldərz/
/dʒd/ + C	He managed to do it.	/hi ˈmænɪdʒ tə ˈdu ɪt/
/vd/ + C	I saved my breath.	/aɪ ˈseɪv maɪ ˈbrɛθ/
/ðd/ + C	She mouthed the answer.	/ʃi ˈmaʊð ði ˈænsər/
/zd/ + C	It amused me.	/ɪt əˈmjuz mi/
/md/ + C	I calmed down.	/aɪ ˈkɑm ˈdaʊn/
/nd/ +C	He fanned the flames.	/hi ˈfæn ðə ˈfleɪmz/
/ŋd/ + C	It belonged to me.	/ɪt bəˈlɑŋ tə mi/
/ld/ + C	I appealed to them.	/aɪ əˈpil tə ðəm/
/pt/ + C	He stopped talking.	/hi ˈstɑp ˈtɑkɪŋ/
/kt/ + C	He was tracked down.	/hi wəz ˈtræk ˈdaʊn/
/tʃt/ + C	I switched channels.	/aɪ ˈswɪtʃ ˈtʃænl̩z/
/ft/ + C	I stuffed my face.	/aɪ ˈstəf maɪ ˈfeɪs/
/st/ + C	I was forced to do it.	/aɪ wəz ˈfors tə ˈdu ɪt/
/ʃt/ + C	I brushed my teeth.	/aɪ ˈbrəʃ maɪ ˈtiθ/

An exception to this pattern of elision is that /t/ isn't elided in the clusters /lt/, /nt/, /rt/, and /rd/: *I felt sad* remains /aɪ ˈfɛlt ˈsæd/, *front door* remains /ˈfrʌnt ˈdor/, *start the car* remains /ˈstɑrt ðə ˈkɑr/, *hard times* remains /ˈhɑrd ˈtaɪmz/. An exception to this exception is contractions with *not* (see Section 8.16), which frequently lose their final /t/ before vowels as well as consonants (but not before a pause). This is particularly true of the disyllabic contractions: *I couldn't say* /aɪ ˈkʊdn̩ ˈseɪ/, *I shouldn't ask* /aɪ ˈʃʊdn̩ ˈæsk/, *I hadn't known* /aɪ ˈhædn̩ ˈnoʊn/, *It hasn't changed* /ɪt ˈhæzn̩ ˈtʃeɪndʒd/.

A less frequent kind of consonant elision is the elision of /k/ in final /sk/ clusters when a consonant follows: *masked* /mæst/, *risked* /rɪst/, *tasked* /tæst/. Although there are few words ending in /sk/, this kind of elision is common in the word *ask*: *I'll ask them* /aɪl ˈæs ðəm/, *They asked us* /ðeɪ ˈæst əs/.

Note the /v/ of *of* is often elided when a consonant follows, particularly before /ð/ in high-frequency words like *the, this, that, these, those, them* (e.g., *the back of the truck* /ðə ˈbæk ə ðə ˈtrək/, *one of these days* /ˈwən ə ˈðiz ˈdeɪz/).

12.2.2 Vowel elision

One kind of vowel elision has already been described under syllabic consonants (see Section 8.2). Words such as *deafen* and *cycle* have the basic form /ˈdɛfən/ and /ˈsaɪkəl/, which usually results in the pronunciations /ˈdɛfn̩/ and /ˈsaɪkl̩/ with syllabic consonants. When a suffix beginning with a weak vowel follows, the syllabicity of the consonants can be lost, *deafening* and *cycling* becoming /ˈdɛfnɪŋ/ and /ˈsaɪklɪŋ/. Through this process, a schwa is elided from these and other words that fulfil these conditions.

A similar process occurs when schwa is followed by /r/ and then an unstressed vowel (e.g., *history* /ˈhɪstəri/ becomes /ˈhɪstri/, *separate* (adj.) /ˈsɛpərət/ becomes /ˈsɛprət/). If the following vowel is strong, the schwa is not elided: *hyphenate* = /ˈhaɪfəneɪt/ or /ˈhaɪfn̩eɪt/, not */ˈhaɪfneɪt/, *idolise* = /ˈaɪdəlaɪz/ or /ˈaɪdl̩aɪz/, not */ˈaɪdlaɪz/, *separate* (v.) = /ˈsɛpəreɪt/, not */ˈsɛpreɪt/.

12.3 Assimilation

Assimilation in English is most often **anticipatory**, meaning that a sound is influenced by a sound that follows it. Less often, assimilation in English is **perseverative**, meaning that a sound is influenced by a sound that precedes it. In the case of anticipatory assimilation, the change happens because the articulators are getting ready to make the next sound while still articulating the present sound (i.e., they anticipate the following sound). When the assimilation is perseverative, the articulators are still in the position for the earlier sound when they are articulating the present sound (i.e., some aspect of their position perseveres into the following sound).

12.3.1 Place assimilation

English alveolar plosives /t, d/ and the alveolar nasal /n/ take the place of articulation of a following plosive or nasal. This means that:

*   /t/ (voiceless alveolar plosive) → /p/ (voiceless bilabial plosive) before /p b m/ (bilabials):

    wet paint /ˈwɛp ˈpeɪnt/   *jet black* /ˈdʒɛp ˈblæk/   *white mice* /ˈwaɪp ˈmaɪs/

*   /d/ (voiced alveolar plosive) → /b/ (voiced bilabial plosive) before /p b m/ (bilabials):

    a bad person /ə ˈbæb ˈpərsn̩/   *a loud bang* /ə ˈlaʊb ˈbæŋ/   *red meat* /ˈrɛb ˈmit/

*   /n/ (voiced alveolar nasal) → /m/ (voiced bilabial nasal) before /p b m/ (bilabials):

    brown paper /ˈbraʊm ˈpeɪpər/   *a thin book* /ə ˈθɪm ˈbʊk/   *lean meat* /ˈlim ˈmit/

*   /t/ (voiceless alveolar plosive) → /k/ (voiceless velar plosive) before /k g/ (velars):

    hot coffee /ˈhɑk ˈkɑfi/   *quite good* /ˈkwaɪk ˈgʊd/

*   /d/ (voiced alveolar plosive) → /g/ (voiced velar plosive) before /k g/ (velars):

    a red gate /ə ˈrɛg ˈgeɪt/   *a bad group* /ə ˈbæg ˈgrup/

*   /n/ (voiced alveolar nasal) → /ŋ/ (voiced velar nasal) before /k g/ (velars):

    green covers /ˈgriŋ ˈkəvərz/   *twin girls* /ˈtwɪŋ ˈgərlz/

In the case of /t/, this is also the context where glottal replacement or glottal reinforcement (see Sections 2.7.2 and 2.7.3) can take place. In which case, instead of assimilation taking place, [t] could be replaced by [ʔ], or assimilation could take place with the resulting voiceless plosive being accompanied by glottal reinforcement.

The alveolar fricatives /s/ and /z/ also frequently undergo assimilation. When they are followed by palato-alveolar /ʃ/, their place of articulation changes to palato-alveolar:

- /s/ (voiceless alveolar fricative) → /ʃ/ (voiceless palato-alveolar fricative) before /ʃ/ (palato-alveolar):

  this shop /ˈðɪʃ ˈʃɑp/   *nice shoes* /ˈnaɪʃ ˈʃuz/
  a famous ship /ə ˈfeɪməʃ ˈʃɪp/   *a close shave* /ə ˈklouʃ ˈʃeɪv/

- /z/ (voiced alveolar fricative) → /ʒ/ (voiced palato-alveolar fricative) before /ʃ/ (palato-alveolar):

  is she /ˈɪʒ ʃi/   *his shirt* /hɪʒ ˈʃɔrt/
  Lee's short /ˈliʒ ˈʃɔrt/   *because she* /bɪˈkəʒ ʃi/

When /ən/ follows the velar plosives /k g/ or the bilabial plosives /p b/, the plosives can be released nasally (see Section 2.9) and the tongue remain in position, resulting in a homorganic syllabic nasal (i.e., [m̩] after /p b/ or /ŋ̍/ after /k g/).

/ən/ → /m̩/   *happen* /ˈhæpm̩/   *ribbon* /ˈrɪbm̩/
/ən/ → /ŋ̍/   *taken* /ˈteɪkŋ̍/   *pagan* /ˈpeɪgŋ̍/

The more frequent a word is, the more likely this assimilation is to occur, but the variant with /ən/ is still more usual, and it's this form that learners are advised to use. This is an example of perseverative assimilation.

12.3.2 Coalescent assimilation

The assimilations we have looked at so far involve a phoneme changing into another phoneme under the influence of a following phoneme. In the case of coalescent assimilation, two phonemes influence each other and combine to form a third phoneme: /t/ and /d/ combine with /j/ to form /tʃ/ and /dʒ/. In such cases, we transcribe the two words as one. This process is most common and most complete when it involves *you* or *your* and is frequently heard in *could you, couldn't you, did you, didn't you,* and so on.

/t/ + /j/ → /tʃ/   *I know what you said.*   /aɪ ˈnoʊ wəʧu ˈsed/
   I've bought you a present.   /aɪv ˈbəʧu ə ˈprɛznt/
   Can't you wait?   /ˈkænʧu ˈweɪt/
   Why don't you go?   /ˈwaɪ ˈdoʊnʧu ˈgoʊ/
   He said that you did.   /hi ˈsɛd ðəʧu ˈdɪd/
   Get your key.   /ˈgɛʧər ˈki/
   Couldn't you try?   /ˈkʊdn̩ʧu ˈtraɪ/

/d/ + /j/ → /dʒ/   *Did you see it?*   /dɪdʒu ˈsi ɪt/
   Could you wait?   /kʊdʒu ˈweɪt/
   They made you do it?   /ðeɪ ˈmeɪdʒu ˈdu ɪt/

	Would your brother try?	/wʊdʒər ˈbrəðər ˈtraɪ/
	He said you did.	/hi ˈsɛdʒu ˈdɪd/
	I found your key.	/aɪ ˈfaʊndʒər ˈki/
	I've read your book.	/aɪv ˈrɛdʒər ˈbʊk/

12.3.3 Voicing assimilation

Unlike many other languages, English has very few examples of voicing assimilation. This is a phenomenon whereby a voiceless consonant becomes voiced under the influence of an adjacent voiced consonant or a voiced consonant becomes voiceless under the influence of another voiceless consonant (perhaps more correctly termed "devoicing assimilation"). English doesn't have the former, and learners should therefore take care not to say *jukebox, scapegoat, white-collar* as */ˈdʒugbaks, ˈskeɪbgoʊt, ˈwaɪd ˈkɑlər/. Devoicing assimilation is rare in English, occurring in only a few common phrases such as *have to* /hæf tu/, *has to* /hæs tu/, *had to* /hæt tu/, *used to* /jus tu/, *supposed to* /səˈpoʊs tu/.

12.3.4 Manner assimilation

Manner assimilation involves the voiced dental fricative /ð/ becoming identical to a preceding /n/, /l/, or alveolar fricative. This is an example of perseverative assimilation. It is most common in unstressed positions (e.g., *on the, will they, that's the, was the* /ɑn nə, wɪl leɪ, ðæts si, wəz zə/) but is also heard in stressed syllables (e.g., *and then, although, what's this, how's that* /ən ˈnɛn, ɑlˈloʊ, ˈwəts ˈsɪs, ˈhaʊz ˈzæt/). Since many learners pronounce /ð/ as /d/, it can be a useful strategy to employ these manner assimilations. Remember to lengthen the assimilated sound, as there's a clear difference between elision and assimilation of /ð/. If you don't lengthen the consonant, *on the table* will sound like *on a table*.

/ð/ → /n/	It's on the table.	/ɪts ɑn nə ˈteɪbl̩/
	And then it rained.	/ən ˈnɛn ɪt ˈreɪnd/
/ð/ → /l/	Will they manage?	/wɪl leɪ ˈmænɪdʒ/
	Although it's sad.	/ɑlˈloʊ ɪts ˈsæd/
/ð/ → /s/	That's the idea.	/ˈðæts si aɪˈdiə/
	What's this?	/ˈwəts ˈsɪs/
/ð/ → /z/	Was the baby healthy?	/wəz zə ˈbeɪbi ˈhɛlθi/
	How's that?	/ˈhaʊz ˈzæt/

References and suggested reading

In addition to reading the following works, those wishing to take their phonetic studies further can consult the IPA website at www.internationalphoneticassociation.org for information regarding its Certificate of Proficiency in the Phonetics of English.

Dictionaries

Jones, D., Roach, P., Esling, J., & Setter, J. (2011). *Cambridge English pronouncing dictionary* (18th ed.). Cambridge: Cambridge University Press.

Perrault, S. J. (Ed.). (2008). *Merriam-Webster's advanced learner's English dictionary*. Springfield, MA: Merriam-Webster.

Upton, C., & Kretzschmar, W. A., Jr. (2016). *Routledge dictionary of pronunciation for current English* (2nd ed.). Abingdon: Routledge.

Wells, J. C. (2009). *Longman pronunciation dictionary* (3rd ed.). Harlow: Pearson Education.

English phonetics

Carley, P., Mees, I. M., & Collins, B. (2018). *English phonetics and pronunciation practice* [British English]. Abingdon: Routledge.

Collins, B., Mees, I. M., & Carley, P. (2019). *Practical English phonetics and phonology* (4th ed.). Abingdon: Routledge.

Edwards, H. T. (2002). *Applied phonetics: The sounds of American English*. Clifton Park, NY: Delmar Learning.

Kreidler, C. W. (2004). *The pronunciation of English* (2nd ed.). Oxford: Blackwell.

Wells, J. C. (1982). *Accents of English 1: Introduction*. Cambridge: Cambridge University Press.

Yavaş, M. (2016). *Applied English phonology* (3rd ed.). Chichester, UK: Wiley-Blackwell.

General phonetics

Ashby, P. (2011). *Understanding phonetics*. Abingdon: Routledge.

Catford, J. C. (2001). *A practical introduction to phonetics* (2nd ed.). Oxford: Oxford University Press.

Ladefoged, P., & Disner, S. F. (2012). *Vowels and consonants: An introduction to the sounds of language* (3rd ed.). Oxford: Blackwell.

Ladefoged, P., & Johnson, K. (2015). *A course in phonetics* (7th ed.). Stamford: Cengage Learning.

Zsiga, E. C. (2013). *The sounds of language*. Chichester, UK: Wiley-Blackwell.

Index

Note: Page number in *italic* denoted as figure and in **bold** denoted as table.

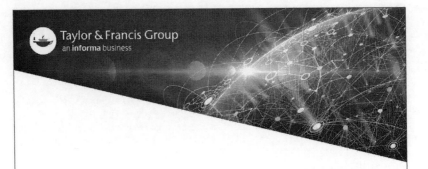

Printed in Great Britain
by Amazon